AUTHENTIC PERSONAL DEVELOPMENT

Realizing Your Potential for Effectiveness

Also by Surinder Deol

Managing Intercultural Negotiations
(With Pierre Casse)

Japji: The Path of Devotional Meditation
(With Daler Deol)

The Summit: A Fable About Integral Transformation

A Moment in the Universe
(Poems)

AUTHENTIC PERSONAL DEVELOPMENT

Realizing Your Potential for Effectiveness

SURINDER DEOL

ATLANTIC

PUBLISHERS & DISTRIBUTORS (P) LTD

Published by

ATLANTIC

PUBLISHERS & DISTRIBUTORS (P) LTD

B-2, Vishal Enclave, Opp. Rajouri Garden,
New Delhi-110027
Phones : 25413460, 25429987, 25466842

Sales Office
7/22, Ansari Road, Darya Ganj,
New Delhi-110002
Phones : 23273880, 23275880, 23280451
Fax : 91-11-23285873
web : www.atlanticbooks.com
e-mail : info@atlanticbooks.com

FIRST EDITION

Library of Congress Cataloging-in-Publication Data

ISBN 978-81-269-0833-2

Printed in India
at Nice Printing Press, Delhi

Your true nature is that of infinite spirit.
The feeling of limitation is the work of the mind.

Ramana Maharshi

Preface

This book has been written with the objective of helping you realize your dream. If you are ready to walk with me, I will show you how you can be more effective in whatever you are doing, no matter the constraints. The book does not contain any secret recipes for success. The knowledge on which the structure of this work rests has been known for thousands of years. This is the wisdom that has been passed on from one generation to another. What makes this book worth reading is how some well-tested ideas regarding personal development and change have been contextualized and applied to the globalized world, the world of 24/7 connectivity, constant innovation, ruthless competition, but the world that also generously rewards highly effective individuals.

I talk about your dream because we all aspire to go some place in life. All the ideas and best practices contained in this book have only one objective—to assist you in becoming an exceptionally well-functioning human being. The most critical element in authentic personal development, we should remember, is starting and sustaining "a set of practices." Mental understanding of models and theories, though a desirable pursuit, will not on its own bring any noticeable benefit. It is only through the act of systematically renewing ourselves that we can create a new future for us as well as for the world we live in.

I take this opportunity to thank numerous friends and associates who have provided support and encouragement to me to creatively express myself, including those whose commitments to causes higher than themselves have had great influence upon me. My sincere thanks to Dr. K.R. Gupta, Chairman, Atlantic

Publishers and Distributors (P) Ltd., for his comments and advice. I would like to express my gratitude to my wife, Daler, and our children and grandchildren for their affection and care. The joy of living lies in exploring and discovering new facets of reality. I would be truly handicapped to do this work on my own without the support of people who are doing all the hard work and letting me run this marathon of life like a cakewalk.

Surinder Deol
Potomac, Maryland, USA

Contents

Introduction

WHY AUTHENTIC DEVELOPMENT?

Every being, according to Buddha, has the potential to awaken. Human beings have capacities that are unmatched in other species. Yet many studies have indicated that large majorities of people anywhere in the world lead their lives at low levels of self-actualization, operating at much lower level than their full potential as human beings. This includes people who are educated and hold professional jobs and responsibilities. Leading management thinker Warren Bennis has mentioned that only one out of four employees works at full potential. One easy explanation for this phenomenon is the "comfort factor" or habits, which once formed are difficult to change. But it does not mean that these people never change; they are subject to the same universal law that says that nothing in life is constant. The change experienced in this case, however, is unmanaged or even unintended. We grow old whether we like it or not. That's a big change. There are other causal factors: change as a result of certain life events; change triggered by past mistakes; or change driven by professional growth or lack thereof. All this is change all right but anything that happens as a result of external pressure does not add up to a life of satisfaction and abiding happiness.

This book is about planned self-development; it is about processes that we can consciously initiate, and change that is managed by us to maximize our effectiveness in our personal and professional lives, based on our dreams and aspirations. It must be "authentic"—genuine or original, as opposed to something that is fake or temporary. Examples of "non-authentic change" are seen in everyday life: New Year resolutions; promises to give up an addiction; and agreements to improve bad behaviors or bad habits. Why do we fail to sustain such changes? Because we have no predefined path that takes us from place A to B to C. Or we just shy away from the effort that is required for making fundamental changes in our behaviors. That's why people laugh and say, "Oh, I tried but it didn't work out." The fact of the matter is that there was no passion in this try; the person was not motivated at physical, emotional, psychological, and spiritual levels to do the heavy lifting required for that change to stick.

Integral Development

Integral is not a new word in our vocabulary, but it has definitely acquired new meaning in recent years. Integral means wholeness that embraces body, mind, heart, soul, and spirit—the whole spectrum of our consciousness. Integral connects different domains of life such as individual as well as collective, interior (subjective) as well as exterior (objective). Such comprehensiveness and inclusiveness leaves nothing out and brings all parts of our being to become whole. This means that an "integral human being" pays attention to keeping a balance between various facets of his or her life within the boundaries of a predefined cultural, social, economic, and political context. We can find the evidence of non-integral development around us all the time. We have seen school and college athletes getting failing grades in their studies. We know people who are brilliant scholars but have frail body structures due to lack of physical exercise or proper nourishment. There are spiritual leaders who are overweight and disorganized and uncouth. While not denying the achievements of these people in their preferred pursuits or occupations, these are not very good examples of integral or authentic development.

Development Needs Transformation

We often use the word "transformation" in lieu of change. Is transformation the same thing as change? It depends. In the ordinary discourse, these two terms are fully interchangeable, but for the specialist these have different connotations, if not different meanings. The word "change" is generally used to describe difference in any situation. Let us take a very simple example. If I rearrange furniture in my apartment, it would have a new appearance. Rearrangement of furniture is the change in this case. Now when I enter my apartment, I may even have the impression that I have entered a wrong apartment because everything would look very different. Transformation, on the other hand, is like moving to a new apartment at a higher-level floor. The reference to higher-level is significant in this example because we have a better view or perspective when we go to upper floors of a building. This means that as we move higher we can see more and as a result our perspective (our way of thinking) changes. This means that when we change, in fundamental and integral ways, our perspective on life and on relationships is enriched. Therefore, in this book I use the words "authentic development" as some other people would use the word "transformation."

Whatever is gained, as they say, is never lost. The same way, the view or the perspective that I gained while living in the apartment at a lower-floor will remain with me as I move to a new apartment on an upper-floor. This is also called "the transcend and include" principle, which means that as we develop integrally, as we move from lower to higher stages of development, we do not lose what we had gained while at the lower stages. Also human development is very linear in many respects. No one is born on day one as a great painter or a musician or a scientist. We go through different stages to master different skills that make us one day a great artist or a scientist. The point is that there is no shame in being at a lower stage, but there is shame if we do not understand our potential for greatness, or if we do not appreciate the effort needed to realize the great dream that we secretly carry in our heart. Life places many barriers in our path, but human potential is a great force that once activated can cross any hurdle and break any barrier.

The Path of Authentic Development

If we want to change our life deeply and meaningfully, how do we go about achieving this objective? This question brings us to the fundamental truth of life: personal development is hierarchical. This means that there are levels, layers, and stages of development. The path to self-development is like climbing a ladder. Consciousness or awareness gets deeper and more pervasive as we climb each step on the ladder. Think of a primitive man living in a bear cave. I can have his attention if I talk to him about food, but if I give him a lecture on non-violence he would probably hit me on my head with his baton. Why would he do that? Because I talked to him about something that makes no sense to him, which means my communication in this case was much above his level of consciousness. We do not live in bear caves any more, but try talking to a fundamentalist about his belief system (like "God wants me to destroy His enemies"), you will meet with the same violent reaction. A fundamentalist is someone who has rigid views on how he sees the world and in his thinking there is no other view that is equally valid. In a way, this person is stuck. If we cannot make him aware of other possibilities and points of view (like "God loves everyone. God has no enemies."), we cannot contribute to his self-development. There is a close relationship between our thinking and our behavior. If I have to behave differently in any situation I need to change or develop my thinking or self-awareness. Any development effort that does not strongly impact my consciousness or self-awareness is not going to be sustained.

The Map

In this book we follow a clear map of development; this map takes us from lower levels to higher levels but what is higher or lower is defined strictly in terms of the contents of our awareness. The movement from any one level to the next level happens only when we develop the new awareness about self, about others, and the world that comes with the higher stage. Authentic development is a movement towards higher meaning and greater fulfillment. It is not about acquiring more knowledge. It is about the awareness that would then help us to gain the knowledge that we need. The process is evolutionary. We learn to do something and then build on it. Our focus is always on what we have within us that we have not put to any practical use. It is simply about realizing our unrealized potential.

What changes is our consciousness or awareness of who we *really* are, the level of self-understanding, and our capacity for love and compassion. Authentic development is, therefore, a fundamental shift of consciousness from a lower biological state to a higher awareness consistent with our potential for completeness. It is a step forward in our evolution to achieve fullness that we lack in our ordinary life and, perhaps, liberating ourselves from daily sufferings that arise from failures driven by ineffective choices and ineffective implementation of ideas.

Why Should I Care?

Why is authentic development important? We can lead our life the way we like it. That's what most people do in fact. Yet how vehemently people complain of lack of happiness or fulfillment and a sense of void in their lives. They complain of being stuck in their unproductive routines. They are frustrated because their dreams remain just dreams. Also, there is a feeling of disconnect between what the mind aspires to achieve and what the body can physically sustain. Mind and heart often get conflicted. There is a tension between cognitive or mental and emotional aspects of our personality. How many times have we seen people who have great potential for achievement, but who do nothing about it except complain about their bad luck. On the other extreme, we also find people who have moved ahead in life, materially speaking, much beyond their talent or capacity, but they are unhappy because they see other people who are equally talent or values deficient command even more wealth and fame. Some people are unhappy because they didn't make it, others are unhappy despite the fact that they made it. Material success is no guarantee of satisfaction, though money is a major source of empowerment in today's world.

Effectiveness vs. Efficiency

Effectiveness consists of successfully producing a desired result in a timely fashion with positive and sustained *impact* on one's immediate environment. The concept of efficiency, in contrast, has to do with input-output ratios: if A completes a task in two hours while B takes three to do the same, then we can say that A is more efficient than B. There are many ways to look at our latent abilities, but in this book we are looking at our potential as a synonym of our "potential for effectiveness." Therefore, we can expand the dictionary meaning of effectiveness to include achieving success coupled with satisfaction in whatever we do; attaining the desired results in the most efficient manner; and fully engaging our body, heart, soul, and spirit in the pursuit of the desired ends. This implies that anything done in a casual manner or at the surface without deep involvement is highly unlikely to result in effective outcomes.

What Do We Need to Do Differently?

What does authentic development entail? It demands attention to several things at the same time—it means taking care of our physical well-being, building and sustaining strong relationships, embracing different approaches to good health and healing, recognizing and honoring our bonds with nature, and adoption of some regular practices. In the words of Rabbi Nachman, the most important thing in the world is to be willing to give up who we are for who we might become.

Once we are focused on seeking wholeness based on a strong inner commitment, our difficulties start to dissolve. As we move closer to our goal, our needs and aspirations change qualitatively. We are not simply seeking perfection; we are mirroring unparalleled beauty in all our words and actions. This form of change is about knowing ourselves fully and deeply. It is a discovery of the ever-present strengths hidden under layers of thoughts, experiences, and false impressions.

As we evolve, moving from one level to another, new ways of thinking unfold in a sequential, yet highly interactive manner.

Each higher level of consciousness brings with it higher degrees of ego-deficiency, openness to new experiences, and the ability to live in a timeless universe. Each newly unfolding level of consciousness includes the lower level as a realized capacity and the higher level as a potential to be actualized. As we develop the higher capacities they are more representative of our true nature. We did not get life and other attributes of humanness to operate suboptimally. We do that as a matter of choice. A commitment to authentic development, however, offers another choice and this is the choice that must become our destiny.

The Seven Levels Framework

The Seven Levels Framework for authentic development, presented in this book, derives inspiration from an ancient source, namely chakra system from India, which for 3,000 plus years has worked as a cornerstone for individual personal development and spiritual transformation. The seven chakras are centers of subtle energy that impact, positively or negatively, specific parts of human body. They also contribute in many ways to our physical, emotional, mental and spiritual strengths and dysfunctions.

Each chakra symbolizes a unique universal principle like grounding, sexuality, power, love, creativity, intuition, and unity. While chakras themselves are not specific physical entities, their predetermined locations provide a pathway from our lowest life energies to our highest spiritual potentialities, from hate and anger to love, compassion, and our connection with the unknown. Lower chakras represent human or ground-centric energies and thus assist us in horizontal transformation, whereas higher chakras are sources of spiritual energy and thereby they are effective tools of vertical transformations. Whatever way we look at them, chakras are the evolutionary path of authentic development. Figures 1 through 3 which appear at the end of this Introduction provide the reader a quick overview of the framework, especially highlighting the stages or levels of personal development, shifts in our consciousness, and opportunities and challenges faced by us at each level. Figure 4 provides some measures of effectiveness that work as guideposts in our developmental journey. These measures are important for monitoring our progress as well as treating them as gifts to be had if we succeed in our change efforts.

Let me highlight a few key features of the Seven Levels Framework:

- Our map recognizes a fundamental truth that our awareness is spread widely and on a typical day we have experiences that touch most, if not all the seven levels.
- All of us however start at the lowest point of our consciousness called the ground of our being (level one) and then slowly move upwards. If we make no effort at all, with the passage of time, our consciousness will settle down around levels three and four, without realizing the full development potential however of the first four levels. The fact that our consciousness touches higher levels as well for brief periods of time on any given day gives us no durable advantage.
- How can we raise the level of our consciousness and thereby the whole spectrum of personal development? That is the issue of "trainability" addressed in a number of components in this book, namely development challenges, developmental interventions, exercises and guided meditations. Personal effort is the sole motive power for initiating and sustaining authentic development.
- Individual differences such as gender, ethnicity, preferences, etc. matter the most at the lower as against the higher levels of awareness. Every higher stage is a solid step towards unity, harmony, and oneness where inner and outer, subjective and objective, higher and lower realities come together and merge into one all-embracing wholeness.
- The chakra system is unique in the sense that it not only describes the seven levels or stages of human development, each level has a distinctive state of mind

or consciousness that is different both from the previous and the next level. The seven levels are therefore state-stages, which means that when we reach a particular *stage* (or level) we automatically gain a *state* of consciousness attached to that stage.

- The levels are not without corresponding pathologies. Reaching a particular level by itself will not confer all the benefits. It is using strength of each level effectively and not allowing the "shadow" (repressed negative energies) aspects of our personality take control of us. "The Living Stories" in each chapter provide examples of effective and ineffective responses to one's current reality.
- Each level carries with it a color code that is consistent with the color that is usually assigned to the comparable chakra. Taken together these are seven colors associated with the rainbow. Use of color makes the map visually more appealing, but we should not see too much into the color scheme. As every human being is unique because of his or her life history, it is common for aura readers to see more than one color in each chakra when they look at specific individuals. The color scheme is, however, logical in the sense that lower three colors, namely, red, orange, and yellow vibrate at a slower frequency than the green, blue, indigo, and violet used for chakras four through seven. This rainbow pattern was confirmed in a pioneering study conducted by Dr. Valerie Hunt at the UCLA in 1970s.

The book is divided into two parts and an appendix.

Part I includes detailed explanation of the Seven Levels Framework and suggests a number of practices and exercises. This part, consisting of 7 chapters, is strong both in theory and practice. While explaining different theories I have made an assumption that this stuff would be new for the reader though from the perspective of any one individual reader it might not be so. The advantage of this assumption is that I was forced to write in a style that is engaging as well as self-explanatory. It is hard to avoid the jargon completely while writing a book on human development, but I have tried that the written word makes ordinary "real-world" sense. Whether I failed or succeeded in doing this, I will await your assessment.

Part II of the book is of special interest because it is an animal story drawn from *Panchatantra* with which both children and adults in India are quite familiar. But the story has been substantially expanded here as well as adapted for specific pedagogic purpose of demonstrating different shifts in the awareness of two animal characters and what those shifts mean for their behaviors or their overall effectiveness.

The fable helps us in deepening our understanding of the Seven Levels Framework in a developmental context. There are several good reasons for a quick read of this story before going in more deeply into individual components of the Seven Levels Framework, but let me mention one. Stories are great attention grabbers and a very productive pedagogical tool. People will perhaps learn more about personal change by reading this story than from anything else in the book. It is highly recommended that you read the fable in Part II before you engross yourself in the concepts described in Part I.

Appendix contains a number of additional activities and exercises relevant to your personal, professional and organizational needs and challenges. The material contained in the Appendix is for an advanced practitioner and it is recommended that you come to this part of the book only after you have tried out most of the suggestions contained in Part I.

FIGURE 1: The Seven Levels Framework

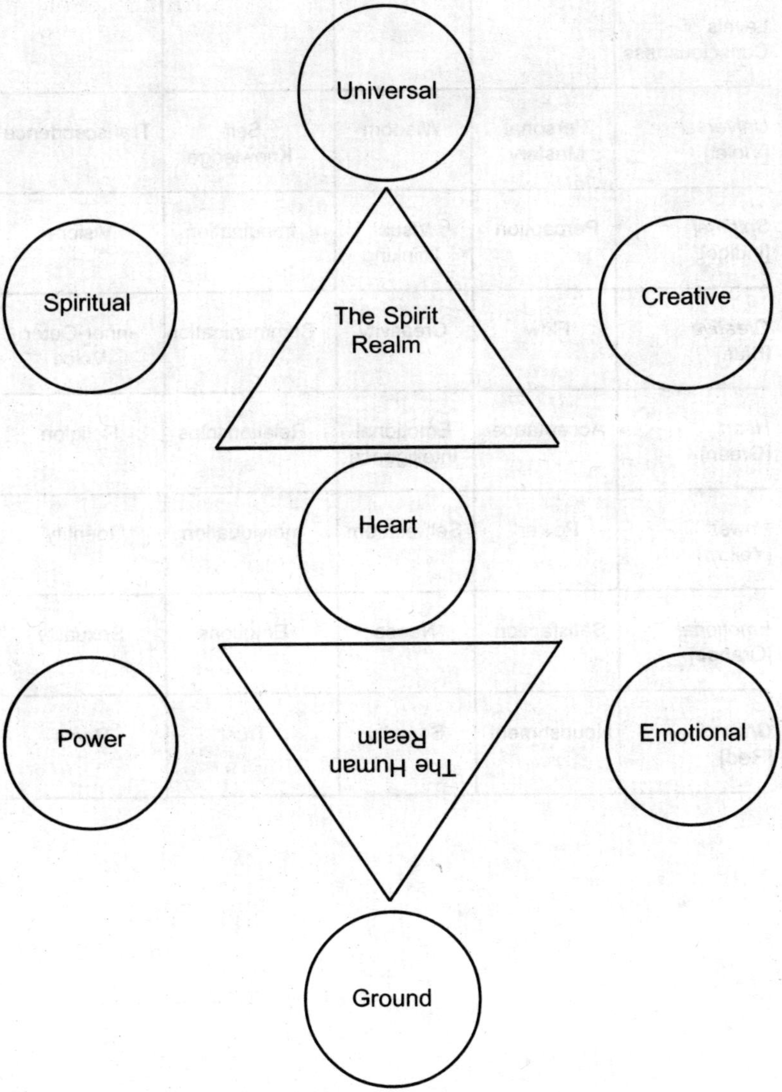

FIGURE 2: The Radiant Map of Authentic Development

Domains of Being Levels of Consciousness	Body	Mind	Heart	Soul or Spirit
Universal [Violet]	Personal Mastery	Wisdom	Self-Knowledge	Transcendence
Spiritual [Indigo]	Perception	Visual Thinking	Imagination	Visions
Creative [Blue]	Flow	Creativity	Communication	Inner-Outer Voice
Heart [Green]	Acceptance	Emotional Intelligence	Relationships	Religion
Power [Yellow]	Power	Self-esteem	Individuation	Identity
Emotional [Orange]	Satisfaction	Needs	Emotions	Sexuality
Ground [Red]	Nourishment	Security	Trust	Roots

FIGURE 3: The Seven Levels Framework

Definitions and Explanations

Ground Level

It is the most important manifestation of our physical reality, our needs and necessities for survival and basic pleasures of life. It is our connection with our family and community, our sense of belonging. We need ground to stand on. We need to be fully grounded for stability. At this level:

- Our body is essentially looking for food and nourishment.
- Our mind is asking questions about security: Is my future secure? What happens if there is a crisis tomorrow? Who will stand with me and who will provide the needed support?
- The heart is focused on trust issues. In this world where everyone is looking for his or her own interest, who can I trust?
- The soul or spirit is pondering some fundamental questions: What am I doing here? Where are my roots? Who can answer the questions for which I have no answers?

Emotional Level

At this level, we confront our basic emotions in a raw form. These emotions may have something to do with happiness, sadness, composure, curiosity, pride, anxiety, confusion, frustration, embarrassment, nervousness, and passivity. This emotional level does not include what is often called the "emotional intelligence," which shows up much later in our development. There are a number of emotions at this level that cluster around relationships, especially sexual relationships. A common experience for people at this level is to find release through fantasizing and living in a world that is unconnected with reality. Some of the common concerns and questions that arise are:

- The human body seeks pleasure and avoids pain. Therefore, there is lot of concern with seeking satisfaction. The questions that arise are: What would give me the greatest satisfaction? Why do I look for *more* satisfaction when I *already* have everything? Why do I look for satisfaction outside of myself?
- At this level, we process information that has to do with our needs. We also use our cognitive capacity to rank needs in some logical order. We make life decisions (like taking up a new job) based on this analysis. The common questions that call for response are: What are my needs? How do I satisfy them? What would best work for me? What are the risks and rewards?
- Another concern deep within our heart is to deal with emotions. Since emotions come and go in rapid succession, we try to find a stable emotional state for us. Our questions may lead to some probing: What is love? Why do I hate some people and love others? Why do I get frustrated when I fail to learn something new? How do I control my anger?
- At the deepest level, our thoughts gather around issues of sexuality. This concern becomes even more important in cases where people have unmet sexual needs. A survey of young male college students showed that they think of sex very frequently of their waking life. This may not be true about adults in later years, but sex is still a very important issue and people struggle a lot in bridging the gap between their worlds of fantasy and reality. One opportunity here is to channel one's sexual drive to something more sacred as in ancient traditions like the Tantra.

Power Level

This level is primarily about personal identity and self-esteem. When they arrive here, most people feel empowered for the first time. Initially, it is only the sense of physical power, the capacity for assertiveness or aggressiveness. But at the deeper level, this is about inner power—how much strength people find within themselves, something that must be developed is the form of self-esteem. Lack of self-esteem could become a major blockage in later years if this issue is not addressed early on. The relevant questions at this level are:

- How strong do I feel physically? Can I stand up to my opponents? Can I survive an attack? Can I beat up others?
- Do I lack self-esteem? Am I easily pleased by others? Do I seek others' approval? Do I have problem asserting myself? Can I clearly present and defend my viewpoint?
- We become a person through a process called "individuation." This is a process that helps us in developing individual characteristics. Individuation also helps in integrating different aspects of our personality in a single, recognizable whole. Following Swiss psychologist Carl Jung we can ask ourselves several questions to know our personality type. Am I an extrovert or an introvert? Am I a sensor or an intuitor? Am I a thinker or a feeler? Am I a judger or a perceiver? Taking Myers-Briggs Type Indicator (MBTI) questionnaire can help a person get answers to these questions.
- The most important question at this level is about identity. Who am I? But this is such a complex question for which there are no reliable answers at this stage of our development. Many other things need to happen before we get an answer to this question. But it is a good thing if this question catches our attention early on.

Heart Level

This level is a bridge between higher and lower forms of our being. As it is clearly shown in Figure 1, heart level is located in-between human and spiritual realms. It, therefore, draws energy from the currents floating upwards to the spiritual realms and downwards to the human realms. When we substantively gain access to this level, there is a qualitative shift in our perception. The answers we are seeking are:

- Who do I accept and who accepts me?
- Do I have the "emotional intelligence" to deal with difficult emotional issues of my life?
- What is the state of my relationships? Who *really* loves me? Who do I *really* love?
- What are my religious beliefs? What god or gods do I worship? What is the ultimate meaning of life? What happens when we die?

Creative Level

At this level, our inner voice gets its most authentic expression. A unstoppable urge to follow a personal dream gets stronger at this level and one starts to ask questions like:

- Do I live and work in a state of flow? Flow, according to psychologist Mihaly Csikszentmihalyi, is a mental state of operation in which the person is fully immersed in what he or she is doing, characterized by a feeling of energized focus, full involvement, and success in the process of the activity. Flow includes clear goals; a high degree of concentration on a limited field of attention; direct and immediate feedback; balance between ability level and challenge; and a sense of personal control over the situation or activity. Flow, in simple words, is an effortlessness of action.
- Am I creative? Do I think out of the box? Creativity as a concept has to do with original and appropriate responses to situations. It is also identified with divergent

thinking—thinking broadly in all directions, leaving nothing out.

- Am I a good communicator? Do I speak from the heart? Is my communication making a positive difference in the lives of others?
- At the soul or spirit domain, the important question is: Am I listening to my inner voice? Am I making a connection within my inner and outer realities?

Spiritual Level

Spiritual is not the same thing as religious. Religion is a belief in a particular dogma, while spirituality is an open-ended inquiry about the unknown. Spirituality is an openness to trans-body experiences; movement away from limiting faith-based practices to genuine inquiry, readiness to embrace the unknown, a realization of oneness of things around us, and above all a belief in the oneness of all humanity. The questions at this level include:

- What is my perspective on different things? What has influenced the shape of my perception? Am I capable of having second or third person perspectives, meaning can I put myself in the shoes of others?
- Can I think visually? Visual thinking is a special capacity where cognitive and perceptual factors are united to create a visual representation of our thinking. It is the difference between Word and PowerPoint software applications.
- Spirituality has close relationship with the use of imagination. Several spiritual practices require the use of mental imagery for guided meditations. The power of imagination is a special mental capacity to play with different images and to run mental simulations to solve difficult problems. Therefore, the questions relate to: Do I consider myself to be an imaginative person? How can I use the power of imagination in my daily life?

- Visioning is the capacity to see the future in the present time. People who do self-reflection or meditation can easily engage in visioning. They can easily ponder questions like: What is my vision in life? What do I want to become? How do I go from here to there?

Universal Level

At the universal level, all parts of our being become whole; there is the birth of an integrated self-awareness; there is an overarching sense of higher connection; wisdom coupled with personal mastery makes it possible to gain universal worldview where body, mind, heart, and soul are aligned with the unknown. There are no questions at this level. When we reach the universal level, we have resolved most of our life issues. Therefore, questions do not bother us any more. We want to live in a state of blissful perfection, beyond self-doubt, beyond skepticism, and it is possible to do so only if we stay in a state of flow—taking things as they come, finding the missing harmony in every situation, and creating a better world not only for ourselves, but for all humanity. We therefore pursue with passion and commitment ideals like personal mastery, wisdom, self-knowledge, and transcendence:

- The concept of personal mastery was popularized by Peter Senge in the 90s. It can be applied to any of the domains—body, mind, heart, and soul. The three elements of personal mastery are current reality (the present state), creative tension (tension that generates fruitful action), and the vision (the desired future state).
- Mind is the center of logical thinking. But at this level we are not seeking analysis; we are seeking wisdom. Traditionally defined, wisdom is the capacity for insight, reflection, the practice of virtue, and the ability to distinguish between the good and the bad.
- Self-knowledge or self-realization is the capacity to know oneself. This capacity is gained over a number of

years through rigorous practice of meditation and contemplation.

- Transcendence has to do with a philosophical belief that there is an ideal spiritual state that "transcends" the physical and the empirical state that we are most familiar with. This belief raises a number of questions: Is there another life that awaits us after death? Can I experience that other-worldly spiritual feeling in this life?

FIGURE 4: The Seven Levels Framework

Measures of Effectiveness

Ground Level

Sense of Security: Having a feeling of physical and emotional security

Self-Preservation: Withstanding pulls and pressures of life with equanimity

Healthy Food Habits: Making a willful decision to eat healthy foods

Home and Family: Taking care of one's obligations to family members

Trusting Self and Others: Putting confidence in self and the others to do the right thing

Stress-free Living: Keeping stress out of one's life and being fully relaxed in all circumstances

Satisfaction With One's Body: Maintaining pride and a sense of satisfaction with one's physical endowments

Emotional Level

Healthy Body: Keeping one's body free of injury and disease

Rational Need Analysis: Looking at one's needs through the lens of reason and logic

Quality of Emotional Life: Managing the impact of one's emotions, especially negative emotions, and staying positive about one's future

Healthy Sexuality: Accepting sexuality as a sacred act; finding fulfillment in healthy relationships

Nurturing Attitude: Developing an attitude of helping others; providing coaching and mentoring

Seeking Pleasure Without Guilt: Accepting pleasure as an essential part of life and not suffering from a sense of guilt for leading a good life

Managing Change: Thinking about personal change and managing it

Power Level

Sense of Power: Feeling empowered and not entertaining the feelings of powerlessness

High Levels of Energy: Sustaining high levels of energy through proper nourishment and physical exercise

Self-esteem: Feeling confident and acting appropriately in all situations

Knowing Self: Knowing one's inner motivations and purpose in life

Willpower: Directing one's impulses and inner motivations to cope with extraordinary challenges

Predictability: Predicting the outcomes of one's actions

Self-confidence: Trusting one's abilities, qualities and judgments

Heart Level

Attitude of Acceptance: Trusting and accepting others; trusting essential goodness of human nature

Emotional Intelligence: Making effective use of one's emotions in four personal domains such as self-awareness, self-management, relationship management, and social awareness (Daniel Goleman perspective)

Strong Relationships: Building and sustaining strong relationships

Healthy Interest in Spirituality: Understanding the differences between religion and spirituality; cultivating a spirit of openness and healthy inquiry into questions that have no ready answers

Gender Sensitivity: Understanding and developing a sense of appreciation of gender roles and perspectives

Compassionate Nature: Showing care and compassion for those who need help

Self-sacrificing: Sacrificing one's self interest for the benefit of others

Creative Level

Flow: Developing a sense of effortlessness in pursuing different tasks of life; being fully relaxed and easy to work with

Creativity: Bringing novelty to one's humdrum existence; seeking beauty in ordinary things; thinking out of the box

Speaking from the Heart: Speaking one's truth; not lying or willfully misrepresenting

Being the Voice of Wisdom: Giving sound advice to others; sharing eternal truths; being virtuous in thought and action

Listening: Giving full attention to the words spoken by others and the bodily gestures

Personal Resonance: Giving a sense of deep and full connection with others

Musical Intelligence: Appreciating music and its impact on human cognition; ability to differentiate between different sounds (notes, tones, and pitches)

Spiritual Level

Perceptive Body: Having a body that is open to new experiences; showing sensitive insights; very intuitive and observant

Visual Thinking: Seeing images or objects in great visual clarity; looking at the future in vivid details

Imagination: Forming new ideas, or images or concepts of external objects not present to the senses; creating or imagining new realities

Intuition: Thinking outside the domains of formal reasoning; having a sixth sense; getting insight or gaining information with suddenness and without anticipation; in Carl Jung's typology it is the opposite of sensing as a way of gaining information

Strong Sense of Being: Enjoying the fullness of life; being filled with spirit and optimism

Healthy Dreaming: Subtly but consciously directing one's dreams to reflect one's current passions and endeavors

Sense Making: Making deeper sense of ordinary phenomena; finding meaning in mundane things

Universal Level

Personal Mastery: Knowing one's purpose; cultivating a vision; using creative tension to realize that vision (Peter Senge perspective)

Non-dual Awareness: Having a sense of oneness with Infinite Spirit

Innate Wisdom: Having wisdom that is inborn and not dependent on one's experience; spiritual wisdom that is more a gift of Spirit

Self-awareness: Knowing one's strengths and weaknesses; being aware of one's potential

Connecting With the Unknown: Experiencing the unknown in a personal way; listening to the inner voice

Seeing Truth in All Spiritual Traditions: Accepting the fact that different spiritual paths lead to the same destination

Non-Judging Attitude: Non-judging others' motivations

Openness: Having an open mind; exploring new possibilities; being ready to be surprised

Part I

The Seven Levels of Personal Effectiveness

1 The Ground of Our Being

THE MAP

As electrical gadgets are grounded to ensure personal and gadget safety against external forces like lightening, human beings have to ground themselves to ensure safety against external forces, including other people who are contemplating doing harm; situations that arise without anticipation like political upheavals; or unexpected natural disasters like Tsunami or Katrina. A grounded person with a strong sense of purpose or meaning of life will withstand these onslaughts with strong will and confidence, whereas an ungrounded person caught in the cobwebs of meaninglessness will lose heart and courage and would fall a victim to circumstances. The ground level confers on the individual the power to shield self against problems, possible threats and potential enemies. The success, however, depends on how effectively this shield is used to protect self against harm and how quickly we move ahead to higher levels of consciousness instead of staying stuck at the ground level and thus open to all kind of risks and uncertainties.

Victor Frankl (1905-1997), Austrian psychiatrist, was transported to Auschwitz and later to two other concentration camps where he lost his wife and both his parents. He survived the Holocaust because of his inner strength and grounding. He strongly believed that his life had meaning and even Nazis could not shake his will to survive.

What Does It Mean To Be Well Grounded?

The single most important indicator of good grounding is sound physical health. Healthy body is a gift that we give ourselves. Nature gives us the genetic makeup and physiological systems that keep us going. But that is just the beginning. We must build on this foundation and maintain what nature has given us. For this we need to pay attention to our diet and regular physical exercise. The second requirement for good grounding is our inner sense of safety and security. Our life conditions change constantly; we lose jobs and careers; we lose friends and relatives; and we go through several transitions in our lives. In the midst of all these ups and downs, we need to stand firmly. That is possible only if we feel strong internally, which has less to do with our external circumstances than what we have inside our own heart. Only our inner self can provide the stability and solidity that we need. The next requirement for good grounding is the pursuit of a right occupation—something in which we are investing our best talent and energies. The last and perhaps the most important condition is our state of mind—for a true experience of good grounding we need to inculcate a quality of stillness. The seasons of life change and new challenges arise like weed in the grass, but we need to keep our mind still, unruffled, sharply focused on our broader purpose, not being too excited or depressed, and always ready to cope with the unexpected.

David Allen, in his book *Getting Things Done: The Art of Stress-Free Productivity*, talks about an aviation analogy: the plane needs ground (runway) to take off and land. But the real excitement of aviation is in flying high (30,000 feet and above). In the same manner, the excitement of life is also in flying high and not being grounded, but ground is essential for refueling (regaining high levels of energy), mapping the course (life planning), and taking off in the right direction (the purpose or vision). We need to keep the ground strong and clear of obstacles, but the last thing that we want to do is to stay on the ground for more time than necessary. Also when we are at the runway we have a limited view (perspective). Once we are airborne and reach an altitude of 30-40,000 feet we see more and our perspective is much wider. The same is true of life. The higher levels of consciousness enrich our perspective and thus we become more effective human beings.

The Shadow

Carl Jung uses "shadow" archetype—a primitive mental image that is present in our unconscious, something like a template—to highlight the power of our unconscious mind. Shadow contains our basic animal nature as well as what we reject in our conscious life. As we know, animals either pick up a fight or run away from a fight, they either cause fear or let fear numb their senses. In order for us to become fully civilized we have to suppress our animal nature, but we can also go too far in this endeavor and suppress spontaneity, sense of wonder, capacity to enjoy life, and thereby become spiritless. Also, what we have rejected or denied at the conscious level does not disappear into a black hole. It stays somewhere inside and is eventually embraced by the shadow. What is repressed may come back in our dream state or as a nightmare that constantly haunts us. That is why shadow becomes the repository of our fears and anxieties, of bad things happening to us or those we love.

Shadow cannot be completely suppressed. Jung reminds us that animal in us only becomes more beastlike when it is repressed. Any such attempt will make us insane. But what we can do is to befriend our shadow, acknowledge its existence, and get to know its contents. When our conscious mind (ego) stays connected with our unconscious, we experience high levels of self-awareness. Shadow adds vigor and vitality to our life, but it is also symptomatic of our animal nature—our ability to commit heinous crimes against fellow human beings. Therefore, self-awareness is our only way of knowing the good and the evil that resides in our heart. Shadow work is important at any level, but it is most essential at the ground level. When we are not fully grounded, shadow has greater ability to do us harm. A regular meditation practice is helpful in raising our self-awareness and thus harnessing shadow's positive side.

Values and Needs

As we are a body composed of flesh and bones, the call for grounding—digging our feet firmly into the ground—comes naturally. There is an urge to find a voice that speaks of physical being—the need for food, shelter, intimacy, and community. Having a body causes awareness of separation from others and consequently it is the cause of anxiety, the fear of alienation, of being left alone, of not being cared for. The body wants to protect itself against all kinds of threats, and it does so through a series of fight or flight responses. Groundedness symbolizes concerns for personal safety and security, continuous supply of nourishment, and a yearning for companionship of the mythic Mother (a protector), of guarded connectedness, which means neither being too close to others nor too remote. There is also the feeling of being a victim of circumstances, the world being an unfriendly place where survival is the biggest challenge of all.

Physical needs speak loudly and demand immediate satisfaction. There is no patience to wait. It is always now or never. What gives pleasure is eagerly sought, and what is uncomfortable is carefully avoided. Ego-self is the center of one's personal universe. Selfishness is not just a behavioral trait; it is the overarching need that drives everything else. Other people are important as long as they are part of the need fulfillment equation. They are means to personal ends, very narrowly defined, not as something sacred or worthy of respect for their unique humanity and compassion.

Communication and Leadership Style

Ground awareness does not provide adequate preparedness in terms of communication ability to connect with other people as equals. Therefore, communication is highly defensive, aggressive, or self-serving. Favorite expressions include: "What can you do for me?... Do you understand what I need? ...How can you get me what I want?" Those who are well-grounded may express the same wants and needs, but they communicate them in a more sophisticated language. Generally, people at this level have short attention span and as a result they are unlikely to make or understand a complex presentation. The lack of moral development makes it difficult for the person either to be a good exemplar, or to be restrained in personal actions. Deceptive and manipulative behaviors are common at this level. Perspective is first-person singular, meaning self is the sole focus of attention. Personal beliefs are unsupportive of inner growth and development. Feedback from others is either not valued or rejected out of hand. Conflict is either not managed or avoided. The inability to mediate differences limits options for reaching a compromise. There is no inner motivation for change, unless strongly pressured by circumstances or guided by a strong mentor.

LIVING STORIES

These are real stories of real people that will appear with some regularity in all the 7 chapters of Part I. My objective in including these stories is to demonstrate the fact that the Seven Levels Framework is not an academic model. It accurately mirrors the challenges in the lives of people in different parts of the world. I have either personally known these people or heard their stories from reliable sources or read about them in media reports. I have changed the names, locations, and in some cases occupations to respect their privacy.

There are possibilities for effectiveness or ineffectiveness at any level. The level itself does not guarantee success or failure. What it means is that when we are at a certain level we have an opportunity to inculcate new values and behaviors that would make us more effective than before. What if we do not embrace those opportunities and instead move in a completely wrong direction? The result would be negative. Ground level is a special case because this is the starting point for all human beings. More people are getting stuck at this level than at any other. Here are stories of two individuals who are at the same level of consciousness but, as you can see, they are leading very different lives.

John is always hungry; he is all the time looking for food and he consumes it wherever he finds it. His wife is always complaining about his eating habits and his weight problems.

She thinks that her husband is in poor health and he needs to do something about it. John thinks he's just fine. He is little bit lazy or laidback, nothing else. John is not known for self-control. If some information is shared with him, he cannot keep it to himself. He feels the urge to talk about it with outsiders who have no reason to have that information. As a result, his supervisor does not trust him. Many a time, he is left out of the loop. John interprets this as willful discrimination.

John has poor relations with his parents. He complains that they didn't raise him very well. When he visits them, he ends up spending more time in useless arguments and fights instead of providing emotional support to them which they require in their old age. His relationship with his wife is no better. On several occasions, his wife has threatened him with divorce unless he mends his ways.

The problems at workplace are becoming more severe. No one wants John to be in their work team. His annual evaluations are getting worse. In response to these challenges, John is trying to please all his colleagues and bosses. He doesn't say no to any kind of work for fear of annoying other people. This strategy is not working. In this confusing state of affairs, John has lost all perspective and this lack of focus is not doing him any good. He has these nightmares that he is going to lose his job; his wife is going to leave him; and his children are going to be ashamed of their father when they grow up.

Jane's is a very different story.

Although she has moved from one job to another in recent years, Jane feels very secure. She has that rare instinct for self-preservation. She is very proactive in her thinking. She invests herself in acquiring skills that are going to be in great demand in her workplace.

Jane is meticulous in her eating habits. She reads all the labels before buying any food. She avoids foods that are rich in fat and carbohydrates. She buys organic foods whenever she can afford it. She spends 15 minutes every morning in self-reflection followed by 45 minutes of Yoga exercises. She goes jogging every weekend. She takes care of her family and her relationship with her spouse is most productive. Both of them value each other's contributions.

Jane is a trusting individual. She puts lot of trust in her work colleagues and as a result she gets lots of trust and respect. Her stress-free lifestyle has kept her in good health. Although in her early 30s, she looks much younger than her biological age. She has never been happier than at the present time.

What's going on here?

Jane is building a strong foundation for herself; John has no focus and no priorities. He is in a confused state of mind and losing it both at home and at workplace. Is there any hope for John? Sure, there is if he is willing to invest in his future. He has to move beyond instant gratification of physiological needs. He can probably partner with his wife, who can help him get on the track and get properly organized for challenges in his life. A very little effort on his part can make a lot of difference.

John needs to regain his sense of security. His insecurity is at the root of most of his problems. He wants to survive the crisis in his life, but he does not have a plan. He has not shown any real commitment to change. He should take care of his biological needs. He should be more selective in his eating habits. He should consume smaller quantities of healthier food. His wife can help him in achieving this goal. But he has to take an initiative to start regular physical exercise.

He needs to be more productively involved in his family life and be a good role model for his children. He has to demonstrate that he is a trustworthy individual. John is in the habit of creating stress for himself and for others when there is no need for it. He must start with 15 minutes of self-reflection every morning. Instead of just trying to please others, John should focus on doing his job well. He seems to be unhappy with his physical state. He should realize that his eating habits and his lack of physical exercise has brought him to this state. He should start loving his body, but the body needs good nourishment and regular workouts.

DEVELOPMENT CHALLENGES

Necessary, but not sufficient

Ground awareness is inadequate to meet the full complement of basic human needs. Therefore, it is natural for people to search for alternative ways to lead their lives. We do not live by food alone. Having a sense of security is valuable, but clearly not enough. The focus at this level is very individualistic, which is not bad because groundedness is an individual attribute. But the greatest achievements in life occur when we work with others. Teamwork and companionship are necessary conditions for a contented life. The ground level, however, does not support building strong partnerships.

Evolution brings new possibilities

When the individual cognitive ability develops as a result of evolutionary processes, human brain is able to consider new options. Doors to higher levels of awareness are opened. The need to heal the split between the mind and the body assumes importance. What this means in practice is that as we grow older, as we gain more experience, our mental capacities expand. As a result, we are able to consider more options for enhancing our effectiveness. Evolution gives us the opportunity, but we need to exploit new options.

We need strong and supportive relationships

The inability to form and sustain supportive relationships is recognized as a major drawback of the ground level awareness. We need strong relationships for ensuring greater security to self and safeguarding our personal possessions. Once people start making some progress in forming simple support organizations, they unknowingly release forces that lead to new learnings, greater self-organization and emergence, and the ability to organize more complex support groups.

Emerging emotional needs

Sometime during our struggle with groundedness a realization dawns that we are concerned more with biological issues at the cost of other emotional needs such as romance, companionship, recognition, teamwork, and collaboration. It is not that these needs are not important at the ground level; people are generally not equipped to process and handle these emotions in a competent manner.

The need for alternative ways to manage conflict

The only way people manage conflict at the ground level is through mutually assured destruction (MAD). If you hit me, I will hit you back. If you slap me once, I will slap you twice. This is called tit for tat or two tats for one tit. Limitations of managing conflict only through sheer force become apparent. The development of verbal ability provides choices to people to solve their problems through arguments, if not through full-scale reasoning. People come to a realization that bad behavior does not pay. A connection between behavior and need satisfaction is established opening up new ways of interacting with others.

The need for a well-functioning social organism

There are other drivers of change that operate at more systemic or organizational levels. If everyone existed at the ground level, the state of the social organism will be primitive. This was the case during the initial development phase of human societies. In this situation, individual was solely responsible for ensuring safety of life and property. But as societies evolved, certain functions like fighting aggression by other tribes or nations were assumed by the social or political institutions. In today's world the role of society or state is not a settled issue philosophically, but in reality all societies provide varying degrees of care and comfort to their members or citizens. The effectiveness of social organism, however, rests a great deal on public participation—people electing their leaders and legislators, people paying taxes, people debating issues and finding solutions. Since the ground level is so much focused on fulfilling individual needs, a person at this level, though a member of the social organism, is not contributing his or her full potential for the good of all. And this incapacity can't last for very long without hurting effectiveness of individuals who are stuck at ground level.

The need for personal organization

Some understanding of causes and effects, at the ground level, makes people realize not only that actions have consequences, but also how to avoid adverse consequences by doing different things. Thus the concept of planning is born in its most elementary form. Lack of proper self-organization is a great challenge at the ground level. Typically low performers suffer the consequences of poor organization. A book on the subject of personal organization sums up the problem by its evocative title *It's Hard to Make a Difference When You Can't Find Your Keys*. Think about it: If you are spending all your time in unproductive pursuits like searching for your keys, your shoes, and other necessities of life, how can you sustain the highest levels of personal productivity? For no reason your life turns into a big struggle.

The emergence of follower-leader roles

The importance of managing and leading becomes important because almost nothing of great significance can be accomplished with people living in atomistic isolation. When we work with others we accomplish more. We can show leadership only in meeting a team or a group challenge. Leader-follower roles start to emerge only in a context of collective action. It is harder to work with others than on our own, but the real rewards are earned when we come out of the cocoon of our lonely existence and stand in front of others with confidence. This change requires moving upward to higher levels of effectiveness.

DEVELOPMENTAL INTERVENTIONS

The Foundation of Yoga Practice

The science of Yoga is a great gift of India to the world. Yoga is not only a set of physical exercises; it is a new way of leading our life. Before we make any effort to learn basic Yoga postures, we should pause and fully understand the basic principles of Yoga that were enunciated by the great sage Patanjali in his *Yoga Sutras*. These principles are popularly referred to as "Eight Limbs of Yoga". You can read about these principles in greater detail in any good book on Yoga, but here is a short description to get you started.

Yama is the starting point which means how we behave with other people. Do we treat others with kindness and consideration? Do we show compassion? Do we communicate correctly and accurately? Do we control our anger while dealing with others? *Niyama* is the reverse of *Yama*. It is how we treat our own self. Do we take care of our daily hygienic needs? Do we lead a disciplined life? Do we have a positive attitude? Do we think optimistically about our future? Are we able to control our destructive emotions? Do we value a feeling of calmness and stillness? Do we respect our inner self?

Asanas refer to the correct postures while we are engaged in our Yoga workouts. This has to do with minute technical details. Therefore, whenever you select a Yoga exercise for daily practice please do read very carefully about the right posture, or seek guidance from a qualified teacher. Doing things the wrong way will not yield any positive benefit.

Pranayama is the breathing practice. There is no life without breath. Daily breathing exercises are required for meditation, self-reflection, contemplation, or for the simple reason of keeping a healthy mind in a healthy body. There are techniques of breathing correctly that we need to learn. Good breathing does not come to us naturally.

Pratyahara is the practice of controlling our senses. We live in a world of myriad temptations. Things go on sale in the department stores all the time. New models of cars show up every fall. New electronic gadgets appear every Christmas season. We are tempted by the advertisers to have sensual gratification all the time. The fight against senses is not easy to win. It requires a lot of self-discipline, which needs to be developed gradually over a period of time. This is not an argument against sensual pleasures; it is an argument for moderation, simplicity, and self-control in life.

The next three principles have to do with mind concentration. *Dharana* is focusing our attention on an object. This object could be a flower, a painting, a statue, or any other thing of interest. Concentrating on an outer object helps us in creating a feeling of stillness in our mind. *Dhyana* is uninterrupted concentration on the object. When we concentrate on a flower or a burning candle successfully we think of nothing else. *Samadhi* is the last principle and it denotes the highest state of our mind. When we are in a state of *samadhi* we are not just concentrating on the object; we are in a state of oneness with the object. There are no other thoughts, no distractions. The seer and the seen are one. This is the state of pure awareness and freedom.

Walking

Walking is different from running. Not everyone can run, but all of us, in the absence of any physical disability, can walk. There is an endless variety of physical exercises, but there is nothing as simple and as satisfying as walking. The only item that you need to acquire is a pair of comfortable walking shoes. Walking is also a great social activity because you can walk with a group of friends or family members. More than 50,000 people walk the magnificent Chesapeake Bay Bridge in an annual ritual that is an uplifting experience, physically and spiritually. In this book I will be recommending a number of daily physical exercises, but walking is a basic recommendation: You must walk for at least 30 minutes every day of your life starting today. You can listen to your favorite music or your favorite Podcast on your iPod but walk you must. If it is rainy, walk on a treadmill; if it snowing, go to a public place where there is covered space for walking. You should never miss your daily walk. If you do this, and do no other physical exercise, you have already built a foundation for healthy living.

Alternate Nasal Breathing

There are many breathing exercises, but alternate nasal breathing, also called *Nadi Shodana Pranayama,* is without a parallel. It is also a very simple exercise. To start, sit in a comfortable posture. Exhale and inhale repeatedly through both the nostrils keeping a paper tissue handy in case of need. Now lift your right hand to your nostrils and place your thumb on your right nostril and your ring finger on your left nostril. Keeping the left nostril open completely block your right nostril. Inhale through the left nostril. Hold your breath as long possible and then gradually and fully exhale through the right nostril. In the next round, inhale through the right nostril while keeping your left nostril blocked fully and when you cannot keep the breath any longer completely exhale through the left nostril. This alternating process should be repeated 5-6 times every morning. This technique helps us connect the left and right sides of the brain. We also learn to regulate the flow of *prana* (the life energy).

Conscious Breathing

Conscious breathing is exactly what its name suggests—we are consciously aware of the breathing process and as a result we are able to guide it. Conscious breathing helps in integrating mind and body. The breathing cycle itself has four components:

- Exhalation—moving the breath outward
- Inhalation—moving the breath inward
- Suspension—suspending breathing
- Retention—retaining the breath after inhalation

In *pranayama* or conscious breathing based on Patanjali's *Yoga Sutras*, the main emphasis is on the exhalation because of its use of the lower abdomen. You must completely exhale before beginning to inhale. These four components of breathing are well integrated and they do impact one another. A very long inhale causes exhale to become short and fast. Retention (after the inhale) helps develop the inhale itself. Excessive retention can disturb exhalation, shortening it and disrupting its smoothness. Similarly, excessive suspension can disturb the inhalation. While selecting a particular breathing ratio, you must take into account your physical comfort. Under no circumstances, you should force yourself or cause stress. Breathing practice can be done standing upright, seated, sitting in a chair, or lying down.

Some people believe that because breathing is something that we do all the time, learning to breathe well and accurately requires no effort. This is a wrong notion. Conscious breathing is a three-step process. First, we need to clear our head of all distracting thoughts and emotions. Therefore, play with the thought: *I have no head. If I have no head, how can there be any thoughts?* Second, when thoughts do not exist, there is emptiness, but in this emptiness there is real and genuine fullness. Once the thoughts disappear, then we "focus" on our inhalation and exhalation, suspension and retention, as described above. In the last step, we go beyond mere "focus": We become the breath. Nothing remains of us except the breath. A few minutes spent on this three-step process every day will regulate our breathing and will make us more conscious, more awake, and more focused individuals.

Vipassana Meditation

Vipassana in the Theravada Buddhist tradition means clearly seeing things as they are. It is believed that Buddha discovered and taught vipassana meditation. In the modern times, vipassana owes its popularity to the collaborative workings of two great teachers, Sayagyi U Ba Khin and S.N. Goenka in the Theravada tradition. In Mahayana tradition, however, vipassana is meditating on two truths—the world, as we know it, and the absolute truth—the world without any inherent existence (emptiness or *sunyata*).

Vipassana is a non-sectarian technique. You don't have to be a Buddhist to practice the technique. In fact, it requires no religious beliefs at all. Based on S.N. Goenka's teachings, vipassana involves the following five elements: (1) Self-observation—observing your own self in all its facets. (2) Paying attention to the deep interconnection between the mind and the body. What sensations are we experiencing? This involves reflecting on physical, mental and emotional experiences without making any judgments. (3) Seeing the connection between our actions and their consequences. Realizing how our own actions are responsible for our sufferings. (4) Knowing and putting into practice three foundational truths about vipassana: moral conduct *(sila)*, concentration of mind *(samadhi)*, and the wisdom of insight *(panna or prajna)*. The practitioner stays in a detached observation of the mind-body connection from moment to moment. (5) During periods of vipassana practice, the practitioners are required to observe five abstentions: precepts which are in the nature of no killing of any living creatures; no stealing; no sexual activity; no telling of lies; and no consumption of intoxicants.

Here is a simplified version of vipassana for daily practice: Sit in a quiet place. The exercise can be completed in as short a time as 15 minutes or it can go on for a much longer time. You can sit on the ground or in a comfortable chair, but you must keep the head and the back straight. Keep your eyes closed. Stay connected with your mind and body—your breathing and your body sensations. If thoughts arise, look at them as an observer; feel them; follow them, but not own them. Go wherever they lead you. If emotions arise, experience them as an observer too. Observe deeply, beyond the confines of visible reality. Feel the emptiness where no thing has any meaning. Actually, there are no "things" in emptiness. Do not try to solve a problem. This is not a problem-solving session. Resolve to lead a moral life informed by vipassana's code of conduct.

Mountain Pose

Grounding has to do with creating a strong bond between our feet and the earth we stand on. We do this through another simple Yoga exercise called the Mountain Pose, also called *Tad Asana*. What do we see when we look at a mountain? The first thing that comes across is the strength and stability. It is fully grounded. Nothing short of a big earthquake can move it. We replicate this quality through our standing posture. We stand firmly with our feet joined together, with our lower body in a straight line, shoulders relaxed, chin slightly raised, arms hanging comfortably on the sides, and the gaze fixed straight ahead. The secret of a good mountain pose is how powerfully and elegantly we manifest our inner strength and stability in our outer body. Once we got the posture right, we should inhale and exhale at least five time. These should be full and deep breaths, no shallow breathing.

The Importance of Personal Organization

For those at the ground level, personal organization is a great challenge. If we can't find the car key, the engine would not start. This is a metaphorical truth about our life. Living a routine but highly disorganized life is an invitation to disaster. Lack of organizing skills is not like a cognitive disability. Most often, extremely bright people are very disorganized. Its genesis more often lies in an attitude to life that is casual and which is fuelled by procrastination: postponing things until they become an emergency. In my view, there are five stepping stones to personal organization:

1. Know your purpose in life. You are not an accident. No one is. There was a reason nature gave us life. We can never know the invisible plan, but we can start asking some important questions: What do I want to achieve in life? What is my vision? What do I need to get in order to realize my vision? What did I do today, yesterday, last week, last month, and last year that helped me move towards my vision? If we are not asking these kind of questions, we are planning to live from one crisis situation to another. And that's certainly not a good use of something as precious as our life.

2. Use a diary or a calendar to organize your daily life events—your appointments, to-do lists, addresses, and phone numbers. You can use an electronic gadget to do the same. Plan everything, but stay flexible. Keep an open mind. Do not become slave of a gadget. Think of the strategic advantage you are gaining by how you are spending your time. You can be in the meetings the whole day, but accomplish nothing much of great value. This brings us to the question of priorities. Establish your priorities every day. Anything that is not within the purview of your highest priorities at any given time should be receiving only marginal attention. Stay focused on the most important outcomes.
3. Modern communication technologies bring us extraordinary conveniences, but they have also given birth to many new distractions that did not exist before these technologies were invented. Telephone, especially the cell or mobile phone, could be a great time waster. People do not realize how much time they waste in highly unproductive telephone conversations. Web surfing is another positive tool that is likely to be misused. While going to web forums and posting your views on issues of the day have some legitimacy, when taken to an extreme it's a dangerous pastime. The same is true of e-mails. It is the best productivity tool ever invented, but writing long e-mails where a simple two line message could be the best response, is another significant time waster. It is a great idea to have some time during the day when you are not on-line, sending or reading e-mails. The world would not come to an end if certain e-mails are not read as they poured into your inbox. Try to keep a part of your weekend gadget-free so that you are able to pursue other interests.
4. Organize your work area: keep the papers in their proper places. Open and answer your snail mail. Pay

your bills on time. If something needs to be done, it is best done early. Procrastination is not free; in today's world there is a heavy financial cost attached to it in the form of penalties and late fees.

5. Although life in the modern world seems like a ride on a roller coaster in the sense that we are engaged in some activity or the other all the time, the richness and beauty of life lies in free and open spaces. We need to look for and cherish those moments of peace and quietude that provide us spiritual sustenance. In order to organize our life and our priorities, we need to have these moments when we do nothing and think of nothing in particular. This could be 15 minutes of reflection or meditation in the morning or stretches of 5 minute breaks when we stop everything—just being still while we are deeply connected with our heart and soul.

A Few Other Things

Learn to pay attention to small things and practice active listening. Not listening or listening while you are evaluating what the other is saying is nothing short of a social disability. Various studies have shown that the most effective managers and team leaders, above all, are exceptionally good listeners. Developing strong inner focus makes us better listeners.

Any effort to cultivate self-critical attitude and actively seeking constructive criticism from others is a great habit. People who are sensitive to criticism or who only love to collect glowing tributes will have problems in improving themselves. Constructive feedback from friends and work colleagues is a valuable tool for sustaining a self-improvement plan.

Pursue right occupation and a supportive work environment with a view to having productive interactions with other people. Never choose an occupation or a job if your heart is not in it. Don't do it to please other people. You need to follow a path that energizes you, that makes you passionate about achieving extraordinary success in your chosen profession. Once you are in an occupation that appeals to you, learn to work with other people. Be a good teacher or a mentor to younger workers. Reach out to those who need help. We can practice compassion at our workplace by doing simple things. And in the long run these simple things yield us greater benefits because these days organizations are promoting only those workers to higher level positions who are exemplary role models and mentors, who are improving the quality of results not through sheer hard work but through innovation and by engaging others for delivering quality results.

Create a supportive home environment involving caring and compassionate relationships with other family members. It is the first business of every adult, male or female. Your job is not the only important thing in your life. You need to seek a better balance between personal and professional dimensions, between work and play.

Manage your finances wisely. Save for the future. Invest cautiously. There are people out there who are all the time thinking of schemes of robbing you of your hard earned cash. Beware of their schemes.

Pursue hobbies and interests aimed at enhancing self-esteem and providing a feeling of fulfillment like writing a journal, writing poetry, drawing and painting, music and dancing. The more we express ourselves through any of these hobbies, greater is the opportunity for us to develop our inner self.

Never feel shy of seeking help when needed. Problems do not disappear simply because we deny their existence. Seek psychological counseling aimed at easing the burden of difficult childhood issues and steps needed to promote healthy parental or spousal relationships.

Visit places of historic or spiritual significance and seek connectedness with sacred places. These journeys are very rewarding and greatly assist in our spiritual development.

A Poetic Interlude

The Present Moment

There are two worlds
for us to lead our life.

The world within us is bigger
a[illegible] brighter.
It has no boundaries,
no fences, no barriers —
it is a big open world
for us to travel,
move around, stop and go.
There are no soldiers
guarding the iron gates —
no prisons with concrete walls.
It is a world where there is
little pain or suffering.
It is a world of great serenity —
it has the music
of slow moving symphonies.
It is a world of meditation,
of being in touch with infinity.

If this world ceases to exist,
we would lose touch
with our own sacredness
and spirituality.

The world outside is much bigger
and brighter,
but its bigness reminds us
of our own smallness.
Sometimes its brightness is too oppressive
for our naked eyes.
It is a world of people,
some known but many unknown.
It is a world where people wear masks
of politeness through which
real faces and real people are hard to see.

It is a world where people play games
with words.
They don't mean what they say
and not say what they mean.
It is a world that raises questions
for which there are only incomplete answers.
The feeling of incompleteness
haunts us and
makes us hide in the empty corners
of space
where no one can find us.
Good or bad, nice or nasty —
this is the real world
with a real sun and stars.
And this is the world
where we need to stay in touch
with the present moment.

Our hidden self is the work
of these two worlds:
internal and external,
inner and outer.

When we are fully in touch
with the inner world
while mindful of the outer,
we understand the way things are,
and in this balancing act ends
our striving for defensiveness.

When we master the present moment
and withdraw into our deeper selves,
we express ourselves creatively
and meaningfully, and it is in this
present moment of convergence
of inner and outer that
our true self finds a voice —
loud and clear.

From *A Moment in the Universe* (2006, pp. 19-21)

1. A SUMMARY OF KEY IDEAS

- The single most important indicator of good grounding is sound physical health, which is the function of healthy nourishment and regular physical exercise. When both these things are not taken care of at the same time, health starts to deteriorate.
- Once we are airborne and reach an altitude of 30-40,000 feet we see more and our perspective is much wider. The same is true of life. The higher levels of consciousness enrich our perspective and thus we become more effective human beings.
- Self-awareness is our only way of knowing the good and the evil that resides in our heart.
- Lack of proper self-organization is a great challenge at the ground level. Typically low performers suffer the consequences of poor organization.
- There is an endless variety of physical exercises, but there is nothing as simple and as satisfying as walking.
- Conscious breathing is exactly what its name suggests—we are consciously aware of the breathing process and as a result we are able to guide it. Conscious breathing helps in integrating mind and body.
- Vipassana is a non-sectarian technique. You don't have to be a Buddhist to practice the technique. In fact, it requires no religious beliefs at all.
- Any effort to cultivate self-critical attitude and actively seeking constructive criticism from others is a great habit.
- Problems do not disappear simply because we deny their existence.
- The present moment is a moment of convergence—of inner and outer in which our true self finds a voice.

2 Our Emotional Self

THE MAP

The birth of emotional self brings with it a sense of balance between the inner and the outer energies that shape our life. Emotions arise from deep within us. No one really knows where they come from. It seems that we have a sea of emotions within us, a constantly functioning sprinkler system that throws up new emotions every minute of our waking life. Emotions show up even in our dreams and often give us nightmares. Their complexity often makes us pause and think about the inner workings of our mind. This is a radical new development for most people because at the ground level our attention was so much focused on the challenges and threats posed by the outside world.

A Typology of Emotions

Emotions by their nature come and go. They are like waves of the ocean. They come and recede. There are some emotions that we experience more frequently than others. The following chart identifies 36 positive and negative emotions that most normal human beings would experience within short spans of time. The duration and intensity of each emotion, however, differs from one person to another.

Most Frequently Experienced Emotions

Appreciation	Fear
Composure	Agitation
Bliss	Anxiety
Calmness	Annoyance
Happiness	Concern

(Contd...)

Contentment	Depression
Confidence	Despair
Curiosity	Detachment
Enthusiasm	Disappointment
Excitement	Pain
Inspiration	Guilt
Gratitude	Fatigue
Optimism	Frustration
Pleasure	Helplessness
Pride	Hostility
Satisfaction	Hatred
Affection	Loneliness
Fascination	Sadness

Because of the variety and their latent ability to do good or bad, there is need for managing emotions. The management in this case, however, is not "direction" or "control." Generally, the more we try to control our emotions, the more uncontrollable they become. One strategy that works well is that of mentally distancing ourself from the ebb and flow of emotions. In practical terms, it means adopting an "observer stance"—being an observer of what is going on inside our heart, just noticing but keeping our normal state of mind.

According to one survey, the most successful CEOs of large corporations have one thing in common: they are very competent in managing the flow of their emotions. They do not jump on the couch when they are happy, and they do not show their intense grief in public. It does not mean that they are trying to hide the authentic expression of their feelings; what they are doing is trying to manage the "self and nonself" emotional boundaries in view of their public stature. When you are in a position of authority, you can very easily impact the environment by sending out unguarded emotional signals.

Relationship as Energy

People at the emotional level get moving, which is quite a contrast from the ground level where lack of mobility is such a constraint. This mobility has a lot to do with our ability to build relationships. Alan Watts, Buddhist teacher and philosopher, used to say that if we place one ball in the outer space, we would never know whether it has any motion because there will be nothing else to compare this ball with. But if we place a second ball close to the first ball, then we would know whether the first ball is in motion or is stationary. In this case, we would have established a relationship that would tell us something about their latent energies (motion is a form of energy). Our entire existence is made of this relational energy.

Resistance to change decreases significantly as people are able to see themselves in relation to others. Emotions play a very important role at level two, and our personal effectiveness depends very much on how we deal with them. As long as people understand their emotional states, they are able to make a big jump in getting clarity on their inner motivations.

A Need for Boundary Management

Emotions require competent boundary management. I have the right to be angry or sad, but I must learn to keep it to myself. Lack of boundary management often leads to complications in interpersonal relationships. Emotional dependency always results from poor boundary management. Approval seeking behavior is another manifestation of the same problem.

Emotions and Sexuality

In many ways, the first experience of mating with another person makes people think that life is not simply pain and suffering. Healthy expression of one's sexuality opens possibilities for more balanced personal development. Yet when sexual energy is uncontrolled and unchecked, it turns itself into an addiction or an obsession, which is potentially destructive.

Values and Needs

Emotional level creates feelings of outer fullness and wholesomeness, of being fully connected with deepest desires of finding a place for self and seeking the companionship of another. There is less guilt about finding ways to enhancing one's sense of joy in everything, including matters pertaining to sexuality. At a more advanced level, sexuality could manifest itself as the celebration of a loving relationship, a carefully orchestrated embrace of male and female principles. But initially it is more of an obsession; a way of satisfying a physical need. Emotions are rarely stable; there are peaks and valleys of living experiences that create joy and abandonment as well as pain and frustration. There is symbolic death and martyrdom in the pursuit of a pleasurable life inasmuch as one dies to one's peak experiences and is reborn to go through the cycle once again.

Needs at emotional level center around satisfaction—physical, mental, emotional, and psychological. But these needs can be met only by moving outside of one's physical space, one's comfort zone. Personal boundaries are, therefore, expanded to include other people. Change and movement that new relationships bring into one's life open up new opportunities for learning, and the new learning allows satisfaction of higher level needs.

Communication and Leadership Style

Communication is more direct and purposeful. Words carry emotional content that was missing before. The focus of communication may include diversity of interests, including issues of personal well-being, intimacy, and material prosperity. Favorite expressions include: "I have a feeling... I don't want to hurt your feelings.... We need to work together...." The language of platitudes and clichés is commonly used. The person really tries hard not to show emotions or hurt others' feelings. At a deeper level, there is a strong desire to be liked by others. Therefore, it is normal for the person to seek others' approval before taking any action. Change is managed smoothly but not without some effort. Failure to change could be frustrating. Individual perspective now includes the second person, which means there is the ability to put oneself in another's shoes. The birth of empathy as an emotional competence is one of the major accomplishments at this level. Conflict management could still be a problem because rational ability to examine different viewpoints is not yet fully developed, and emotionally driven conflict resolution brings mixed results at best.

LIVING STORIES

Kumar and Sheila live in two different metropolitan cities, several hundred miles apart. They have some similarities in the sense that both of them earned degrees in engineering with reasonably good grades. Both of them have semi-technical managerial jobs in large corporations. But both of them operate with different levels of effectiveness as revealed by their life stories.

Kumar has always been conscious of maintaining a healthy body. Proper diet and exercise are things that he has always attached great importance to and he has taken care of his physical fitness at all times. He has a probing mind and asks lot of questions. He has no problem in admitting his ignorance about things that he does not know. Recently, when his wife suggested that they replace an old 27 inch TV with a new Plasma TV, he admitted that he didn't know enough about Plasma technology to make an informed decision. But he surfed the web and collected lots of information about new flat-screen TVs and eventually he decided to buy a 42 inch Plasma TV from an internet retailer. He respected the wishes of his wife, but he used his analytical skills to narrow his options to obtain the best price-performance combination.

At his work, Kumar gets lots of good press for his emotional stability and his ability to stay calm under the most stressful conditions. It is not that he does not experience strong emotions; he has mastered the art of being an "observer" of his own emotional state. He knows when he is angry and, therefore, he is quickly able to control his anger.

He has a deeply loving relationship with his wife. They have postponed having a child for now. They enjoy having a warm and intimate relationship, which is not just limited to sexual attraction, but a relationship in which there is lot of caring for the other. It is this kind of nurturing attitude that has allowed their relationship to deepen and become more authentic. Both Mr. and Mrs. Kumar are looking for ways to improve themselves and become more effective. They have no hesitation in trying out new things—new outfits, new gadgets, and even new restaurants. But they do think a lot about maximizing the return on their investment—money, time, and tradeoffs.

Sheila's story is quite the opposite.

When she was in college, she started to smoke a few cigarettes each day because she wanted to make some kind of a statement to her parents who were very controlling and who never allowed her the freedom to make her own choices. But smoking became a permanent habit and now she smokes a pack or two a day. She has resolved several times to give up smoking but without any success. Some years ago, she decided not to marry the boy her parents had selected for her. Since then she has entered into short term alliances with several men. For the last one year, she has been meeting men through on-line dating services. She starts a relationship because she finds a man attractive, but the real physical contact leaves her very unsatisfied. As a result, she has developed negative feelings about men she has known and about her own emotional self.

At work, she is known to show great sensitivity to gender issues and sees a gender bias in almost every situation. Her direct reports have given her feedback about her mood swings; she can be nice and nasty within a matter of minutes. Lately, she has had serious fights and conflicts with her work colleagues and personal friends. As a result, she has lost a good deal of sympathy and support. She has also been accused of practicing emotional manipulation. In short, every day ushers in a new challenge. She always wanted to be a happy and a carefree person, but that's not the way things have turned out for her.

What's going on here?

Kumar is aware of his emotions and as such he shows great self-mastery in dealing with others. On the other hand, Sheila has never tried to find out what she really wants in life. Kumar attaches great importance to building a warm and self-sustaining relationship with his spouse. Sheila has focused on physical pleasure as the glue that joins men and women in relationship. But she also finds physical contact very unsatisfying because there is not enough emotional support for it. Kumar has used his intellect to channel his emotions; Sheila is using temporary emotions to deal with long-term issues. Kumar values good health; Sheila is damaging her health through her addiction. Kumar is a people-centered manager; Sheila is exploiting others for her own needs.

What can Sheila do to renew herself?

First and foremost, she must find her life mission and purpose. What does she *really* want from her life? She has serious behavioral issues that she must address with strong will and determination. For the sake of her long-term health she has to consider giving up smoking. She needs deeper understanding of her emotions: why she feels certain ways in some situations; and how can she enhance her self-awareness. A more viable philosophy about human relationships would be of help to her. You can't get more from a relationship than you are willing to invest in it. Using other people for one's pleasure does not help in the long run.

DEVELOPMENT CHALLENGES

Emotions and creativity

Emotions release our creative energies, but unfortunately we tend to express them in limited ways such as pursuit of pleasure for its own sake, or building relationships on the basis of personal need satisfaction. This limiting view of creativity turns frustrating because what is attained in the moment is really shortlived.

Coping with negative emotions

Emotions are a double-edged sword. Positive emotions provide rich nourishment for the body and soul, but negative emotions cause stress and drain our energies. At this level, the individual has limited control over how the emotional life is experienced or managed. Some emotions like selfishness can make us "controlling" in terms of our communication and leadership styles. We tend to approach others with a strong need of our own ego satisfaction that only yields very limited results.

The presence of negative emotions often creates feelings of frustration, alienation, and hopelessness. People can get upset by simple events in their lives like flunking an examination and contemplating suicide as an escape. Similarly, one broken relationship can make people think that everything is lost and that life has no meaning left in it. This happens because emotions tend to narrow our focus to just one event or one little thing. People can go crazy laughing at something really silly and then go into deep depression after an event that is sad but not really a great tragedy.

Emotions and spiritual life

People at this level have a vague idea of a spiritual life. As a result, all spiritual aspirations are soon frustrated because the mind doesn't yet have the ability to conceptualize spirituality as a living force in one's life. Spirituality, therefore, tends to get mixed-up with meaningless ritualism.

Emotions and insecurity

Emotions can produce insecurity for want of a strong anchor. People may worry about their health when they are perfectly healthy; they may worry about money when they have enough cash in the bank. More of anything doesn't equal more satisfaction.

DEVELOPMENTAL INTERVENTIONS

Swimming

Swimming is a highly productive recreational activity. In fact, it is one of the oldest recreational activities known to mankind. Our ancestors had to learn swimming for their self-preservation. As roughly 70% of our body is made up of water, swimming has a natural attraction for the body. One unique characteristic of swimming is that it provides synchronized exercise for the whole body—hands, arms, and legs; front, back, and the two sides. It is a great option for those of us who have problem walking due to arthritic joints. Swimming is an excellent relaxation and a full body workout as also a life saving activity. Staying in water for non-swimmers too is highly soothing experience, especially after a walk. Swimming is best learned during formative years because as the body ages, it loses its flexibility and strength—the two essential attributes of a good swimmer. If you know swimming and you have access to a swimming pool, or a safe natural water body spending 30 minutes a day swimming is an excellent workout.

Mindfulness

There are many ways of meditating, but none so simple and straightforward as mindfulness practice. Jon Kabat-Zinn, a physician by training, has done more to popularize mindfulness than anyone else. Starting with his book *Full Catastrophe Living* in 1990, Jon has built a strong foundation of theory and research that has helped thousands to find a simple technique to gain peace of mind and inner strength. Before we come to the actual practice, which is quite simple, it is important to understand some basic principles that form the foundation of mindfulness practice. In Jon's words, these are: (1) *non-judging*—you have to be an impartial observer to your own experience; (2) *patience*—you have to be open to each moment; (3) *beginner's mind*—you have to see as if for the first time; (4) *trust*—you have to put trust in your own intuition even if you make some mistakes on the way; (5) *non-striving*—you are not doing anything but paying attention to whatever is happening (6) *acceptance*—you have to come around to a willingness to see things as they are; and (7) *letting go*—you are letting things be, accepting things as they are.

The simplified process of mindfulness meditation covers five stages: (1) Select a quiet place in your home where you will not be disturbed for 15-20 minutes. Decorate this place to make it more appealing. You can sit cross-legged on the carpet or on a cushion or on a chair. You can even lie down on your back. Be completely relaxed. It is advisable to keep your eyes closed. (2) One very important part of your posture is that your back is kept straight but not stiff. (3) Become aware of your breathing. Awareness of breathing is not the same thing as thinking about it. Feel your breath. You can feel your breath in your nostrils, in your chest or in your belly. Feeling your breath in your chest or belly is much better. (4) Do not let your thoughts wander away. If they wander away, please bring your attention back to your breath. (5) You can start this practice for a very short time—3 to 5 minutes initially. But as you gain more confidence, you can increase the duration to 15-20 minutes.

One important part of this practice is that it is not limited to one place. Once you are comfortable in establishing a relationship with your breath, then you are free to practice mindfulness anywhere, anytime, in-between breaks at work, and traveling by plane or train. What you are doing in this practice is simply breathing mindfully. There is plethora of information on physiological (health-related), mental, emotional, and spiritual benefits of mindfulness in books on the subject and in websites so that I have not found it necessary to repeat that information here.

Body Scan

Body Scan is a good complement to mindfulness practice. It was again Jon Kabat-Zinn who has popularized its use. According to Jon, "The idea in scanning your body is to actually *feel* each region you focus on and linger there with your mind right *on* it or *in* it. You breathe in *to* and out *from* each region a few times and then let go of it in your mind's eye as your attention moves on to the next region" (1990, p. 77).

The process is as follows: Start with the toes of the left foot and slowly move up the foot and leg, feeling the sensations and directing the breath inward and outward from different regions of your leg. From the pelvis, go to the toes of the right foot and move up the right leg back to the pelvis. Then move up through the torso, through the lower back and abdomen, the upper back and chest, and the shoulders. Then go to the fingers of both hands and move up simultaneously in both arms, returning to the shoulders. Finally, move through the neck and throat, and the regions of the face, the back of the head, and the top of the head.

Body Scan is an excellent way of getting in touch with our body. Our body is always trying to get our attention, but for the most part we are very busy with other things to pay any attention to it. If we can spend some quality time to listen to different regions and organs of our body, we can deepen our relationship with them. Also any part of the body that we pay attention to will feel better. Our attention, which is nothing other than our consciousness, is a great healer. Body scan should be done at least once a week or as needed. The complete process takes no more than 10-15 minutes.

Emotional Scan

Dr. Reuven Bar-On is a leading Emotional Intelligence (EQ) thinker and researcher. EQi, the instrument designed by him to measure EQ, contains 15 EQ factors, arranged in five major categories. We can use these factors to scan our emotions on a daily basis. Emotional scan is like body scan, but instead of parts of our body we focus our attention on our emotional parts (experiences). Systematically, we pick up one emotional factor and then use the following recommended questions for self-reflection. When we are finished with one factor, we go to another one. Don't try to scan all the 15 factors in one sitting. For proper self-reflection limited to one sitting, I suggest randomly selecting two or three factors.

Intrapersonal EQ

Self-Regard: Am I feeling sure of myself? Do I feel fulfilled and satisfied? Is there a feeling of personal inadequacy or inferiority?

Emotional Self-Awareness: Do I know what drives me? Am I connected with my underlying feelings, assumptions, and values? Do I communicate my feelings to others? Do I stay aligned with my true motivations? Do I sometime feel emotionally drained? Can I differentiate between one emotion and the other?

Assertiveness: Do I express my feelings properly? Do I share my thoughts openly? Do I stand up and speak for my beliefs? Do I show my assertiveness as aggressiveness?

Independence: Can I think on my own while being sensitive to the views of the others? Am I a victim of "group think" at times? Am I self-directive? Am I emotionally dependent on anyone?

Self-Actualization: Do I fully use my latent talents and abilities? Am I living up to my potential? Am I true to my nature? Am I achieving the higher levels of my effectiveness?

Interpersonal EQ

Empathy: Can I put myself into the shoes of others? Am I motivated to pay attention to others? Do I understand the distinction between sympathy and empathy?

Social Responsibility: Do I recognize and assume responsibility for the well-being of others? Am I interpersonally sensitive? Do I nurture antisocial attitudes in others and in my own self?

Interpersonal Relationships: Am I able to establish and maintain mutually satisfying relationships? Do I believe in mutual give and take?

Stress Management EQ

Stress Tolerance: Do I feel stressed out? Am I able to cope with stress? Do I engage in fight or flight responses?

Impulse Control: Do I resist the temptation to act or do something without thinking through the consequences? Can I stay composed in the face of aggressive moves by others?

Adaptability EQ

Reality Testing: Can I immediately size-up a situation? What is the evidence that what I feel or think is real (based on real evidence)? Who else sees the reality the same way as I do?

Flexibility: Am I quick to adapt to new situations? Am I ready or willing to yield to the influence of others?

Problem Solving: Can I define problems as problems? Do I know how to analyze a problem situation? Do I look at alternative courses of action before selecting a final course of action?

General Mood EQ

Optimism: Do I take defeat as temporary or final? Do I tend to look at the bright side of things? Do I see the glass as half full or half empty?

Happiness: Am I satisfied with my life? Do I like to have fun? Do I live in a happy state of mind? Am I happy or try to be right most of the time?

A Poetic Interlude

Relationships

To be is to be related.
J. Krishnamurti

I look at myself in the mirror
of relationships
and I see myself as I am.

There are all kind of relationships,
some short lived and others
that last a lifetime.

There are relationships
in which I'm giving,
and truly reaching out.

There are relationships
in which I seek and get
endless self-gratification.

There are relationships marked by
care and compassion, always protecting
the integrity of self and the other.

There are relationships
in which I destroy the blazing field
of tulips in a minute.

Good or bad, nourishing or destroying,
a relationship is an integral part
of the geography of my being.

Helping or hurting, living or dying
it tells me something about myself,
and how I relate with the rest.

And when I look at myself in the mirror
of relationships I see myself
the way I really am, now.

My creative life begins with this perception
of all my relationships and what they tell me
indirectly about who I really am.

From *A Moment in the Universe* (2006, pp. 9-10)

2. A SUMMARY OF KEY IDEAS

- It seems that we have a sea of emotions within us, a constantly functioning sprinkler system that throws up new emotions every minute of our waking life.
- Resistance to change decreases significantly as people are able to see themselves in relation to others.
- Emotions require competent boundary management. I have the right to be angry or sad, but I must learn to keep it to myself.
- Emotions are a double-edged sword. Positive emotions provide rich nourishment for the body and soul, but negative emotions cause stress and drain our energies.
- One unique characteristic of swimming is that it provides synchronized exercise for the whole body—hands, arms, and legs; front, back, and the two sides.
- Once you are comfortable in establishing a relationship with your breath, then you are free to practice mindfulness anywhere, anytime, in-between breaks at work, and traveling by plane or train. What you are doing in this practice is simply breathing mindfully.
- Scanning our emotions from time to time is as important as scanning our body. There is a close connection between emotional well-being and physical well-being.
- A relationship is a mirror in which we can see ourselves.

3 The Road to Empowerment

THE MAP

Power is the storehouse of raw energy, sometimes called "fire in the belly." It is an appropriate symbol for the phenomenal physical strength in human body. In addition to its physical manifestation, power has a psychological dimension. The lack of physical strength can make us dependent on others. The lack of psychological strength, on the other hand, can make us psychologically dependent on others. The latter condition is actually worse than the former. It is also true that sheer presence of any form of power is not enough. The outcome, any goal that we seek, depends on how creatively this energy is harnessed. By using our personal power we can build new avenues for our progress or we can destroy within a short time what has taken us years to build.

The Power of Self-Esteem

When we feel empowered, we actually get a voice. We can then speak our mind without fear of retribution. Our greatest gain perhaps is self-esteem, which is the single most valuable attribute that makes us a fully effective and fully functioning human being. People may have good looks; they may have an intelligent mind, but if they lack self-esteem, they will end up going nowhere. Psychologist Nathaniel Brandon, who has written several books on self-esteem, including *The Power of Self-Esteem* (1992, p. 8) defines self-esteem "as the experience that we are appropriate to life and to the requirements of life. More specifically: (1) Confidence in our ability to think and to cope with the basic challenges of life. (2) Confidence in our right to be happy, the feeling of being worthy, deserving, entitled to assert our needs and wants and to enjoy the fruits of our efforts." What this definition says is something very simple: life brings many challenges—some great, others more trivial. Whatever be the nature of the challenge faced by us, we should be able to stand-up firmly and respond with confidence. The challenge may be being a confident participant in a social gathering in the company of people who are more accomplished. Or it may be addressing a group of people who are critical and demanding. In all these situations, self-esteem is our greatest asset. If we feel good about ourselves; if we can talk about ourselves in an open and candid manner, we can make our presence felt, and we can make an impact.

Writing on the importance of self-esteem in today's workplace, Brandon identifies five essential prerequisites. These are: (1) Trusting yourself—trusting that you are adequate for the job. You can think, you can decide, and you can implement. You don't need someone's opinion to know that you are okay. (2) Approaching others in a benevolent spirit—approaching others with respect, without judging others, and always acting in a spirit of acceptance. (3) The conviction that you are worthy of success—not believing in chance, but firmly believing that you deserve success, happiness, trust, respect, and love. (4) Feeling as if you make a difference—firmly believing that your individual contribution makes a lot of difference to the work in your team, in your department, and in your organization. (5) Continuing to learn and improve. Continuous learning is the cornerstone of all human development.

When power is improperly used it leads to several complications. People may appear as dominating, controlling, and competitive the way they use power in relation to others. When people view you as arrogant, that one perception, can radically change your relationship with them. When we do not use our personal power effectively, we may appear passive, lacking energy, and lacking self-esteem. There is, therefore, need for balance on how we cultivate and use our power.

Will Power

German philosopher Friedrich Nietzsche corrected a view held by his compatriot, Arthur Schopenhauer, that all living things were motivated and sustained by what he called a "will to live." Nietzsche maintained that it was "will to power" and not just "will to live" that was needed in order to grow and sustain oneself. "Will to power" is also a "free will" because it is based on internally motivated actions and not on those which are caused by external pressure. In recent times, psychologists have used the term "internal motivation" to convey the same idea. People freely make decisions to take up challenges that are extremely difficult. They work very hard to train themselves. They go through lot of pain and suffering in the process. And ultimately they succeed in accomplishing something which was until then considered as something impossible.

Two well-known stories to demonstrate the importance of will power and internal motivation are about Mount Everest and one-mile run. Edmund Hillary and Sherpa Tenzing were the first humans ever to climb the Mount Everest in 1953. But within 50 years (by the end of 2003) nearly two thousand people had climbed the Everest (and nearly two hundred had died in their attempts to do so). Until 1954, no one had run a mile under 4 minutes. Roger Banister, a British athlete, was the first one to accomplish this feat. But within few months another person improved the record by one second. And by mid-1999 18 other athletes had run a mile under four minutes. Similar examples are found in all areas of human endeavor. Pioneers pave the way and others follow. But in every case there is a story of exceptional will power and fortitude that rejects the reality and thereby motivates others to follow in their footsteps. From a spiritual standpoint, there is a view that when one person learns to accomplish a particular task it becomes easier for others to do the same. It seems that when one person opens a new door, spirit keeps it open for others to pass through the same door.

Values and Needs

Power is an interesting blend of material richness and raw idealism. Self-esteem expressed through assertive behaviors together with self-confidence and freedom of choice is highly valued. The warrior archetype—representing physical strength and the ability to protect, defend, and fight for one's rights—is the positive driving force giving one confidence and courage, but on the down side there may be inner emptiness that no amount of physical valor can fill. These contradictions make one roar like a lion at one time, and be subservient like a mouse at another. What one wants to do is to succeed, but very rarely is there a clear concept of success. As a result, doubt coupled with skepticism diminishes the positive energy giving rise to despondency and pessimism.

The gaining of personal identity and showing it off is the greatest need. Ego inflation is a common occurrence together with overbearing self-confidence. The positive outcome is the emergence of selfhood, but on the negative side there is the problem of misuse of power, especially actions devoid of ethical or moral content.

Communication and Leadership Style

People who feel empowered use power-driven communication and generally seek compliance. The relations between the one who is wielding power and the other against whom the power is being used are generically unequal. Common expressions include: "I want you to do this.... Listen to me what I'm saying.... There will be consequences if you don't follow orders...." The leader is authoritative and commanding, but generally ineffective in terms of listening to others and showing sensitivity. Learning generally takes a back seat disabling the person in terms of managing change.

Third person perspective, looking at self through the eyes of a third person, shows up here for the first time in both positive and negative aspects. The positive aspect has to do with the recognition of third parties (absent selves) who are being talked about, but the negative aspect is linear causality, the straight-line cause and effect thinking and the possible use of force to solve all disagreements. We have often heard people say, "I don't care what people think of me. I will do what I want to." There is a strong tendency, therefore, to manage interpersonal conflict through sheer force, which is imposition of one person's viewpoint on the other, resulting in hidden resentment and creative non-compliance. Personal loyalty is thus valued more than competence. Power driven leaders are obsessed with their legacy, but the truth is that they are soon forgotten once they are out of power.

LIVING STORIES

Let us look at two stories—Jennifer and Mark's.

Jennifer comes from a large family—three sisters and two brothers. Her father worked as a supervisor in the county's sanitation department, earning enough for a decent living, but no extra cash for vacations in the Caribbean or fancy dresses or other forms of expensive entertainment. Jennifer knew it even when she was very young that she would have to work hard to make a place for herself in life. She attended a community college on a scholarship and then she went on to earn her graduate degree in psychology in a prestigious state university.

She took up several jobs on her way to establishing herself in a career, but finally settled into the position of an HR manager in a large energy related corporation. What kept her going was her immense inner strength, the sense of power within and high levels of personal energy. Although she always sought high outcomes, she never compromised her self-respect and self-esteem to gain anything. She became a strong role model for her younger sisters and brothers, who went on to distinguish themselves in different occupations. She always felt a sense of gratitude towards her parents who had encouraged her to be a strong person.

Jennifer made it a practice to sit for periods of 25-30 minutes a day each morning for self-reflection. As a result, she gained great insights into her own strengths and weaknesses. She also developed a proactive attitude towards life that made her a highly successful manager. At 26 years, Jennifer looks forward to building a strong career and a strong family. She plans to get married at 30 and have at least three kids before she is 40.

Now let us look at Mark.

Mark's family ran a successful small business. They lived in a large house in the suburbs, a house surrounded by pristine natural beauty—hills in the background and a large national forest reserve within a short walking distance. Mark had two younger sisters and he tended to control and dominate their work and play. As a result, the sisters had little respect for him. They called him a "bully." But Mark was not a bully in his school; in fact, he was like a little mouse. He always felt inferior to others. He earned good grades, but never stood out in a crowd. He yearned to have friends but he had few friends, if any.

Mark went to a reputable business school for his MBA. He worked in several companies, but did not distinguish himself in any of them. In his latest job as a sales manager in a relatively new outfit, Mark has lot of real authority, but he tends to misuse his power. Instead of building strong relations with his staff, he tends to dominate over them. As a result, he has created a climate of fear and mistrust. There is little warmth the way he interacts with others. He was married at 25 but got divorced at 30. His emotional deficiency has always stood in his way of building strong personal relations with others. Mark's coach has identified lack of self-esteem as a key problem in his work and personal life. But Mark has refused to accept this assessment and, consequently, he has made no progress in renewing himself.

What's going on here?

Jennifer saw challenges in her early life and decided to take charge; Mark had everything going for him but he never identified his real challenges and thus he has lived a life of denial. Mark's inferiority complex has very deep roots and he needs to consult a therapist, but when you are in denial there are few viable options.

Is there any hope for Mark? We cannot be certain because we are dealing with a very difficult character. He has power, but only external power. He has not internalized the fact that inner power makes a greater difference in one's life than position-based power. He has power of expertise (he knows his job quite well), but even that cannot be used without great self-confidence, which is again the byproduct of self-esteem. Mark is still young;

he has a bright professional career ahead of him, but he needs help and he should have no hesitation in accepting help. He can change the future course of his life by developing inner power, the feeling of fullness within, and the world will listen to him.

DEVELOPMENT CHALLENGES

Individuation

Carl Jung wrote about the process of "individuation," which is the process of a child becoming an adult, and an adult becoming a person. This process is inborn and natural. We all go through it with the passage of time, but the process itself does not ensure that the "person" eventually becomes a "healthy person." Our mental and emotional health depends on many factors, the most important of which is integration of the entire personality into a single whole. In simple terms, this is the integration of body, mind, heart, soul, and spirit. Jung uses the technical term "transcendent function" to indicate the individual capability of uniting all of the opposing trends in one's personality and of working toward the goal of wholeness. What comes together is our ego (sense of self), mingling of our male and female sides (all gender differences disappear except in the biological sense), our persona, and our shadow self. In all of this, the gradual sense of empowerment—self-confidence and self-esteem play an important role. A person who lacks self-esteem is less likely to integrate parts of his or her self into a fully functioning whole.

Personality Types

Jung also made another unique contribution to sharpening our understanding of human personality, and this relates to his work on "personality types." This framework is extremely useful in understanding attitudes and mental functions of human beings in real life. The first major difference, which Jung mentioned, relates to two polarities called *extraversion* (objective) and *introversion* (subjective). Extraversion has to do with the world that lies outside of and surrounds the person; a world of people and things. Introversion is the inner and private (invisible) world of human psyche. These two attitudes are mutually exclusive; they cannot coexist simultaneously in the same person, although they can and do alternate with one another. However, one attitude predominates over one's lifetime.

In addition to these two attitudes, Jung also talked about four mental functions. There are two modes of how human beings get information. The first one is *sensation* (or sensing), which is sense perception that includes all conscious experiences produced by stimulation of the sense organs—sights, sounds, smells, tastes, and touch as well as sensations originating inside the body. The second mode is called *intuition.* It comes from inside, or at least that is what we think. Intuition is an immediate experience that appears "out of the blue," so to say. The main difference between sensation and intuition is that in the case of former we can always pinpoint the source, while for intuition we can never be certain. Both sensation and intuition are called irrational functions because they require no reason at all. They are just there.

The second mental function pair is thinking and feeling, and these are two modes that help us decide things. *Thinking* consists of connecting ideas with each other in order to arrive at a general concept or a solution to a problem. If you are offering me an investment opportunity, I will have to think about it. I may ask you many questions before accepting the offer. That's how thinking works in day-to-day life. *Feeling* is an evaluative function; it either accepts or rejects an idea on the basis of whether the idea arouses a pleasant or unpleasant feeling. If you invite me to go for a movie, I can say no in a second. I could use the thinking function, however, and ask several questions about the movie before accepting or rejecting your offer. But when I am suddenly accepting or rejecting a proposition, I am using my feeling function. Thinking and feeling are both rational functions because they both require an act of judgment.

If you are already familiar with the MBTI (Myers-Briggs Type Indicator) you will understand these differences quite well. Two American women, Katherine Briggs and Isabel Myers, mother and daughter, built on Jung's work and created this instrument that helps people discover their attitudes and mental functions (also referred to as preferences). In my own training experience, I have found MBTI to be extremely useful for self-knowledge and self-awareness.

Power Related Developmental Challenges

There is a very thin boundary line between power and powerlessness. To avoid this confusion, power must be deeply rooted in ethics and spirituality. When people, who have no moral intuition and no moral considerations, get hold of power, they do awful things. History is witness to mass murders and genocides that could be traced to highly unethical use of power by just one person.

In certain ways, power encourages people to adopt commanding styles of communication and leadership which are ineffective for achieving lasting results in today's world. Power is known to generate several undesirable behavioral traits such as aggressiveness, manipulation, temper tantrums, stubbornness, and blind ambition.

While power is an extremely important developmental need (the birth of self-esteem), people who define themselves in terms of the "raw power" (unlimited power to reward or punish) are ticking time bombs. They not only self-destruct themselves, in the long run they destroy organizations and countries they lead.

DEVELOPMENTAL INTERVENTIONS

Influencing Others

One question that seminar participants have repeatedly asked me over the years has to do with their ability to influence others. "How can I influence those who do not care about me? How can I influence when I have no authority?" We need to be clear about what we mean by influence. It is our ability to influence the thinking, values, behaviors, and decision-making styles of another person (including decisions actually made), who is not obligated to comply with our wishes legally or personally or organizationally. Wouldn't it be wonderful if we could make our bosses do what we want them to do? While there is no magical trick involved in this, there are some people who wield a lot of influence through the sheer power of their presence. How do they do it?

As always, we need to start with our self-perception. If I view myself as an influencer, I will always have influence. If I view myself as a helpless victim, I will have no influence at all; it's that simple. When I have no formal authority, I have to use the force of my personality. I must have some power and that power could be the power of expertise, or the power of information. I must display a positive attitude, that is not only talk about my own interests but the interests of others too. As long as I am addressing a broad array of interests and concerns, I am exerting a great deal of influence on others.

Those people who are great influencers invariably display great communication skills. They are extremely competent in presenting their viewpoint. They show a lot of enthusiasm when they speak. They speak with a voice that commands respect. People who talk too much lose their influencing ability because they do not grab anyone's attention.

Great influencers are not shy of speaking to power (or higher level officials). Because they can speak with confidence not only to their immediate bosses, but several levels up in the organizational hierarchy they command great respect. These people always use departmental meetings and townhall meetings to make weighty comments on the organization's core business. These are the people who are always taken seriously by everyone.

Ethical considerations are extremely important if you want to be an authentic influencer. Never try to influence others for wrong (meaning unethical) reasons. And never use negative tactics like lying, making up information, asking for unreasonable favors, and talking against others at their back. In the long run, such tactics prove extremely harmful and you will end-up minimizing your influence instead of enhancing it.

To summarize, the most important actions for enhancing personal influence are:

- Establish your credentials and credibility.
- Know what you are talking about: what's your purpose; what do you want to gain; be precise and not just being ambitious.
- Make a logical and compelling case; rehearse your arguments well.
- Anticipate criticism and be ready to respond with sound counter arguments.
- Build trust and respect others' viewpoints.
- Appreciate others' needs and concerns.
- Be inspiring in your speech and thinking.
- Know the organizational priorities and let your concerns align with organizational concerns.
- Don't create the impression that you are pushing your own (meaning selfish) agenda.
- Be an active part of a network, build coalitions and alliances to enhance your influence.

Building Sustainable Relationships

Healthy and supportive relationships are our greatest asset. Our effectiveness depends a large part on the kind of relationships we have sustained over time. Building a new relationship comes to us naturally, but sustaining a relationship over a longer period of time is an art. Philosopher J. Krishnamurti repeatedly mentioned that a relationship is also a source of our self-knowledge, a mirror to see our self. "Self-knowledge comes into being when we are aware of ourselves in relationship, which shows what we are from moment to moment. Relationship is a mirror in which we see ourselves as we actually are. But most of us are incapable of looking at ourselves as we are in relationship, because we immediately begin to condemn or justify what we see" (1995, January 31). One thing that harms a relationship, therefore, is our tendency to judge the other person, to "mind read" and to evaluate others. What are some of the other do's and don'ts of building and sustaining productive relationships? Think about the following things:

- Show respect, project warmth, and sincerity. Extend normal courtesies and greetings.
- Listen actively and keep a cheerful profile while talking with others.
- Signal your ability to help others, if help is needed.
- If you make a mistake, apologize. Justifying a wrong action does not help the relationship.
- Make use of every opportunity to build trust. Absolute trust is the foundation of a strong and lasting relationship.
- At work, keep your office door open (if you have a closed office), walk around several times during the day to connect with others.
- Keep appointments and promises. If you are late for a meeting or break a promise, apologize profusely.
- Appreciate others' contributions. If you receive help from anyone, acknowledge it openly and sincerely.
- Ask for feedback how you're doing. Use this information to make improvements.
- Use "mirroring," which means adjusting your style to that of the other. If the other person speaks very slowly, speak slowly. If the other person shows some anxiety, be anxious yourself. Mirroring the body posture of the other person also helps in building rapport.
- Keep confidences. If someone has shared a secret with you, keep it to yourself. When mutual confidence is hurt, the relationship is no longer a trusting relationship.
- If there are difficult issues in a relationship, attack the issues and not the person.
- Keep room for little surprises: a gift when none expected, a "surprise" birthday party, and doing things which the other values but never asks for.

- Stay active in informal and formal networks; show your presence through the strength of your ideas and contributions.

The Art of Collaboration and Alliance-Building

We can extend our influence through collaboration with others. All teamwork in organizations is basically a collaborative effort. Why do we need to invest time and energy into this endeavor? The most important reason, of course, is the fact that we live and work in a highly uncertain and highly networked world. The days of the lone ranger doing great feats are virtually over. The most significant achievements in our personal and professional life require teamwork, collaboration, and alliance-building. Large corporations are seeking alliances, often with their rivals, to strengthen their own expertise base (value creation) and market power. Not all such alliances work well, but many do.

The seven-step approach described below, if properly followed, can assist you in building cooperation, collaboration, and sound alliances:

1. Invest your energy into building trust and confidence. Show strong commitment. Give up one thing to gain another. Demonstrate loyalty to the relationship.
2. Make your own expectations very clear at the outset. Also take the time to understand the other party's expectations. The two questions to ask are: What's in it for me? What's in it for the other?
3. Know your own perspective (worldview) and that of the other. Two parties that do not share the same worldview are very unlikely to cooperate fully. If perspectives do not match, find out the key differences. Invest time in minimizing those differences. Build a common ground on the most significant issues.
4. Talk about the skills—technical and interpersonal. Know what the other party is good at. Are the skills complementary? Are there critical gaps in terms of skills and competencies?

5. Talk about the objective and the task. What do you really want to achieve together? What's the goal? What's the purpose? Any alliance that does not have a meaningful outcome for the two parties is unsustainable and an exercise in futility. It does not mean using the other party for your own ends. What it means is that the relationship should add some value somewhere. Benefits in such relationships are often unequal, but would you continue to invest time in a relationship that is yielding no positive outcome at all?
6. Learning and continuous development are extremely important goals in a working relationship,—between two individuals, members of a team, and two organizations. People and organizations must grow in a productive relationship. If they are not growing, then it means that something is not working.
7. There is no relationship that lasts forever. Things change over time. Circumstances change, and so do mutual expectations. Therefore, there is a need to invest in the "renewal" of an ongoing collaborative relationship. Without the renewal effort, the relationship runs the risk of withering away.

Managing Conflict

Life is full of suffering. Buddha shared this fundamental truth with his followers many centuries ago. Suffering has many sources and interpersonal conflict is certainly an important one. There are conflicts in relationships. There are conflicts in cooperative alliances. Several surveys show that managers in organizations are spending as much as 20% of their time managing interpersonal conflicts. This is a huge waste of valuable time. What can we do about reducing conflict and creating greater harmony in relationships? Some people by nature and temperament avoid managing conflict. But the conflict does not go away by our act of avoiding it. In fact, more it lingers, the more damaging it becomes.

The first thing we need to learn is that, pleasant or unpleasant, conflict should not be avoided or shoved aside. We must address the underlying reasons. Why is there conflict in place of cooperation? Finding the reason itself is a challenging task because most conflicts have multiple causes, or causes so deep-rooted that it is very difficult to get the total perspective. That's why one has to ask many questions. There is also the need for deep self-reflection. Ask yourself: In what ways am I responsible for this conflict, or have my actions in any way contributed to the severity of the conflict? If we fail to acknowledge our own part in a conflict, the resolution can become very difficult. It will simply turn into a "blame game."

Here are some useful tips based on my personal experience as a coach and a trainer:

- *Listen very carefully to the other party's story.* Ask open-ended questions that start with what, how, why, when, and where. Do not rush to make judgments.
- *Present your own point of view calmly, using non-defensive language.* Follow Steven Covey's advice, "Seek first to understand and then to be understood." Identify the key issue that is causing the problem, and from then on focus on attacking the problem, not the person.
- *Try to find a win-win solution.* Any resolution that benefits only one of the parties will not stick. Win-win solutions are not simple compromises, dividing the pie into equal parts. They expand the size of the pie so that each party takes home more than what was at stake.
- *Aim at developing a proactive strategy.* It means keeping your relationships healthy and vibrant so that there is little scope for the conflict to arise in the first place. If there is a misunderstanding, take immediate steps to remove it.

Not every conflict lends itself to resolution. There are three situations in my opinion in which the conflict may not be resolved and, therefore, it would be just fine to bring the relationship to a close. These are (1) When one of the parties is making impossible demands—the demands that cannot be met. If there is no room for negotiation and compromise, there is nothing much that you can do about it. (2) Situations where there are strong "values" conflicts. For example, if one of the parties has shown lack of integrity and is in a constant state of denial about it, the conflict will not be resolved. Both parties need to move beyond a state of denial in order to resolve the conflict. (3) If one of the parties is repeating the same behavioral patterns and the same issues that create conflict time and again, it is not a case of simple conflict management. There is need for therapy. Marriages that end-up in divorce go through cycles of repetitive behaviors on the part of one or both the partners that are destructive of a trusting relationship.

A Poetic Interlude

Listening

There are voices
of people talking
in high and low tones.

There is someone
who's saying something to me
and I'm listening.
To me listening is life.

When I fail to listen
I get disoriented, I get confused.

I start doing routine things —
things which do not matter
but which I do mindlessly
and derive no satisfaction, no pleasure at all.

When I listen I get connected with reality,
with people and what they want,
their aspirations, their pains, their joys.

I learn about things and people —
their roadmaps, their life plans.
Listening is a total experience for me.

When we listen, we attain freedom,
we are freed from the prison
of our own beliefs and
we come out of the freeways
of our own experience.

If I don't listen, I don't learn.
Creativity needs listening and learning.
If I don't listen, I'm just there.

From *A Moment in the Universe* (2006, pp. 27-28)
© by Surinder Deol

3. A SUMMARY OF KEY IDEAS

- By using our personal power we can build new avenues for our progress or we can destroy within a short time what has taken us years to build.
- Self-esteem is the single most valuable attribute that makes us a fully effective and fully functioning human being.
- Our mental and emotional health depends on many factors, the most important of which is integration of our personality into a single whole.
- There is a very thin boundary line between power and powerlessness. To avoid this confusion, power must be deeply rooted in ethics and spirituality. When people, who have no moral intuition and no moral considerations, get hold of power, they do awful things.
- If I view myself as an influencer, I will always have influence. If I view myself as a helpless victim, I will have no influence at all.
- One thing that harms a relationship is our tendency to judge the other person, to "mind read" and to evaluate others.
- The most significant achievements in our personal and professional life require teamwork, collaboration, and alliance-building.
- Ask yourself: In what ways am I responsible for this conflict, or have my actions in any way contributed to the severity of the conflict? If we fail to acknowledge our own part in a conflict, the resolution can become very difficult.
- Not every conflict lends itself to resolution.
- Listen very carefully to the other party's story. Ask open-ended questions that start with what, how, why, when, and where. Do not rush to make judgments.

4 Harnessing the Power of Love and Compassion

THE MAP

When you are at the heart level, you are actually deriving energy both from the human and the spiritual realms. The human energetic current brings with it past memories, prejudices, and biases while the spiritual energy propels the person for more universal, more non-egoic acts of unconditional love and compassion. That is why, in popular imagination, heart is always associated with love and compassion. A person who cannot love or show compassion is viewed as someone who has no heart and no feelings.

More than any one else, Mother Teresa has become a symbol of love and compassion due to her extraordinary work in the slums of Calcutta. She received her calling to serve the poor when she was just 12 years old. Although she was admired by millions around the world, she was not without her critics. Once she was criticized metaphorically for giving people fish, but not teaching them how to fish. She responded: "The people I take care—they are disabled, they are hungry, they are sick, they are rejected by society, they have forgotten what love is. They are completely broken. I will give them the fish to eat and then when they are able to stand and hold the rod, I will hand them over to you, and you give them the rod to catch the fish." This is the essence of compassion—taking care of people who are so completely helpless that they can't take care of themselves.

Love is Divine

More has been written on love than perhaps on any other subject. Dictionary defines it as an intense feeling of deep affection for another person. The affection in question may be plain and simple love for someone (love for a family member or a friend), or love that is based on feelings of romantic love for another (which is different from love based on sexual desire). In extreme cases, love can take the form of an obsession. Love in relationship between two people may not be limited to merely physical desire; it can rise to unprecedented spiritual heights. The famous Italian poet Dante (1265-1321) first saw his beloved Beatrice when he was only 9 years old. He fell in love with her without speaking a word with her. He saw her again a few times when he was 18 but never knew her well. It was the case of love at first sight. Love for Beatrice became a reason for his poetry and he imagined her as nothing less than a manifestation of God.

Greek word "agape" symbolizes a special kind of love, meaning divine love. Greeks, in fact, distinguished between three forms of love, namely, *agape* (divine love), *eros* (love based on sexual attraction), and *philia* (a form of brotherly love). In almost all major spiritual traditions, love is mentioned as the force that connects us with the Divine. It is also the force that unites people to care for one another. At the Sermon on the Mount, Jesus said, "You have heard that it was said, 'Love (*agape*) your neighbor and hate your enemy.' But I tell you: Love your enemies and pray for those who persecute you, that you may be sons of your Father in heaven. He causes his sun to rise on the evil and the good, and sends rain on the righteous and the unrighteous. If you love those who love you, what reward will you get?" (Matthew 5-44-45).

Many Christian mystics (the same is true of Sufi and Hindu sages) extended the idea of erotic love to the love of the Divine. Soul is often presented as a feminine entity yearning for union with her Lover (God). In the words of St. Bernard: "O that you would kiss me with kisses of your mouth." St. Teresa of Avila expressed the mystical love in her book *The Interior Castle:* "He has bound Himself as firmly as two human beings are joined in wedlock and will never separate Himself from her." *Gitagovinda,* a poem written by the 12th century poet Jayadeva, celebrates the courtship of divine lovers, Radha and Krishna.

The Psychology of Love

Psychologists starting with Sigmund Freud have struggled with the question as to how much of what we call "love" is just "sexual energy." Freud used the term *libido* to describe the energy associated with sexual instinct, and eventually with all constructive human activity. *Libido* (as also *eros*) is opposed by *thanatos,* which is the urge to die or to destroy. All variations in the development of human beings, according to Freud, are therefore the result of this struggle between *libido* and *thanatos.* Mental development of the child depends very much on healthy libido development.

Compassion

Compassion, as we saw in Mother Teresa's example, means sympathetic concern for the suffering and misfortunes of others. Often, compassion is interpreted as loving-kindness, which in turn is based on the Buddhist concept of *metta* or *maitri,* meaning unconditional loving. Sharon Salzberg in her book *Loving-Kindness* mentions that Buddha had specifically identified 11 benefits of loving-kindness practice: You will sleep easily; you will wake easily; you will have pleasant dreams; people will love you; other sentient beings and *devas* will love you; *devas* will protect you; external dangers will not harm you; your face will be radiant; your mind will be serene; you will die unconfused; and you will be born in happy realms.

What makes us more loving and caring? The question is redundant perhaps because to love and to care is an essential part of human nature. All human beings are endowed with this ability at the time of their birth. How do we then explain evil, hatred, jealousy, mass murders, and other horrible crimes committed by some men against others? This inevitably brings us to the question of values. It's true that when untamed, human nature has great capacity for aggression, violence, and sectarian hatred. It is only through the inculcation of right kind of values that we learn to love and genuinely care for others. Nazi parents were caring parents because they cared for the well-being of their children, but they also taught them racism and racial hatred. Childhood experiences, including the role of teachers, are very important in crafting our loving nature. We can add to this list the power of real life experiences—especially the kindness of strangers. Life teaches us many positive things because there are still a lot of good people out there who make a difference in the lives of others through their generosity and compassion.

When you have love in your heart there is no problem for you to take the perspective of a second or a third person. You accept racial and ethnic differences. All your energies are centered and you show contentment with your life conditions. We may, however, add a cautionary note here: Excess of everything is bad. Excessive love (often called blind love) can create problems like codependency, poor boundary management, jealousy, and the tendency to subjugate self to the whims and fancies of another.

Values and Needs

Heart level is located at the intersection of higher and lower currents of consciousness—a place in our subtle body where they intermingle and go their separate ways. It is the center of love, joy, and peace, but since people express themselves differently, these unique loving expressions could be problematic in some ways. Many people choose to find and express their loving nature through the medium of an organized belief system. Unquestioned obedience to a religious dogma transfers authority over inner transformation to an authority outside oneself. As a result, heart may actually become less open to experiences which are not part of one's own belief system. Rigid or fundamentalist interpretations negate feelings of love and compassion for all beings. On the positive side, the emergence of a loving heart is a major development. If love is the sole driving force and an overarching value, this level is a major transition to a life of spirit that is an altogether new experience.

Heart level offers an opportunity for nurturing belief in a power higher than self; it is an opportunity for those who think alike to find affinity. While this need for deeper connection with those who are liked and loved is visibly expressed, people tend to show varying degrees of intolerance toward those who think and act otherwise. Due to inner conflicts, the heart is not yet ready for unconditional love and compassion. There is something which is lacking, which is a higher realization that every sentient being on this planet is worthy of unconditional love and compassion. There is also a longing for mergence or connectedness with something higher than self. This need is not fully met at this level.

Communication and Leadership Style

Since heart level places love in the center of daily living experiences, the overall personality at this level is qualitatively different. A person who is genuinely able to love self is also the person who is capable of expressing love through one's communication style. Communication is, therefore, more open and is aimed at making clear what one really wants from others. Favorite expressions include: "There is a higher purpose.... My values are more important to me than anything else.... I seek guidance from Higher Power...." This kind of person might not always act morally, but tries very hard to impress others with his or her moral authority. Fourth person perspective (moving from I, we, they to all of us) increasingly shows up as concerns for broader social and cultural issues become important. Personal change is easy in some ways but difficult in others. It is easy to follow one's own belief system, but it is more challenging adjusting to other belief systems that one is less familiar with. The result is imperfect; it is the kind of transformation where openness on one side is diminished by the darkness of the other.

LIVING STORIES

The following two stories illustrate how closely love is aligned with the healthy development of human psyche and how its absence can suddenly take away the warmth and beauty out of human existence.

Katya was born in a small farming community in communist Russia. Like every other girl in the community, she got good schooling. She didn't make the grades for entry into the state college. Therefore, she decided to move to Moscow and got a job as a secretary because of her impressive typing skills. At the age of 23, she married her own boss, a well-educated young man, who traced his ancestry to one of the richest families in pre-communist Russia. When the Soviet Union disintegrated, her husband took up a job with an oil company in Western Europe and the family lived in many fancy places around the world before finally settling down in the US in 1990s. On the surface, the story looks like that of a couple which lived happily ever after!

But that's not the case. Katya is not a very social person. She grew up in an environment where you could never trust another person. One of the things that she learned while growing up was the importance of taking care of one's own needs more than anything else. She was somewhat withdrawn and was a private kind of a person even as a child. But over a period of time, although the communist ideology failed and her sisters who also migrated to the US as well became more open and very social, Katya became more critical and intolerant of other people. She had learned to value material things because there was so much scarcity of everything in the Soviet system, but living in Western countries and the fact that her husband earned six-figure salary coupled with handsome bonuses made no difference in her attitude towards money. Although Katya openly bemoans materialism of Western societies, she is more of a materialist than anyone else in her circle. Her husband has tried to change her views, but without any success. Her children consider her "intolerably selfish and self-centered." She has no friends outside her narrow circle of few Russian speaking families. This has not made any difference to Katya because she is quite convinced about the "rightness" of her own thinking.

Madhav was born in India and his story is very different.

Madhav's father had a small piece of land in an area known for extremely low rainfall. To supplement his income, his father took up a job as a primary school teacher which again didn't pay much. No one in the family had ever gone to college. Madhav was the first one to do so. He was a good student and there was always the state scholarship money to be had. He earned a degree in engineering and headed to America like many other young men of his age group. While doing a part-time job, he earned his doctoral degree in chemical engineering.

He has worked as a professor at a well-known state university for the past 35 years. He holds patents on more than a dozen chemical processes used by some large corporations. He has made millions in his life, but has not accumulated them in a bank account. He has paid for the construction of a school and a health clinic in his village (he used to walk seven miles a day during his own schooling).

Madhav is very active in the local community; he has tutored kids from the minority communities for years. He is one of the biggest donors to environmental and other nonprofits in his state. While moving in the high circles of corporate executives, Madhav has not forgotten his own humble origins. He has silently withstood many tragedies in his life—the death of his son in an auto accident followed soon by the death of his wife by cancer. He lives with his daughter, who is completing her doctorate in her father's specialty.

Those who have known Madhav praise him for his loving-kindness. He always shows an attitude of acceptance. Anyone coming to his house is always welcome. He believes in building and sustaining strong relationships. His address book contains hundreds of names, but he makes it a point to greet each one of his contacts personally, through mail, or internet during the holiday period. He has closely followed the careers of his students and helped them build a place for themselves in life.

There is very little that is common in these two stories, except that these people came to the US from foreign cultural backgrounds, but their lives have taken very different routes.

Katya may not admit it, but she is unhappy and suffering. Something happened to her in early years that has shaped her consciousness in certain specific ways. Whether it was something real or imagined, we cannot say. She is in need of therapy or good counseling, but since she is also in denial nothing can be done to help her. Absence of love and genuine care on the part of one person has robbed this family of its right to happiness.

Authentic development, we should remember, can occur only where there is realization of one's actions and their consequences and the willingness to invest time and energy into various developmental interventions.

DEVELOPMENT CHALLENGES

The lower and the higher

Heart level lies at the intersection of biological self and the start of the higher self with its attendant problems of alignment between the lower and the higher. While something has been left behind (our lower physical urges), the higher possibility (spiritual enlightenment) is yet a dream. There is love but not yet selfless loving-kindness; there is compassion but nested within several boundaries. As we know, physical is not separate from the spiritual. These are parts of the same continuum. Heart, of course, is a very special entity. It has a physical dimension like every other organ in our body. It is after all a pump. But based on poetry, every romantic story ever written, folklore, mythology, and spirituality, heart is perceived as an autonomous entity like the human mind with innate capacity for managing the flow of all human emotions, especially every emotion that has to do with love and sex. Therefore, when we talk of heart we are talking about something that is at the very edge of physical domain. As we rise above the heart, we are in a different realm, which is more spiritual than physical. This is major transition in human development and as such it poses many challenges for our entry into the higher realms.

Higher values and higher abilities

Many higher order values are discovered, but the application of these values is a challenge. When we are fully in touch with our heart, we are also in touch with some of our higher level spiritual capacities. But we face problems in the application of those capacities: How to fully use our creative ability? How to make more productive use of our intuition? For us to become fully proficient in the use of these abilities, we need to make further progress in terms of the levels of development.

The fundamentalist creed

In one respect, heart level is very limiting and that has to do with people's belief systems. When people put their heart, say into worshipping a particular deity, their perspective surprisingly becomes narrower. They tend to move away from other deities or other belief systems. We hear it said all the time: Salvation is only through accepting Jesus as the Lord; or by embracing Islam; or by becoming a Buddhist; or by worshipping Shiva. This is basically the fundamentalist creed. If you don't do what I'm doing you're doomed. There is no solution to this problem at the heart level. We have to move up to higher levels of awareness to fix these problems. But if the fundamentalists are stuck here; everybody else is. That's a big challenge of our time.

The wounded self

When you love someone deeply, there is always a fear of rejection. What if she or he stops loving me. This fear of rejection leads to feelings of being a victim. This could result in self-talk such as: "I give lots of love but I don't get enough." The result could be a wounded self that is in downward spiral. Despite some of the limitations and some of the challenges, heart level is at a higher level of development. Those who reach here move ahead with minimal effort, if they are not caught up in one of the fundamentalist routines.

DEVELOPMENTAL INTERVENTIONS

Tonglen Meditation

For someone who has a stone heart and wants to change fundamentally, it would require nothing short of a miracle. And this miracle will not happen under normal circumstances through divine intervention, though positive stories on this subject serve a very useful purpose. The person who needs to change has to make an effort. Among the many useful tools for this purpose, there is *tonglen* meditation. *Tonglen,* which is a Tibetan word, means "taking in and sending out." We take in the suffering of others and give them peace and happiness. The basic idea behind this meditation is to put others before one's own self. For *tonglen* practice, we need to proceed systematically:

- Find a quiet place. Sit comfortably on a chair or a cushion. Do some preliminary breathing exercises. Once you are perfectly at peace with yourself, start *tonglen* meditation,
- In the first step, take a deep breath and silently say: "With this breath I take in suffering that others feel." It is important for you to take in this breath with openness and compassion. Your acceptance of others is unconditional. You can't say that I take in the suffering of the people who are my loved ones, who are my friends, or who live in my neighborhood. You accept all living beings as worthy of your compassion. Hold the breath as long as it is comfortable.
- When you exhale, you silently say, "I give to all beings good health, happiness, harmony, and peace of mind." You are giving away your pleasure, your happiness and everything else that feels good about your self. Whatever good exists in us, whatever we feel good about, we breathe out to others. In this way, you dedicate yourself to the service of others. This meditation ties in very nicely with the ideas of *metta* or *maitri*, which have to do with warmth, friendship, and compassion.

Do this meditation for 10-15 minutes at a time, as frequently as possible. There are several benefits of *tonglen,* especially it is useful in developing generosity, making people move away from stinginess, something that holds back many people who lack love and compassion for others. In time, it should make us feel less important compared to others, and others' needs will suddenly become more important than our own. That's the foundation of the spirit of service.

Managing with Heart

If you are doing *tonglen* practice, it would make you a caring and compassionate technical professional or a manager who manages compassionately. What if you have no time for *tonglen* meditation, but you want to practice a compassionate management style? Here are several suggestions for you to use in your real life and if you follow them you will see a difference in how others perceive you—

Do not be too possessive or materialistic. If by making any monetary sacrifice, you can benefit more needy people, please consider doing that. It will mean more to you in the long run.

Always try to be a good teacher. Reach out to people who are stuck with something. Guide them to solve problems. Coach and mentor new employees. Support those who are worthy of your support.

Do not accept any undue favors, gifts or bribes from anyone. No one has become rich or contented following this route. Never compromise your personal integrity and reputation for a material gain.

Always apologize if you have committed a mistake, hurt someone's feelings, or done something awful. Defending a wrong action does not help. People do appreciate an apology if it is sincere and comes from the heart.

Share knowledge and information, but make sure that the information that you share is valid. Information hoarding for the purpose of gaining importance is one of the worst behavioral attributes in today's organizations where timely sharing of information with others is extremely important.

Always acknowledge the help that you have received from others. Showing gratitude is the best form of kindness.

Always be humble and gentle. Never allow power to go to your head. Arrogance based on position power is like a disease. It makes people less effective because it encourages negative perception of our self by others.

A Compassionate Business Strategy

Business strategy or strategic thinking, as taught in the business schools, is a highly cognitive subject, emphasizing the use of mainly mental and rational abilities. I feel that leaving the heart out of strategic thinking is a big mistake. The following approach brings the heart and the mind together for a more balanced approach for strategy formulation and implementation. Here's what you need to do—

Have a clear vision of where you want to go. See the destination very clearly. Picture it thoroughly. Use a rich picture full of color in your own imagination. Ask yourself what is so unique about this picture. How is it different from your present state? Note down differences because every little thing matters.

Are you passionate about this strategy? If you do not give yourself at least 8 out of 10 on this one, this is not the best path for you.

Who else shares this picture? Do your stakeholders or customers share this picture? If not, why do you want to go there?

What are the critical success factors involved in the successful implementation of this strategy? List each one of them. Take note of gaps, if any. Try to balance two considerations: what this strategy will do for the business (return on investment, etc.) and what it would do for the people (both within and outside the enterprise).

What skills and competencies will you need to translate this dream into reality? Who else will contribute support when you are executing the strategy? What is your partnership or teamwork strategy? How would you create a worldclass team?

Who are your competitors? Where are they located? What are their strengths and weaknesses? What is your strategic advantage vis-à-vis these competitors? Is there a scope for building an alliance?

How can you add "real value" into the value chain? How can you improve your business processes? How will you motivate your employees? If your employees do not "see" your strategy, you will not succeed.

Identify and bring the best people to work with you at the frontline. Put your heart into building a solid team. Give them training. Give them monetary as well as non-monetary incentives.

Use your intuition. Ask questions and make your intuition work on finding the best answers for you. Do not depend too heavily on analysis. While analysis is important, it can often blind decision makers about non-tangible (human) factors, which is a deadly mistake.

Keep the communication going. You cannot over-communicate in this situation. Give out the most reliable information. Do not make up facts to make people happy. Give them the "brutal facts" and make them use that information productively.

Celebrate small victories and liberally send out "Thank You" notes. Sincere expression of gratitude is one of the finest human qualities. Jim Collins in his book *Good to Great* talks about great leaders looking outside the window when they succeed and inside when they fail, meaning they give credit for success to others and take personal responsibility for failure. Bad leaders of course do otherwise.

A Poetic Interlude

When You're in Love

When you're in love...

Nothing looks and feels the same.
Breathing is heavier. You sleep less and dream more.
Sky is bluer than it usually is.
Birds fly close to you singing romantic melodies.
Memories are sharper and deeper. Pain is unbearable at times.
And you feel your body is on fire.
Nothing looks and feels the same.

When you're in love...

There is only one thing you need.
A loving touch of the one you love.

When you're in love...

You die every minute. You are born anew every day.
You are a new person because love is transforming.
Love is rejuvenating. Love is refreshing. You forget the pain.
You forget the longing. You are in a blissful state.
You are a sacred body because love transforms you.

When you're in love...

Nothing looks and feels the same.
Because nothing is same when you're in love.

From *A Moment in the Universe* (2006, pp. 93-94)

4. A SUMMARY OF KEY IDEAS

- The human energetic current brings with it past memories, prejudices, and biases while the spiritual energy propels the person for more universal non-egoic acts of unconditional love and compassion.
- In almost all major spiritual traditions, love is mentioned as the force that connects us with the Divine. It is also the force that unites people to care for one another.
- It is only through the inculcation of right kind of values that we learn to love and genuinely care for others.
- Personal change is easy in some ways but difficult in others. It is easy to follow one's own belief system, but it is more challenging and adjusting to other belief systems that one is less familiar with. The result is imperfect; it is the kind of transformation where openness on one side is diminished by the darkness of the other.
- There are several benefits of *tonglen,* especially it is useful in developing generosity, making people move away from stinginess, something that holds back many people who lack love and compassion for others.
- Always acknowledge the help that you have received from others. Showing gratitude is the best form of kindness.
- Have a clear vision of where you want to go. See the destination very clearly. Picture it thoroughly. Use a rich colored picture in your own imagination. Ask yourself what is so unique about this picture. How is it different from your present state? Note down differences because everything matters.
- Having a loving heart is one of our most precious possessions.

5 Creative Self-Expression

THE MAP

The three upper levels above the heart are closely connected with the realization of our hidden potential. That's why creativity plays such an important part at the level that we are going to address in this chapter. When we are creative, we are dipping into layers of our unconscious self that is the repository of everything that is good and beautiful. Creativity is popularly understood as something *novel* (new), *useful* (but not limited to the utilitarian sense of the term), and *artistic* (satisfying some basic aesthetic criteria). The creative act itself could be spontaneous (an "aha" moment) when a novel idea suddenly pops up in one's mind. But creativity could also be fostered through ensuring a certain environment supportive of the creative process. Creativity is said to occur in the midzone between total chaos and perfect organization, between insanity and sanity. That's why Peter Senge used the word "creative tension" to describe the journey from the *current reality* (our present state) to *vision* (our future state).

It is also common to decompose the concept of creativity into its identifiable parts: *the person* (the creator); *the process* (the steps followed); *the product* (outcome); and *the environment* (conditions in which the person operates). Arthur Koestler made an important point when he stated that creativity is not the monopoly of people who are formally identified as "artists." He identified two other types of creative individuals, namely, the sage and the jester. All three of them are creative in their own ways.

Some people also draw a distinction between scientific creativity and artistic creativity. A scientist uses logic and analysis to find new solutions to specific problems. There is also extensive use of data in scientific research, including lab or field testing of results. An artistic endeavor, on the other hand, is dominantly expressive, unbounded, flexible, and open to newer possibilities.

Fostering Creativity

One of the most debated questions of the 20th century had to do with whether or not creativity could be consciously fostered. Those people who believed in the power of the right-brain advocated its use to be more creative. Others taught techniques of convergent and divergent thinking. A quick look at the relevant literature shows that fostering creativity is not that difficult after all. Doing some simple things can allow all of us to tap into our creative self—

- Start with the self-knowledge—the more you know about yourself and the purpose of your life, better prepared you will be to start a creative life.
- Develop basic creativity skills like using brainstorming, free association, divergent thinking, etc.
- Start a practice (breathing exercises or meditation) to keep yourself focused on your inner self.
- Always stay focused and relaxed and use every opportunity to think in terms of finding unique and original ideas and images.
- Never get distracted by others' negative comments. Never lose confidence in self to produce extraordinary outcomes.
- Talk about your creative pursuits with friends to share your passion about what you are doing. Positive emotions like joy and happiness play an important part in generating creative thinking. Negative emotions like fear and jealousy drain our creative impulses.
- Manage yourself well. Be creative, but do not get carried away. Always keep yourself firmly grounded.

Values and Needs

When people experience unrestrained creativity at this level they give expression to their values and beliefs through words (poetry), sounds (music), body movement (dance), pure awareness (meditation), drama, painting, sculpture, architecture, and science. The self, the symbol of one's personal identity, is expressed not only as the narrow self serving one's limited purposes but as an all encompassing self, the boundaryless self, the self that reaches out to others, the self that looks for wider spaces to create new forms and patterns of expression, and the self that seeks soulful richness and variety. The inner feelings are expressed not only through words but through subtle expressions such as communicating with the power of one's silence. One is always speaking one's truth without fear or reservation.

Seeking creative self-expression in all situations is a major personal need that must be fulfilled. Communicating with others to build understanding and relationships is another. Creative people tend to live dual lives and therefore they are always challenged to maintain a balance between their practical and idealistic modes of thinking. Creative consciousness makes people do the right thing without expecting a reward or recognition.

Communication and Leadership Style

People at this level express themselves with honesty and integrity. They share their feelings openly with others. Favorite expressions include: "Can we think out of the box?... What's another way of looking at the same thing?... Who has a different solution to this problem?" Communication is highly participative and problem-centered. They manage change through modeling new behaviors and then adapting these new behaviors to interact with others. They manage conflict through innovative ways of reaching consensus on divisive issues because they can look at the same issue from different perspectives, and play different roles. When they are stuck, they do something different. Flexibility becomes part of the art of living creatively. Creative people have the capacity to stand alone to defend their beliefs, and they don't change their commitments seasonally to benefit self or others.

LIVING STORIES

The following story comes from Thailand, but there are people like Lina almost everywhere who keep this world in the balance despite all the craziness and absurdities that seem to have such enduring presence in human nature.

Lina was born in England—the child of an English father and a Thai mother. When she was only few months old, her mother decided to go back to Thailand because although her husband loved her dearly, his parents never really accepted Lina's mother. In the circle of their family and friends, Lina's mother was an odd presence and many a time she was treated no better than a maid. Lina, therefore, deeply missed the presence of her father in her early years. But her mother always remained a great role model for her and did everything to teach her good values. Both mother and daughter lived within a limited income that came mostly from Lina's maternal grandfather, who was a leading public figure at one time. After Lina finished her schooling in Bangkok, she went to Australia for her undergraduate and graduate studies.

Lina got a job in a leading British investment company and worked in Singapore and Hong Kong before finally settling down in Bangkok. Those who have known Lina appreciate her sense of flow. She is a person who is always at peace with herself and speaks from her heart. She has used her English language skills to write and talk about Thai culture and Buddhism. At just 27 years, she is looked by many others as the voice of wisdom.

In her own words, she has crafted her life in a particular way. "I was very unhappy as a child, always missing my father. I also felt sorry for my mother, who had to work so hard to maintain the appearance of a good living standard. I developed my creative abilities by doing many odd things, including listening to birds. I thought that they communicated much better than the humans. Because of my great listening capacity, I am always able to develop high levels of personal resonance. Now I am trying to diversify my interests by learning piano. My mother always reminds me that I have to get married and settle down. I told her recently that it might take years because I am determined to marry only after my first concert hall performance."

Karl is single like Lina. They both share inadequacies of early life in the sense of not having the support of both the parents, but that's where any similarities end between them.

Karl comes from Swiss-German background. He left his home without completing his college education. While he worked for a European airline in New York he attended college in the evening and finally earned a degree in Ethics. There is a contradiction here because according to his own admission, Karl has lived "an unethical life." Although now he occupies a respectable position with a public relations firm, he has never overcome a feeling of insecurity. "My parents were at some stage very controlling, but then I don't know what happened they stopped caring for me and even stopped loving me. They wanted me to just go away and that's what I did. My father died without meeting me again and now my mother lives in a seniors home whom I have seen two or three times during the past 12 years."

Karl's associates complain that he has a tendency to lie or to exaggerate. They do not even believe the stories he has told about his parents. He has two permanent staff who report to him, who have regularly complained about his habit of making them work late in the evenings, and even during the weekends. Because he is very talkative and boastful it has been a problem for Karl to keep secrets. His small talk has landed him in serious trouble on more than one occasion.

He goes to singles parties regularly and has used drugs on several occasions. He does not see any moral or ethical issues in having sex with strangers and indulging in substance abuse. Recently, a friend has tried to help him clean the mess his life has become, but this relationship has not made any difference. The friend has stopped seeing him.

What's going on here?

Both these people are competent in their own ways. They have professional jobs with some public visibility. But while Lina has channeled her life into several creative arenas, Karl seems to be stuck with several unresolved issues. While he talks ill of his parents, he has not acknowledged what he might have done to anger his father who asked him to leave their home. Karl has a theory that when things really go over the edge, nature helps him come out unscathed. Will this continue to happen forever even when Karl evades taking charge of his life?

DEVELOPMENT CHALLENGES

The challenges of creative-self-expression

Creative self-expression provides a very high level of self-satisfaction. People who reach this level do not wish anything more. They wish to stay here and deepen their sense of inner fulfillment. But they also hear a calling, a voice that beckons them to scale greater heights—heights which are more inner than outer.

There are two triggers for change: (a) the urge to make one's creative expressions or experiences more unique and path-breaking; and (b) the urge to reach out to others, to share with them one's gifts, mentor and coach those who need help. These aspirations cannot be fulfilled by staying at this level.

There are four challenges in creative self-expression:

Fear of the unknown. People are afraid to say what's on their mind because they are afraid of the consequences of free self-expression. I won't say it because someone would be offended. I won't say it because I would be misunderstood. Such suppression of free speech is not healthy. In the words of Buckminster Fuller, "Everyone has the perfect gift to give the world—and if each of us is freed up to give our unique gift, the world will be in total harmony."

Speaking from the heart and saying your truth. Speech is not only what we want to talk. It is about our authenticity as human beings. Speaking from the heart means the same thing. Saying our truth is telling what's on our mind; what we really believe in. But this does not mean causing undue hurt. If our "truth" is likely to cause pain to others, we need to handle it differently.

There is a priceless quote from Mother Teresa: "Kind words can be short and easy to speak but their echoes are truly endless."

Understanding the cultural context. All languages are culturally grounded. Whether a particular form of self-expression is valid or not is decided with reference to a specific cultural context and the values held by the people in that culture. Americans use some expressions as a matter of routine that in some other cultures would be unacceptable. When Vice-President Dick Cheney used an F-word in his conversation or lack thereof with a senior Democratic Senator, it was fodder for the late night shows. In another culture, such an expression would have created a thunderstorm of political protest.

Recognizing that emotions play an important part in self-expression. From the evolutionary perspective, all self-expression is emotional. As elegantly explained by Charles Darwin in his work *The Expression of the Emotions in Man and Animals,* published in 1872: "The movements of expression in the face and body, whatever their origin may have been, are in themselves of much importance for our own welfare. They serve as the first means of communication between the mother and the infant; she smiles approval, and thus encourages her child on the right path; or frowns disapproval. We readily perceive sympathy in others by their expression; our sufferings are thus mitigated and our pleasures increased; and mutual good feeling is thus strengthened. The movements of expression give vividness and energy to our spoken words. They reveal the thoughts and intentions of others more truly than do words, which may be falsified."

DEVELOPMENTAL INTERVENTIONS

The Art and Practice of Listening

> "When I ask you to listen to me and you start giving advice, you have not done what I asked. When I ask you to listen to me and you begin to tell me why I shouldn't feel that way, you are trampling on my feelings. When I ask you to listen to me and you feel you have to do something to solve my problems, you have failed me, strange as that may seem.

Perhaps that's why prayer works for some people. Because God is mute and He doesn't offer advice or try to fix things. He just listens and trusts you to work it out for yourself. So please, just listen and hear me. And if you want to talk, wait a few minutes for your turn and I promise I'll listen to you."

Anonymous

Listening is our most important connection with other people and the universe. It is the attribute of our humanness together with our ability to see, to feel and to have compassion. The real mystery of life, as we know, starts with a child hearing voices; the voice of family members, other people, which mean nothing in the beginning but in due course these voices become important emotional nourishment for the child. And as medical science informs us, hearing is the last faculty to die when we die.

Listening means we are paying attention; there is nothing else that is competing for our attention in the moment. To be attentive is to stay focused. How we achieve this state of focus is a matter of personal choice, but there are few things that are quite essential. We need to be awake. A state of sleep or drowsiness minimizes our ability to be attentive. In such a situation it is better to share our state of mind with the speaker and arrange for a different time for conversation. To give a tired look or yawning are unpleasant signals to the speaker that convey lack of attention and possible boredom.

Listening is always in the present moment, and if we are not living in the moment we can't listen. The presence of our body is essential but it is not adequate. We need the presence of our inner body (mental presence) too. There are people who lead a major part of their lives living away from their bodies. And what they miss is the wonderful opportunity to learn and to grow through sheer joy of listening to music, words of a friend or a teacher.

Listening requires openness. It means suspending our judgments of others or of others' values and opinions. "The quieter you become, the more you can hear," says the New Age guru Ram Dass. Listening brings in new ideas thus expanding our mental horizon. Openness requires openness both to the message and the messenger. Rejection of either one could close our mind. Openness enhances anticipation and thus makes our listening more proactive.

Listening requires silence, not just the outer silence, but the inner silence. It needs suspension of our inner dialogue. As we can listen to only one voice at a time, we have to make a choice. And if we make the choice to listen to our inner voice we shall run the risk of getting disconnected with our current outer reality.

There are different ways for people to learn and grow. But listening is the most important and critical channel for learning. There are of course people who suffer from a disability and as a result their hearing ability is impaired. They learn too, but the bar is definitely higher for them.

Listening is spiritual in a very deep and meaningful way. When the first intelligent organism heard a voice, the voice of creation or that of the Creator, a spiritual link was established that continues unbroken billions of years after in the present time, and our longing to hear that voice keeps us going on a spiritual path. Listening to sacred sounds is a spiritual experience. The same is true of listening to the voice and the words of a spiritual teacher.

The work that we do has spiritual dimension too. The word "spiritual" might mean different things to different people, but listening to others in the workplace is an act that directly connects with our deeper values, which some people treat as a dimension of our spiritual self.

Listening becomes more challenging as we leave our own cultural milieu and travel to other countries. The voices of traders in a small town in a developing country may not be familiar to us at first but as we pay attention to the body language and the material objects around these people, the meanings start to become clearer. But it needs more attention and greater effort. It also requires acceptance and appreciation of a different way of life. "Listening is a form of accepting," Stella Terrill Mann rightly points out.

As the world is increasingly turning itself into one large marketplace with all kinds of virtual and video connections, we don't have to leave our own space to experience crosscultural exchanges. Today's workplace is multicultural and its reality is further complicated by virtual teams that extend over geographic boundaries and time zones calling for higher levels of listening and understanding than ever before.

Listening is a bundle of competencies that enables us to:

- Pay attention to what is important
- Comprehend the focus and direction of conversation
- Communicate effectively
- Build bridges with people from other cultures
- Learn and grow as individuals
- Expand and deepen our inner self, and the our connection with the power that lies beyond us.

Building on the work of Ken Wilber (2000a, 2000b) and his four-quadrant model, we get four quadrants of listening consistent with four dimensions of Wilber's model—inner-outer, intersubjective, and interobjective.

Intentional Listening	Behavioral Listening
Cultural Listening	Systemic Listening

Intentional listening: It is subjective, inner and constitutes the realm of thinking and imagination. It is about self and self-consciousness. It is the level where deeper listening occurs. The word "intent" comes from Latin *intentus* meaning stretching out, which in this context means stretching out our purpose, our state of mind, our meaning, and in this act of intending rests the core of our being. Intentional listening is about the meaning and purpose, about what we are trying to achieve. It is personal, transformational, and growth-oriented. Not listening at the intentional level is like building a boundary wall around us and disconnecting from the others.

Intentional listening is a deep form of listening with a clear focus on meaning and purpose, but if this is the only listening we are doing, misalignments can result at the level of our body, our interpretation of the social nature of the relationship with the speaker, and our disconnection with the overall context of the conversation (systemic or organizational).

Behavioral listening: It is objective, outer, organismic and constitutes the visible part of our listening—a signal to the others that we are or aren't listening. It is the level where others see how we conduct ourselves in the act of listening, meaning our response to the others in the form of our body language. It shows how we respond to the external stimulation—the spoken words, the notes of a symphony, or a bird song.

Behavioral listening is most superficial of all because it is nothing more than putting up a show or an appearance. Such listening does not help us and could potentially hurt our image, as someone not interested in listening.

Cultural listening: It occurs against the backdrop of shared worldviews and by its very nature it is intersubjective, meaning it is accessible to or capable of being established for two or more subjects. Culture is interior but it is also collective. It is about shared assumptions and patterns of belief system. Every conversation takes place within a cultural context so as to speak because people bring to the conversation their own worldviews. Myth, magic, metaphors, stories and anecdotes play a role in the broader cultural context.

Cultural listening is a deeper form of listening as we are paying full attention to its relational context and the crosscultural factors, but this one-dimensional focus too is limiting in effectiveness. Relations need to be viewed against the backdrop of their systemic significance unless the conversation is limited to weather or one's favorite TV show.

Systemic listening: It is external but it is also collective and interobjective. We can also call it contextual listening because it occurs in the wider socio-political and organizational context. In today's highly connected world we are never far removed from a "system" of one or another kind. State plays a big role in terms of deciding not only issues of war and peace but also through its economic and regulatory policies that impact the lives of ordinary people and thus determines what they talk about and what they listen to. And then there are organizations, both big and small, that play an important role in the lives of people as employers, providers of services, users of materials and know-how and thus form a significant part of their lives. Therefore, it is hard to imagine a conversation that is absolutely free from any kind of organizational or institutional context or a broader worldview of how things are shaping up for the future. Even a couple planning their summer vacation is faced with questions of personal security, cost of the trip (that in turn is impacted by a variety of economic factors), pressures of competing engagements, and of course the day's newspaper headlines.

It is hard to grade something as "perfect" listening, but if there is anything that comes close to achieving any form of perfection, it is the dynamic balance that we are able to strike between the four quadrants of listening. The distinction becomes clear if we imagine ourselves using only one quadrant (or one channel) at a time.

Systemic listening is hard to do in isolation, but it is not without its merit in some professional contexts. A good example is the bureaucratic, authority focused, conversation where the primary focus is on listening to the message in terms of its organizational implications. The speaker, usually an authority figure, commands attention, does most of the speaking and the listener responds with a "yes" answer without any counter proposal. This form of listening is as superficial as anything else though apparently it serves its intended purpose. But in the end it creates frustration both for the speaker and the listener. No wonder, lack of effective listening is cited as the main reason for bad communication in most organizations. This situation is not likely to change unless we develop capacity for all-quadrant listening, which the above model suggests.

Here are some strategies for improving your intentional listening:

1. **Summarizing:** This is the most important listening strategy that forces you to listen carefully because you

know that in the end you will have to summarize the main points. Summarizing should not be used as a matter of routine because it could become boring or taxing for the other person. But in important conversations, particularly business negotiations, this is a very powerful tool. It is particularly helpful for checking understanding, or laying the foundation of an important agreement. This is sometimes referred to as reframing. There is an ethical issue that is relevant to both summarizing as well as reframing: honesty or integrity of the summarizer or the re-framer. If you change the essence of the speakers' message or put a different spin on the words used by the speaker you will not be summarizing but gaming your way out of a conversation. This will raise some ethical questions. What is your intent? Are you suggesting something that the speaker didn't have in mind? In the latter case, you need to say more in order to clarify your position in terms of why you are hearing the person the way you do and what are the consequences for the person concerned of your understanding.

2. **Proactive Listening:** We listen to the words because words contain meaning. But the problem with this approach is that most of the times meaning is much bigger than the words. Words in fact convey only a small portion of what is being said. Meaning has to do with the perspective or the worldview of the person speaking. We may have great ideas in our head, but words will always elude us. Some people are very good in terms of having a very close alignment between words and meanings, but in most cases words are inadequate and distorted version of one's worldview. An old friend of mine used to say, meanings are in people and not in words. And what is in people is their perspective that they often have difficulty putting into words.

This problem can be addressed in several ways. We suggest proactive listening. This strategy simply takes a higher altitude view of the conversation ("chunking up"). What does this person mean? We look for the perspective ("where is he coming from") instead of narrowly focusing on the words. It is "proactive" because we are constantly validating the meaning we are getting. We get a view but wait for the person to confirm it. We look for the words that would validate our interpretation. Proactive listening is a powerful strategy for important conversations where it is important for us to understand the "mind" of the other person.

3. **Empathetic Listening:** Empathy is a powerful emotion in situations where we have to virtually "put ourselves in another person's shoes" in order for us to understand the special circumstances of the life or environment of the other person. This is not a strategy that we need to use all the time. But there are circumstances where the person speaking to us can't have any deeper meaning for us unless we put ourselves in her position. Imagine talking to a rape victim, or the victim of a terroiist bombing? The spoken words will be few and perhaps sporadic. The only way we can listen to this conversation is to place ourselves in that situation. What would I say if I were in a similar situation? What would be my feelings like? How much of my pain I would convey through nonverbal gestures? Empathetic listening is essentially listening for feelings ("second position listening"), and this could be best done if we can place ourselves in a similar emotional state.

How do you turn your body into a real listening post? Listening to the words is only half the meaning that the other is trying to convey. People speak through their bodies as they do through their speech. The basic listening strategy, combining intentional and behavioral listening, is to pay attention to the words as well as the person in front of you. This could be done in several ways including:

- Maintain good eye contact at all times. There are of course cultural consequences in the sense that a prolonged eye contact is considered rude or intimidating in many cultures. This means that we have to be sensitive to the context in which the conversation is taking place. But let us not forget that the loss of eye contact also means the loss of our ability to monitor the others' body language. There is always a fine balance in these things. Try to find yours.

- Body language should convey interest and engagement.
- A relaxed body posture could help us to get rid of any signs of tension.
- Agreement on different points could be conveyed with a slight movement of our head.
- It is better to take notes if it is an important work related conversation.
- We should keep our face "alive" showing our energy and excitement. Dull or tense facial expressions indicate our loss of interest.
- We should take a physical position directly in line of sight of the person we are speaking with.
- We should pay particular attention to the facial expression of the person who is doing the talking together with variations in the voice tone. We don't have to be face readers to know that people sometimes cut short their speech in the middle of a sentence and convey the rest through their facial expressions.

What are some of the unique challenges posed by systemic listening? This type of listening most often occurs in an institutional or an organizational context. In view of this, the two factors that play an important role are the nature of authority relationship and the fear (both of the known as well as the unknown). Even when the speaker and the listener have the same authority, fear could play a role in the sense that the conversation might involve hidden agendas or power plays. There is therefore need for an innovative approach to systemic listening that separates fear from the act of listening and understanding.

Robert Greenleaf, visionary thinker and founder of servant leadership concept, narrated one such story in his 1977 book

Servant Leadership. "One of our able leaders recently was made the head of a large, important, and difficult-to-administer public institution. After a short time he realized that he was not happy with the way things were going. His approach to the problem was a bit unusual. For three months he stopped reading newspapers and listening to news broadcasts; and for this period he relied wholly upon those he met in the course of his work to tell him what was going on. In three months his administrative problems were resolved. No miracles were wrought; but out of a sustained intentness of listening that was produced by this unusual decision, this able man learned and received the insights needed to set the right course. And he strengthened his team by so doing."

Dialogue: Meaning Beyond Words

Dialogue is generally associated with the practice popularized by Socrates (c. 469-399 BC) and described at length in the works of his disciple Plato (c. 429-347 BC). The origin of the word "dialogue" can thus be traced to the Greek word *dialogos* meaning the process through which meaning of words are found. The process of dialogue is in fact like the unfolding of a musical composition. It is the constant flow of thought and meaning among a group of individuals who may have both common and dissimilar characteristics. These people may belong to one corporate entity, or they may be drawn from a larger segment of society.

Dialogue, says physicist David Bohm, occurs when meaning flows: someone floats an idea, another person adds something new to that idea, little parts start to make the whole, everyone partakes in the whole as the whole, and in this way the process moves along. Bohm was very meticulous about the do's and don'ts of arranging a dialogue session. More than anything else it was a fine balancing act between the sponsor's aspirations and what the group was interested in talking. The rules of thumb, which are to be applied flexibly, would include:

- *Group size.* The process works better with a group of twenty and more. Small groups have a different dynamic that is inconsistent with the processes of an authentic dialogue group.

- *Common broader objective.* Participants in a dialogue session may have wide differences of opinions, but they would be a better group if they shared some common understanding of broader objectives of the conversation. Two warring factions may have different perspectives, but as long as they agree on the long-term need to make peace they will be a good group for a dialogue session.
- *The work environment.* The environment in which the session is conducted is important. What is needed is a peaceful setting without unwanted distractions. Seating in a circle with empty space in the middle is highly desirable.
- *The need for spontaneity.* Sponsors should not worry too much whether they are or aren't going to have a dialogue. Let there be spontaneity in what people wish to talk about. Some conscious risk-taking is better than a rigidly planned approach. Too much concern with failure can make the session mechanistic and less satisfying for participants.
- *Dialogue about the dialogue.* The best way to introduce a group to the intricacies of the technique is to engage them in a dialogue about the dialogue they are going to have (a meta-dialogue). Presenting this as an innovative experiment also helps in lowering the initial expectations.
- *Agenda.* The dialogue session needs no fixed agenda. Sponsors would be better off if they restrain from having a narrowly defined goal or purpose. Also don't even try to bill the conversation as useful since what is and what is not useful could itself be a divisive issue.
- *Leader.* A dialogue session does not need a leader, but an experienced facilitator with a low profile is highly desirable.
- *Coherence.* It is the most valued quality of a dialogue group—going like a laser in the same direction, digging deeper as the laser keeps moving.

- *Language.* The language used by the participants is extremely important. Bohm tells the reframing story pertaining to a seven-year old girl who was extremely hostile to her psychologist.

  Psychologist: Why don't you talk to me?

  Girl: Because I hate you.

  Psychologist: How long will you hate me?

  Girl: I'll hate you forever.

  Psychologist: How long will you hate me forever?

  The girl burst out laughing and the hostility was gone in a minute.
- *Individual versus collective thoughts.* Individual thoughts should shape collective thoughts and vice-versa. There should be continuous interaction between individual and group thoughts.
- *Suspend all assumptions.* If people hold very different positions, there will be some negotiation at the start, but dialogue itself is not another form of negotiation.
- *Trust.* Building a climate of trust is the most challenging task facing a dialogue facilitator. To convey through words and actions that all viewpoints are equally welcome and valid will be a good initial step toward building a climate of trust.
- *Decision-making.* A dialogue group is not a decision-making group. Groups that make decisions are neither free nor open
- *The outcome.* The outcome of a dialogue session is to be treated as a mystery that can unfold in many ways. Bohm recalls the Biblical account of the seed. The seed will grow to be a fruitful tree if it falls on some fertile soil. If it hits a rock, nothing will ever grow.
- *Conclusion.* There is no one best way to end a dialogue session. The group may agree to meet again or do something else. As far as the session is concerned the cup is fully emptied until the time the participants meet again to fill the cup with something else.

Dialogue: The Four-step Pattern

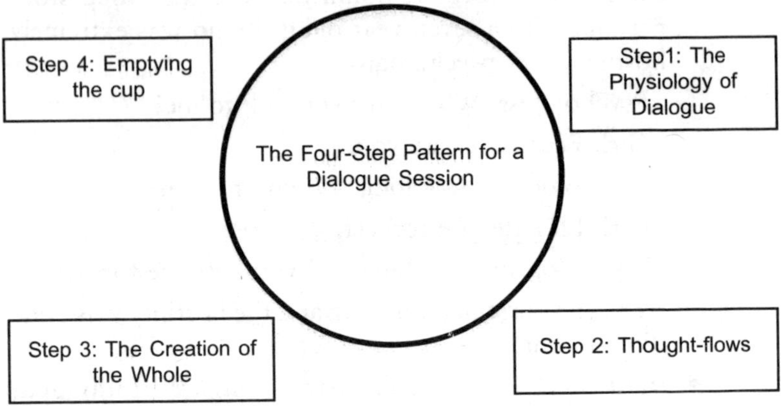

Step 1: The Physiology of Dialogue

Participants are asked to pay attention to their physical reactions. This includes sight, sound, and kinesthetics (feelings). Dialogue requires presence in the moment. Having good eye contact and listening while one has suspended all judgment is extremely important. We can impact our feelings, positively or negatively, by carrying on an internal dialogue that distracts our attention from action that is taking place around us. Feelings play an important part in generating an internal conversation. Words should flow like water in a stream without much conscious attention.

Another helpful suggestion is to ask participants that they adopt the second position. The second position is to look at the reality with another's eyes, to hear the messages that the other is hearing, and to experience the feelings that the other is experiencing. It also means being associated with another person's point of view, assumptions and opinions, and really seeing the world from another person's vantage point. As long as we are dug into our own position (our first position), we are looking at the world through our most preferred perceptual filters. It is therefore difficult for us to escape from our beliefs, assumptions, including our biases.

Step 2: Thought-flows

This has to do with the origin of our ideas in a dialogue session—how are they presented, how do they float from one person to another. Ideas should float like an object floating on the surface of the water—effortless, pleasing to the eyes, overcoming all barriers by going around them, always moving ahead fully synchronized with the speed of the water itself.

We can enhance the quality of thought-flows by understanding the map-territory distinction. We know the reality through the map that we carry in our own mind. There is no absolutely correct map. When we understand the apparent limitations of the map of our mind, we become open to the other maps. Bohm understood this distinction and he talked about it in one of his presentations (Bohm 1985, p. 36). He said, "[The] linear view of time is an abstraction. It's like a map. You can use this map to guide you but the map is not the same as territory. The map may correspond to some features of the territory, but it is never complete, and also it may be distorted." Bohm also validated the view that both mind and body are really one.

Step 3: The Creation of the Whole

This is a natural process. It should happen, says Bohm, if both the individual and the collective allow the stream of meaning to flow unhindered in the center. How can we insure that the conversation will follow the natural course and will stay in the center? Any structural intervention runs the risk of coming in the way of the natural ebb and flow of conversation. Yet an experienced facilitator can encourage participants to use reframing. Reframing shifts the focus of attention from a smaller frame to a bigger frame and vice-versa. The bigger frame widens our vision and we see more details, objects, and people than offered by a smaller frame.

Another relevant intervention will be the use of chunking. This suggests that by slicing information into smaller or larger pieces one can gain a much deeper understanding of the information being shared. Any information can be chunked up (talk about the forest and not the trees), chunked down (talk about individual trees), and chunked laterally (talk about mountains instead of trees). Chunking up and chunking down are inductive and deductive modes of thinking, respectively. Gregory Bateson conceived chunking laterally as an abductive mode of thinking that provokes us to think in terms of metaphors and analogies.

Step 4: Emptying the Cup

This step brings the dialogue session to a close. Unlike other kinds of conversations where the facilitator is required to summarize the main conclusions of the meeting or talk about the next steps, a dialogue session ends without these rituals. The participants should carry the feeling that they have come closer to a shared understanding of some issue. It is the duty of the facilitator to ensure that the "cup" is emptied by saying something on the following lines: "We have had a meaningful conversation that has moved us closer to creating a shared understanding of the issue before us. But let us now empty this cup and fill it with other ideas, thoughts, and meanings when we meet next." People understand the wisdom of not trying to fill the cup that is already full!

Journal Writing

If you are looking for a simple yet highly effective tool for self-reflection, there is nothing better than a simple journal. If you commit yourself to writing your journal regularly, preferably at the same time early morning, you got a great way of gaining greater self-awareness. The process for writing the journal is pretty straightforward. You have to put yourself in a reflective mood and let your writing flow. Do not stop and judge the quality of your writing. The important point is to capture the flow of your thoughts. If you are not comfortable with the free-flowing approach and would like some precise guidelines on how to maintain your journal, here are some good hints: Make a list of things that are most important to you in the moment. Reflect on your most recent personal experiences. Write down a couple of things you have learned. Write down any interesting remarks you have heard, any TV show or movie you have watched and liked, or any book that you have read that left a strong impression on you. Capture reflections on your most important values. Your vision and how you are translating your vision into reality is another important subject. Write about your barriers or challenges. What do they mean to you? Write a short poem about something that touched your heart. Write down any other thoughts that come to your mind.

A Few Other Things

Try to express yourself creatively in all forms—words, drawing, painting, dance forms, vocal or instrumental music. Live life with spontaneity and grace. If the need of the moment is song and dance, sing and dance. If it is prayer and meditation, pray and meditate. Constantly produce results beyond the ordinary. Always go beyond your normal limits. Spend more time in the company of people who are high achievers. Mediocrity pulls us back. Tell the truth and express the voice of your conscience under all circumstances. Model an integral way of life whereby body, mind, heart, and soul are all taken care of in an equal or appropriate measure. Learn to make a connection with one's deepest self while embracing everything that is new and different. Show humility coupled with simplicity. Keep a record of one's dreams. Use intuition for making sense of what's happening around your operating environment. Find beauty in everything, and express yourself beautifully notwithstanding the constraints of time and space.

A Poetic Interlude

Creativity

I need to break myself free
from the web of expectations,
rules of the game, so to say.

Do this, not this,
speak but not too loud,
walk but don't run,
sing but don't disturb those
who are fast asleep.

Laugh but not too loud,
climb high but not too high.
Be kind to strangers, but not too kind,

I need to change myself.
I need to erase
a part of my personal history —
memories, influences of teachers
and caring mentors.
I have to forget the convoluted
pathways of my own journey.

I have to die every day to be born again —
vibrant, fresh and expandable.
When I start this new life —
a life free of do's and don'ts —
I become creative.

To be creative is natural.
Creativity is not yours or mine.
It's truly nameless —
true creativity is anonymous.
To be truly creative we draw from a deeper well —
the well of shared consciousness,
where personal differences are meaningless
and where we are one as humans

and we create new images, new poetry,
we build new minarets for everyone to see,
to cherish and to be at home.

True creativity has no cause and effect;
it's just there.
We can own it or ignore it;
it does not go away.
It stays like a musical note in the air—
unseen yet vibrant when it hits our eardrums.

Creativity is to ask for more —
more of us as humans.
And the world we live in

It is about making demands
that can't be met.
But when we have it—
it is like having a sun,
when a broken candle's light
was enough to look ourselves in the mirror.

From *A Moment in the Universe* (2006, pp. 23-25)

5. A SUMMARY OF KEY IDEAS

- When we are creative, we are dipping into layers of our unconscious self that is the repository of everything that is good and beautiful.
- Creative people have the capacity to stand alone to defend their beliefs, and they don't change their commitments seasonally to benefit self or others.
- Speech is not only what we want to talk. It is about our authenticity as human beings.
- Listening is always in the present moment, and if we are not living in the moment we can't listen. The presence of our body is essential but it is not adequate. We need the presence of our inner body (mental presence) too.
- The process of dialogue is in fact like the unfolding of a musical composition. It is the constant flow of thought and meaning among a group of individuals who may have both common and dissimilar characteristics.
- Reframing shifts the focus of attention from a smaller frame to a bigger frame and vice-versa. The bigger frame widens our vision and we see more details, objects, and people than offered by a smaller frame.
- Chunking up and chunking down are inductive and deductive modes of thinking, respectively. Gregory Bateson, British anthropologist, conceived chunking laterally as an abductive mode of thinking that provokes us to think in terms of metaphors and analogies.
- If you commit yourself to writing your journal regularly, preferably at the same time early morning, you got a great way of gaining greater self-awareness.
- Expressing oneself creatively in all forms—words, drawing, painting, dance forms, vocal or instrumental music. Living life with spontaneity and grace. If the need of the moment is song and dance, sing and dance. If it is prayer and meditation, pray and meditate.

- Finding beauty in everything, and expressing oneself artistically notwithstanding the constraints of time and space is a great personal quality.

6 Our Intuitive Self

THE MAP

In the ascending journey of our consciousness, spiritual level is the first station where we have the experience of pure awareness. There are different ways of defining terms like spiritual or spirituality. But in most definitions, there are references to the existence of the unknown, something which is beyond our ordinary perception. We can know the "unknown" only by the power of inner seeing and there are practices that enable us to precisely do that. The important point to remember is that spiritual is not religious. Religion is about dogma, believing a certain interpretation of nature or God, accepting a certain scripture as Truth, and worshipping in a certain prescribed manner. Spirituality, on the other hand, has to do with believing in oneself, having an open mind about the nature of reality, being inclusive and pluralistic in one's outlook, and accepting the existence of many paths to spiritual enlightenment.

According to a landmark research study published in The Journal of Nursing (Number 27, 1998), researchers D.S. Martsolf and J.R. Mickley hypothesized that spirituality is closely related to personal well-being. It has to do with:

Meaning: significance of life; making sense of situations; deriving purpose.

Values: beliefs, standards and ethics that are cherished.

Transcendence: experience, awareness, and appreciation of a "transcendent dimension" to life before self.

Connecting: increased awareness of a connection with self; God, Spirit, Divine and nature or Nature.

Becoming: an unfolding of life that demands reflection and experience, including a sense of who one is and how one knows.

At its core, spirituality is a deeper awareness of things, people, or nature and this awareness often comes to us through intuition. The basic problem that philosophers have struggled for ages to resolve is: *how do we know what exists.* French philosopher Rene Descartes distinguished between two sources of knowledge: intuition and deduction. Intuition, according to Descartes, is unmediated mental seeing or direct apprehension. Czech philosopher, Edmund Husserl, known for his work on Phenomenology, called intuition a "primordially given act" upon which all the rest is to be found. On the other hand, philosophers like John Locke stated that what we know can only be explained in terms of our experience. Yet even Locke recognized the existence of something outside the perception of external objects, which he called "reflection"—doubting, believing, knowing, and willing.

The Power of Intuition

Intuition is an act of knowing outside the realm of our sensing experiences, observation, or inference. Over time, intuition has gained the reputation of being an independent source of knowledge. True intuition bypasses logical, sensing, and analytical process of gaining knowledge of reality. Intuition is not based on experience, though our life experiences may have some deep rooted connections with intuitive insights that come to us. Although reason plays little or no part in intuition, people tend to "rationalize" their intuition, taking a particular insight as a validation of a certain course of action. Brainstorming is a more organized form of intuition whereby we try to get new ideas around a well-defined theme or topic. What is generally known as the "sixth sense" or "extrasensory perception" (ESP) is a form of intuition that is deeply grounded in our unconscious. Intuition in this sense means something that has no connection with our waking reality.

Some earliest references to the power of intuition were found in the *Yoga Sutras* of the great sage Patanjali. A disciplined yogi, according to Patanjali, could easily attain states of awareness by loosening restrictions of the egoic mind. In this state of non-egoic awareness, we can observe reality that is beyond the power of ordinary seeing.

Carl Jung recognized intuition as one among the four mental functions besides sensing, thinking, and feeling. "The primary function of intuition," says Jung, "is simply to transmit images, or perceptions of relations between things, which could not be transmitted by other functions, or only in a roundabout way. These images have the value of specific insights which have a decisive influence on action whenever intuition is given priority." Jung's reference to *synchronicity* (you think of a friend, the phone rings, and the person you thought about is calling you) as uncanny coincidences that have no apparent causal connection, but can turn out to be very influential in the lives of people experiencing them, is another example of how intuition works in our life.

How can we improve our ability to make our intuitive self work for us? There are several ways of doing this including:

- Do not deny the existence of intuition as a productive force in life, which also means: do not put too much store on sensing experiences. In real life, both sensing and intuition have a role to play.
- Look out for information that is beyond what is seen by the naked eye. Search for deeper meaning and deeper explanations, why certain things happen.
- Maintain a diary or a learning journal and record your reflections on a regular basis.
- Actively listen to your inner voice. Spirit talks to us all the time. Inner messages are drowned out by the noises of our daily workings. That is why taking a walk or finding some quiet time is so essential for inner listening.
- Suspend your judgments about people and things and develop the art of looking at things as they are. Judgments and beliefs disable our ability to gain intuitive insights.
- Pay attention to coincidental happenings, or what Jung calls *synchronicity*. Keep an open mind—a mind that is

willing to take risk and accept unconventional ways of doing things.

- Engage in a spiritual practice like vipassana or mindfulness meditation. Or simply do breathing exercises. Any time we are in touch with ourselves we nurture our ability for intuition.
- Literary pursuits like story writing or poetry recitation are other excellent ways for reinforcing our intuitive self.
- Intuition can play an enormous role in promoting business success. Michael Ray, professor of creativity and innovation at Stanford and author of *Creativity in Business,* talks about five truths about intuition in business. These are: intuition is a gift that must be developed; intuition complements reason; intuition is unemotional; intuition demands action; and intuition is mistake-free (having faith that intuition is part of us that never makes mistakes).

Values and Needs

Spiritual level consciousness is like knowing and experiencing the unknown from a distance. Intuition is a special quality of this consciousness that helps in bridging the gulf between our aspirations and hidden potentialities. There is also an emergence of the visionary outlook that helps us in making a connection with the unseen and the unknown. Visual imagination makes things transparent which are not part of our reality and which we can only dream of. Insightful thinking gives rise to ideas that have no identifiable form or shape but have depth that is hard to measure. Self-reflection is deeper and fuller and therefore richer because of its affinity with spirit. There is a merger of rational with spiritual whereby intuition informs logic, and heart speaks to mind. There is a sense of completeness and wholeness, not experienced before. Information gives way to knowledge, knowledge turns itself into wisdom, and wisdom madly seeks to find oneness—an elusive target, reachable but quite distant still.

The needs at this level are subtle and non-material. Examples would include recognizing patterns in a messy situation (pattern recognition), seeing oneself and others in great clarity, experiencing the surge of spiritual energy within, opening self to scriptures and other forms of spiritual awakening, and seeing one's smaller self as part of a bigger unified whole.

Communication and Leadership Style

People who have attained this level of consciousness are known for the purity and simplicity of their thinking. They can break very complex formulations into simplest routines. Serving a broader global, national or a communitarian goal is what really motivates them. They provide a vision to their followers that is highly empowering and energizing. Most often, they combine exceptional cognitive abilities with impeccable personal character and moral values. Their favorite expressions include: "We want to create a new world.... We have a vision of where we want to go.... Working together we will create a better future for all of us...." Managing change is not a problem because these leaders are masters of adapting to different circumstances painlessly and smoothly. They are also great modelers of change that they wish to bring about in others. Any conflict situation is an opportunity for expanding the range of options available for action. They always aim at creating win-win solutions and desist from imposing partisan viewpoints on minorities and non-followers. People like Gandhi, King, and Mandela immediately come to mind, but there are many less known examples of spiritually-informed leaders who are making a difference in various walks of life—science, education, healthcare, community service, government, journalism, and economic development.

LIVING STORIES

Kirk and Katie are two very talented individuals. They have inborn qualities that make someone an artist. But they lead very different lives. While one is on the way to becoming a self-actualized person, the other is losing faith in herself and not going anywhere.

Kirk is a fashion photographer. His work regularly appears in magazines and his photographs have been featured in several documentaries. Kirk's father was an engineer and he naturally wanted his only son to follow in his footsteps. But engineering was the last thing on Kirk's mind. He wanted to go to an art school, which meant his father would have to support him financially for several years. Kirk didn't like the idea of any dependence on anyone once he was out of high school.

He started his work life in a typical downtown photo studio, first taking care of the owner's expensive photographic equipment and then taking all kinds of pictures, from passport photos to fancy portraits, and outdoor shoots for sports and wedding functions. When the owner retired, Kirk bought the studio with some help from his father. Meanwhile, the science and art of photography was going through many revolutionary changes, from B & W pictures to color, from bulky studio camera to very powerful portable cameras for outdoor photography. Kirk made many experiments, including a two year stint in Africa taking pictures of birds and animals. Nude photography attracted him for some time because he wanted to work with beautiful women. But this didn't last very long. Kirk started to specialize in photographing models for ad agencies, fashion shows, and magazines. By mid-1980s he had enough name recognition to start taking pictures of famous people—rock stars, stage and film stars, politicians, literary figures, and "people who just looked damn good."

Kirk attributes his success to his ability to visualize things and people and faith in himself. He is not religious but his unceasing search for the unknown has made him a very spiritually driven person. "I first photograph people in my mind. I let my intuitive mind work on different possibilities before I start the shoot. Pictures are ready in my mind and then the rest is just loading the film and pressing the button. I make a good living, but that's not why I'm in this business. My work provides me with a strong sense of being." Kirk looks forward to a day in the near future when he would collect his best pictures and put them into a coffee-table book. "What I visualize always becomes a reality," he says with great amount of confidence.

Unlike Kirk, Katie went to a prestigious art school in France.

She wanted to be a great painter and make lots of money. She had all the good qualities that would have made her a great artist, except that she was always very impatient. She didn't stick to one thing for very long. She was frustrated when her work was criticized in newspaper columns or it failed to get the price that she expected.

Over the past few years, Katie has really lost touch with her current reality. She is a very intuitive person and gets great ideas for her artwork, but she is a poor implementer. She lived with a man for several years without realizing that he was only interested in stealing her money and not marrying her.

She went to South America to spend some time with a community service organization, but that has not helped her in any significant way. She is as indecisive as ever. She relies on her intuition, but this is like too much of day-dreaming. Many of her friends have deserted her lately because they found her becoming too inflexible and arrogant.

What's going on here?

Intuition is a great quality—a great spiritual quality because it helps us open closed doors; it helps us make sense of what is confusing and incomplete. Kirk has found his spiritual fulfillment in his work because he sees himself as a doer, a kind of modern day Karma Yogi. Katie has many things going for her and potentially she could go much farther than Kirk, but something has held her back. Her mind runs faster than her hands. She wants to do many things in too short a time. Her lack of achievement is frustrating Katie inasmuch as that she is now losing confidence in herself. What can she do to help herself? She needs to better control her imagination running off in different directions. If she can balance her intuition with visible results, she can still get on track. Intuition is a great spiritual gift, but it needs to be managed. The essence of artistic life lies in the act of giving birth to objects or performances that others can see and appreciate. What plays in our mind stays with us.

DEVELOPMENT CHALLENGES

Spiritual "disconnection"

Spiritual orientation can under certain circumstances lead to "disconnection" with reality. People can experience extreme forms of obsessive introversion. This is a state in which people become susceptible to hallucinations and delusions. Spiritual awareness that one is experiencing becomes an end in itself and the bigger picture is lost for gaining proficiency in tools and techniques for empowering self in a very narrow sense. The end result is the fear of losing this limited influence. This is not the true spiritual path and those who realize this fallacy move on to the next stage.

Spiritual "materialism" or "arrogance"

There is a broader concern with what is called "spiritual materialism" or "spiritual arrogance." There is an urge for making the self more powerful and thus one is seeking spiritual authority with the same passion as some other person is chasing material wealth. The arrogance shows up in "I have answers because I know everything" kind of attitude. These tendencies are real path blockers; they can in fact take a person down to lower levels of consciousness. On the other hand, realization of one's contradictory pursuits and taking some corrective actions can bring the person back on track.

Spiritual archetypes

Spiritual intelligence, if rightly pursued, is a key to finding one's archetypical identity. We personify some archetypes (or primordial forms) consciously or unconsciously—like Mother (the nourisher), Father (the protector), Warrior (the fighter for noble causes), Magician (someone who can suddenly change the shape and form of things), or Victim (someone who is unfairly accused of wrongdoing). There is no limit to these archetypes and our life stories are in some ways repetitions of these archetypes. The real insight here is the realization that every life story is part and parcel of the bigger story, the universal story. This perspective is helpful in restoring our universal connection.

DEVELOPMENTAL INTERVENTIONS

Imagining Possibilities

We often hear messages that say to us: use and build the power of your imagination; imagine possibilities, imagine a life beyond your self-imposed boundaries. It shows very simply the role that imagination plays in our life. What is imagination? It is the power of seeing something that does not exist in reality. It is the act of reaching out to an idea or an image in the context of a future situation. Imagination is thus the essential requirement for creating works of art and literature—a representation of life in some aspects, but it is reality solely seen through the eyes of its creator. By its very nature, imagination involves an associative process, whereby experience evokes ideas and thus it becomes one with the idea.

According to German philosopher Immanuel Kant, imagination is a synthesis of two processes. First, it is seeing something in real experience. Second, it is imagining its possibilities in an abstract sense. When these two things are joined together, imagination is born. The process is in the nature of a free-play with sudden leaps and jumps. George Santayana and Jean-Paul Sartre presented the same idea when they stated that imagination is a "fusion" of content and experience, in which case "content" could be anything—real or imagined.

We should not confuse imagination with fancy. Imagination is certainly a higher form of abstract thinking than fancy. Poet Samuel Taylor Coleridge was right when he differentiated between the two. Imagination is a form of creativity, the power to shape reality and unify that is separative, while fancy is purely associative thinking.

There is a close connection between dreams and visual imagination. Therefore, paying particular attention to our dreams is very important. It is even suggested that you consider maintaining a dream journal. While we think about our dreams we should remember that this is one way our unconscious is trying to communicate with us. Learning about dreams is a way of establishing a relationship with one's inner self.

For success in life and business, we should use our imagination to think about possibilities, new ways of doing things and leading our lives. Sometime this is called "thinking outside the box" or right-brain thinking. There is some evidence that the two sides of our brain are distinctive hemispheres with distinctive functions. Right side of the brain is more prone to emotional expressions, including leaps of fancy and free-plays of our imaginative thinking.

Developing Visual Imagination

How can we enhance our capacity for visual imagination? The capacity to visualize a certain future is a very powerful tool in achieving extraordinary outcomes. Generally, it is believed that it is a gift of nature. Some people have it while others don't. But the good news is that the capacity for visual imagination can be developed with little effort.

One very special ability for visual imagination is called *synesthesia*. A person shows signs of synesthesia when he or she reports that stimulation through one sense organ leads to experiences in another sense organ. A popular example is a person who while listening to Beethoven symphonies sees waves of color rise and fall. It is a condition in which two sense organs are coupled or they work together. Successful visionary leaders often use language that combines the use of two or more sense organs. Dr. Martin Luther King was master of using language that appealed to several sense organs at the same time. We see the demonstration of this in business world quite frequently. While you can find one business leader talk about strategy in dull numbers of market share and gross margins, another leader paints a picture of a very successful future that "makes people listen through their eyes."

Research has shown that there are measurable benefits of using more than one channel to filter our life experiences. We become more creative and gain greater degree of confidence to handle associative thinking. Using language that contains elements of synesthesia is highly effective in conveying powerful messages. NLP trainer Bill Thomason quotes the following sentence to show the power of synesthesia: *Tell me the flavor of what you were seeing when you first tasted your eyes on the fragrant land of rhythms and form not found in every day experience.* This sentence is very powerful because it appeals to all our five senses.

Cultivating Optimism

People with optimistic disposition symbolize hope and positive outcomes in every situation. They shed skepticism and cynicism in favor of a brighter tomorrow. Cultivating optimism is accepting the power of one's mind to generate happiness and satisfaction in place of fear and rejection. It is like seeing the world in bright and shiny colors instead of a black and white view of things. Every color holds the key to certain hidden energies. Learning to unlock those energies is a crucial step forward in our self development.

Martin Seligman, who has written extensively on optimism, has pointed out that the academic world is obsessed with depression (pessimism). During the last three decades of the 20th century, he mentions, 46,000 research papers were published on depression and only 4,000 on joy (optimism). Seligman together with S.F. Meir has also done seminal research on what is called "learned helplessness." When people go into depression, they experience helplessness that is epitomized by three conditions:

Personal: I am the problem.

Pervasive: The problem affects all aspects of my life.

Permanent: The problem is unchangeable.

In order for us to experience optimism, we have to come out of this vicious cycle of "explanatory style" (the state of learned helplessness).

Evolutionary biologist Stephen Jay Gould has developed a theory called "Tragic Optimism." By this he means our inability as a society or as a nation to do the right things at the right time, though we have the capacity to avert the tragedy that strikes us.

There were enough lifeboats available, but ships didn't carry enough supplies until the tragic sinking of Titanic and the loss of nearly one thousand lives. As pointed by economist Amartya Sen, people died during famines not due to shortage of food but due to the lack of transport systems to carry enough food to the affected areas. We have the capacity to stop genocide related killings, but we do not act until a big one comes around. Katrina related disaster was avoidable if levees were strengthened on a regular basis. All the major disasters in Iraq war (looting of the museum, prison abuse, etc.) were avoidable if there was proper planning and implementation of the plans for occupation.

Optimism as a philosophy of life has several well-documented benefits. For example, it is observed that optimists live longer than pessimists and even suffer less from serious body ailments. Optimism brings a special mood that is helpful in enhancing personal effectiveness.

How can we enhance our sense of optimism? Books on the subject contain a number of suggestions. Here is a sampling of few:

- Fight pessimism, skepticism, and cynicism in every form.
- Do not accept a negative thought as a best solution to a problem.
- Believe firmly in human goodness, but use your common sense before placing blind trust in others. Some checks and balances are essential for healthy relationships.
- Always focus on possibilities. There are choices that we do not generally make use of.
- Cultivate values of humility, gratitude, interdependence, and harmony.

A Poetic Interlude

Emergence

We live in a universe of emergent novelty.
Karl Popper

People talk about emergence —
emergent leadership,
emergent learning,
emergent solutions,
though they do not understand
what it means.

Emergence is not a thing
that is felt
with our bare hands.
It is a process,
a self-organizing process.

Emergence is everything.
It is not the whole,
it is not the part,
it is bigger than both,
the whole or the part.
It is a pattern
and it is a set of properties.
It is coherence in all its beauty
and grandeur.

We watch and wonder
and see nothing of the process.
We see only the end result,
a qualitative novelty,
much arising from little,
perfection unleashed by nature.

If we cannot define it,
how do we know it is there?
If we cannot see it,
how do we know it is there?

Emergence is beyond knowing,
beyond understanding.
It is part of the magic
and dance of life.

It arises out of the complexity
of life, and is slowly
consumed by the simplicity of life.

Emergence is about acceptance,
accepting life as it is,
without a question,
in all its glory, in all its misery,
and in all its sublimity.

Emergence is within our body
and in our relationships.
It is in our actions and in the systems
that drive us crazy most of the time.

Emergence is living,
loving and leading.
It is living with new eyes of wonder
and excitement,
seeking fulfillment
in every little thing that we do.

From *A Moment in the Universe* (2006, pp. 159-161)

6. A SUMMARY OF KEY IDEAS

- We can know the "unknown" only by the power of inner seeing and there are practices that enable us to precisely do that.
- Spiritual is not religious. Religion is about dogma, believing a certain interpretation of nature or God, accepting a certain scripture as Truth, and worshipping in a certain prescribed manner. Spirituality, on the other hand, has to do with believing in oneself, having an open mind about the nature of reality, being inclusive and pluralistic in one's outlook, and accepting the existence of many paths to spiritual enlightenment.
- True intuition bypasses logical, sensing, and analytical process of gaining knowledge of reality.
- The capacity to visualize a certain future is a very powerful tool in achieving extraordinary outcomes.
- Cultivating optimism is accepting the power of one's mind to generate happiness and satisfaction in place of fear and rejection. It is like seeing the world in bright and shiny colors instead of a black and white view of things. Every color holds the key to certain hidden energies. Learning to unlock those energies is a crucial step forward in our self development.
- "We live in a universe of emergent novelty." (Karl Popper)

7 The Self-Actualized Individual

THE MAP

Universal consciousness illuminates both the body and the mind. Together, they shine in the light that burns inside and is seen from the outside. This is the illumination of awareness, the awareness where all distinctions between the one who is loving and the one who is being loved fall by the wayside. There is no difference between the earth and the sky, between what the eye can see and what the eye cannot see; between what is love and what is non-love. Everything falls into its rightful place. Everything has a purpose. Everything is one.

What is Self-Actualization?

The idea of self-actualization, in its present form, comes from Abraham H. Maslow, American psychologist and the founder of humanistic psychology. The important question for us to consider is not only what self-actualization means, but, more importantly, what values and practices actually lead to self-actualization. In other words, what should I be doing in order to be self-actualized. As explained by Maslow in his book *The Farther Reaches of Human Nature* (1971, pp. 40-51), self-actualizing people are, without one single exception, involved in a cause outside their own skin, in something outside of themselves. They are working at something which fate has called them to somehow and which they work at and which they love. Self-actualizing individuals cherish and put into practice, what Maslow calls Being Values or just B-values. These are ultimate values which are intrinsic, which cannot be reduced to anything more ultimate. Maslow specifically lists several of them together with their metapathologies (pp. 308-309):

Being Values	Metapathologies
Truth	Dishonesty
Goodness	Evil
Beauty	Ugliness
Unity: Wholeness	Chaos, Atomism, Loss of Connectedness
Dichotomy Transcendence	Black or White, High or Low, Near or Far, Now or Never
Aliveness	Deadness, Mechanizing of life.
Uniqueness	Sameness, Uniformity.
Perfection	Imperfection, Sloppiness, Shoddiness
Necessity	Accident, Inconsistency
Completeness, Finality	Incompleteness
Justice	Injustice
Order	Lawlessness, Chaos
Simplicity	Overcomplexity, Disconnectedness, Disintegration
Richness, Totality	Poverty, Uneasiness, Loss of
Comprehensiveness	Interest
Effortlessness	Paranoia
Playfulness	Humorlessness
Self-sufficiency	Dependence
Meaningfulness	Meaninglessness

Maslow also addresses the question of specific behaviors that lead to self-actualization. First, *self-actualizing moments are those when we are fully experiencing life.* Therefore, let us not hold back. We should live in the moment, experiencing the pleasure in each moment, not thinking of the past or the future. Second, *we should realize that life is a matter of choices, one choice after another.* At each point there is a progression choice and there is a regression choice. Progression choices move us forward. Regression choices take us back. Self-actualization never stops; it is an ongoing process but the choices we make hinder or facilitate our progress. Third, *self-actualization cannot occur without a self that needs to be actualized.* We are not a *tabula rasa* (a clean slate) or a lump of clay. We are born with self and we should let it emerge. Fourth, *when in doubt, be honest rather than not.* Frequently, when we are in doubt we are not honest. Looking within oneself for hard answers implies taking responsibility. That is in itself a great step towards actualization. Each time we take responsibility, this is an actualizing of the self. Fifth, *we can make right choices or take responsibility for our actions only if we listen to our self.* That is why self-awareness is such important part of self-actualizing process. Sixth, *self-actualization is not only an end state but also the process of actualizing one's potentialities at any time, in any amount.* To become second-rate anything is not the right thing to do. We should try to attain perfection in whatever we do. Seventh, *Maslow also popularized the term "peak experiences"* (see the box below for more detailed explanation) *by which he meant transient moments of self-actualization; moments of ecstasy which cannot be bought, cannot be guaranteed, cannot be sought.* Peak moments occur when we are ready to be "surprised by joy" and set up conditions so that peak experiences are more likely than conditions that make them less likely. Last, *self-knowledge is extremely important for becoming a self-actualizing person.* We should find out who we are, what we like, what is good for us, what is bad, where we are going and what our mission is. By opening our self to our inner self, we can overcome our defensiveness.

ASPECTS OF PEAK EXPERIENCES

The whole universe is perceived as an integrated and unified whole.

Figure and ground are less sharply differentiated.

We are more detached, more objective, and are more able to perceive the world as if it were independent not only of the perceiver but even of human beings in general.

Perception is relatively ego-transcending, self-forgetful, egoless, and unselfish.

Peak experiences are end-experiences rather than means-experiences.

Disorientation in time and space, even the lack of consciousness of time and space.

The world is seen as beautiful, good, desirable, worthwhile, etc. and is never experienced as evil or undesirable.

Evil itself is accepted and understood and seen in its proper place in the whole, as belonging there, as unavoidable, as necessary, and, therefore, as proper.

Facts and values are not totally different from each other; under certain circumstances, they fuse.

The dichotomies, polarities, and conflicts of life tend to be transcended or resolved. We move toward unity and integration.

The profound fear of disintegration, of insanity, of death, all tend to disappear for the moment.

There is a tendency to move more closely to a perfect identity, or uniqueness of the person to his or her real self, to have become a real person.

In a peak experience, the person becomes less an object, less a thing living under the laws of the physical world, and becomes more a psyche, more subject to the psychological laws, especially the laws of what people call the "higher life."

What has been called the "unitive consciousness" is often gained in peak experiences, namely, a sense of the sacred glimpsed *in* and *through* the particular instance of the momentary, the secular, the worldly.

Source: Adapted from Maslow, *Religion, Values, and Peak-Experiences* (1970).

The idea of self-actualization, in its deepest form, is at the very core of the Vedantic thought. Vedantic sages believed that our real nature was divine, pure, and perfect. God is not outside; we are God (Brahman) but we do not know it because maya has covered our true divine nature with a cloud. We can't see the distinction between the rope and the snake. But when we gain real knowledge the cloud of ignorance is lifted. Shankara, the great Indian sage and Vedantic philosopher of the 8th century India, mentioned seven great values or virtues of a spiritual student fervently looking for solving the mystery of here and hereafter. These are the aspirations of someone who is worthy of attaining the highest spiritual illumination in one lifetime. Those at the highest levels of their consciousness demonstrate several of these values in their interactions with other people.

Viveka: The ability to discriminate between what is real and what's not; what's true and what's not. Real is eternal whereas unreal has a short span of life. Real is divine whereas unreal is maya or illusion. Pleasures and attractions of this life fall into this category.

Vairagya: Detachment or renunciation from the bondage of life, the desire to give up our compulsive extraversions, sublimating our lower level desires to higher level aspirations.

Sama-Dama: Calmness and tranquility of mind coupled with self-discipline or self-control, which means objects come to us but we don't go to objects; we respond to life's challenges but not react to them.

Titaksha: The ability to bear the pinpricks of life without complaining. Accepting difficulties as consequences of one's past actions. Getting rid of resentment as a negative emotion. Resentment is the poison that we brew for others but we drink it ourselves. Acting from the sense of righteousness and not revenge.

Shraddha: Having full faith in one's values and aspirations; having full faith (but not blind faith) in one's ability to make a difference.

Samaadhana: A state of mental equilibrium which comes to one who has reached the highest levels of intellectual, emotional, and spiritual heights.

Mumuksutva: A burning desire for liberation and to rid oneself of all worldly limitations.

Communication and Leadership Style

Universal or self-actualizing consciousness makes communication easier though somewhat riskier. When one is committed to telling the truth, nothing but the truth, it is not an easy choice. You can hurt sensibilities of friends and well-wishers because truth can be painful to hear. Your primary purpose in communicating with others is to create circumstances that help and empower others. It is not about serving any personal agenda. Therefore, words are never used to hurt anyone else. Words are also not meant to spread rumors or engaging in gossip. More importantly, communication is about giving voice to others, actively listening to others, without any judgment.

The self-actualizing leadership style is leaderless leading. One is not seeking followers or fame, but people follow and fame comes on its own. Leaderless leading is based on the following four principles: (1) There is always the commitment to the highest entity within a pyramid of entities, community as against an individual, nation state as against a community, well-being of the planet as against the well-being of individual nations. Welfare and well-being of the greatest number is always the goal. (2) Personal or parochial considerations take a back seat. The focus is never on the "self" or the leader. It's on the issues, work to be done, results to be achieved, or simply making a difference. (3) The leader leads from behind. He or she is the path-maker, but rarely is the person in the forefront. Commitment flows from the leader to the masses easily and painlessly so that those who are actually leading have no direct relationship with the leader. The leader is, of course, the custodian of values and makes decisions and takes ownership when circumstances so warrant. (4) The leader's mission is truly a "work in progress." The leader's work in most cases is not completed in his or her life.

The great avatars and prophets revered in different spiritual traditions exhibited such a style of leadership. But this leadership style is not only about history. There are people who are making a difference in their communities even today, embodying the principles of leaderless leading, and mercifully our world is a better place because of the work they are doing. Their names will never appear in any history books, but the world would be a more cruel place to live in without their specific contributions.

LIVING STORIES

The self-actualizing path is not for the faint-hearted. There are challenges and frustrations on the way to becoming a self-actualizing individual together with moments of great satisfaction. As she grew up in a small town in North Carolina, Rubina never thought of anything other than having a decent job and a husband and a couple of kids. But with time she became a very different person, serving not only her own interests but also those who lived in distant lands and benefited from her creativity and passion in charting an original and unique path for herself. This is her story.

Rubina earned her degree in textile design in late 1980s when textile industry was on the decline in the US and there was not much demand for new design talent. She was fired twice within the first three years of her work life as a designer because the companies she worked for filed for bankruptcy. Rubina didn't lose her heart and courage. She took up some odd jobs to keep herself going, but she started to spend most of her time in self-development activities. She began a private study of Sanskrit because she was very interested in sacred texts like the Bhagvad Gita and wanted to study them in their original form. As her interest in spirituality gathered momentum, she went on yearly trips to India and Nepal.

On one of her trips to India she was fascinated by the textile designs she saw in the Tibetan refugee community in Dharamshala. She liked those designs and started to dream once again of becoming a textile designer while using her creativity to produce modern designs drawn from ancient traditions. With a portfolio of her work she traveled to China in 1999 and found to her surprise that several textile manufacturers were willing to use her designs. Rubina was, however, not ready to give her work to large-scale commercial manufacturers. She saw an opportunity to work for a higher ideal. She set up a small company in her native North Carolina for textile printing and garment making.

As US labor costs are high compared with other countries, Rubina outsourced some of her work to a factory in India. She has not become rich as she once dreamed of. As a young entrepreneur Rubina has struggled to keep her manufacturing operation going, but whatever she has earned she has shared with charity organizations on projects varying from primary education to preservation of Tibet's cultural heritage.

Those who have met Rubina have been greatly impressed by her sense of personal mastery and idealism. She has found a vocation as well as a mission. She is using ancient knowledge about human nature to run a modern business. She possesses high levels of self-awareness; she correctly identifies her state of mind and talks about it. Although she has worked closely with the Buddhist community both in the US and India, Rubina has not become a Buddhist. She is regularly seen in the small church in her own suburban community. As a self-actualizing individual, Rubina sees herself as a student of different spiritual traditions. She likes Vedanta, Kabbalah, Sufism, Buddhism, and of course her own brand of homegrown Christianity. She is perfectly at home with all universal truths irrespective of the source or the label. In terms of her business enterprise, Rubina sees many possibilities. She is keen to work with some African women and bring the traditional African textile designs to the fashion world of New York and Paris.

One could say that Ted was self-actualized at an early age if we pay attention to his achievements. There was virtually nothing that he could not accomplish. He also got a head start in a large corporation. He could have rapidly climbed the corporate ladder while using his potential for doing great things in life as he matured. But unfortunately Ted failed the basic values test—

personal integrity, respect for others, humility, and non-egoic outlook. The following story has a somewhat different ending.

Ted was an exceptionally bright student. His father was a community newspaper editor and the mother a freelance writer. Both of his parents had only one dream—to see their only son become an extraordinary achiever in all walks of life. Ted was living that dream to a great extent. In high school he was so ahead of the class that the guy or gal who was second didn't matter at all. One year he was captain of the soccer team and that was the only time in years when his school won the county soccer tournament. He went to a prestigious New England College and an Ivy League Graduate School.

At 26 he became the youngest manager in a large consumer goods company. The person who always spoke from the heart; who was humble and respectful of others; who offered tons of new ideas in any company meeting slowly started to become a different kind of person. People noticed and complained of his impatience and arrogance. As he was in great demand by the senior management to work on companywide projects, he started to spend relatively little time on his own job. At 30, Ted was appointed VP of HR function, a job that was traditionally held by an aging bureaucrat and was never given to a younger person. Everyone expected Ted to bring a breath of fresh air to the HR function, but in reality he was not interested in that job; he was already dreaming of becoming the youngest CEO of this 100-year old company.

A young female staffer complained of sexual harassment but the complaint was dismissed by the ethics office for lack of any concrete evidence. Everyone thought that since Ted was an attractive young man on a fast track many females were attracted to him. Anyone complaining against him would be the one who was frustrated in her attempts to gain his attention. Then over the next one year three more staffers lodged similar complaints and this time with proof that Ted was misusing his position to gain sexual favors. The company CEO saved him after gaining a private assurance from Ted that he would stop indulging in such degrading behavior. But Ted didn't show any change at all. Two more complaints reached the ethics office within the next six months. But this time there was a new CEO—a woman who was hired from the outside to provide new direction to the company that was losing revenues at an alarming rate. Ted lost his job. He was devastated. He could not imagine that this could happen to him. At the intervention of some of his friends, Ted was rehired at a junior position in the public relations department. Ted may work with this company but he has no future there. Within few years Ted has gone from a high achiever to a sexual predator with a very uncertain future. In self-defense Ted says that he was not the only person engaging in this kind of behavior. The older male executives were the worst culprits but they were spared because they had a network of support that he had lacked.

What's going on here?

Rubina and Ted are enormously gifted individuals. While Rubina got little support from her parents because she was part of a large family, Ted got star quality treatment from his folks and he benefited greatly. But where Ted's parents went wrong was the domain of values (or B-values as Maslow calls them). He was told that since he was the highest achiever in every endeavor, he would conquer the whole world and thereby deserve everyone's unconditional obedience. He was never told that he had to show respect to others and not use his power for self-gratification. Even after suffering great humiliation, Ted is not able to see the consequences of his own behavior. He thinks that he suffered because he didn't have a network of support within the organization. Ted has to go back to the basics. He has to start his life all-over again. There is time and there are opportunities for him to explore, but if he continues to hold the same beliefs there is little hope that he would get on the self-actualizing path very soon. As far as Rubina is concerned, her investment in her self-development is paying high dividends. She has the right values and the right motives. There is nothing to stop her from becoming a global visionary—the kind of leadership the world badly needs today.

DEVELOPMENT CHALLENGES

Metapathologies

People who are on the path to self-actualization have to be specially careful about certain metapathologies. These metapathologies, according to Maslow (1971), diminish human potential, they destroy our creativeness, and generate a state of helplessness. Some key metapathologies mentioned by Maslow included:

Alienation: Loss of identity in which the self seems unreal.

Anomie: Lack of usual social or ethical standards.

Loss of zest in life: Lack of enthusiasm and energy.

Meaninglessness: Having no meaning or significance; having no purpose or reason.

Inability to enjoy: Not able to relax and have a pleasant time.

Boredom and ennui: A feeling of listlessness and dissatisfaction arising from a lack of occupation or excitement.

Existential vacuum: Not finding any meaning in existence.

Apathy, resignation, fatalism: A belief that all events are predetermined.

Valuelessness: Having no values.

Desacralization: Not respecting the sanctity of life.

Death wish: Wishing to die or ending life.

Helplessness, apathy, defeat: Lack of interest or concern.

Ultimate doubt: Questioning the worth of everything.

Despair and anguish: Loss of hope and onset of suffering.

Futility: Pointlessness.

Cynicism: Subscribing to a philosophy of doubt and distrust.

Once we have crossed these hurdles, an extraordinary outcome has been achieved. As a result, there is the birth of a new relationship with the others and with our own self. This new relationship is formed on the basis of complete transparency, honesty, and authenticity.

Once we are self-actualized, we stop seeking anything. We want to move beyond all experiences and stay in the realm of experiencing, being in the present moment, freed from the tyrannies of the past and the future. Everything starts unfolding on its own—all the teachers, all their teachings. We become a bowl in which everything falls of its own accord. This effortlessness is fully complemented by nature in unseen ways because nature wants us to stay the course.

DEVELOPMENTAL INTERVENTIONS

The Affirmation Practice

Affirmation, derived from Latin *affirmare,* is a statement that declares a certain outcome to be true. However, the real meaning of "true" in this case may be an aspiration rather than a fact. By declaring something to be true and already happening, we are making *autosuggestion*—sending a message to our inner self about an outcome that we desire to achieve. Our unconscious makes a note of our intent and works on making our intent a reality while we are busy doing other things.

The technique was first used in therapy by Emile Coue, a 19th century French psychologist and therapist, who is also known to have popularized the following affirmation: *Day by day, in every way, I'm getting better and better*. In order to be effective, an affirmation must be stated in the present tense; it should express a positive intent; and it should be verbally repeated several times.

Several affirmations, divided in seven distinct clusters, are being presented here. Cluster 1 contains affirmations for someone who is working on his or her awakening at the ground level. Someone else may use Cluster 5 to strengthen his or her ability to communicate and to be creative and so forth.

You may select one or more affirmations from the cluster of interest to you. Please sit in a comfortable meditative posture, close your eyes, clear your mind of all other thoughts, and repeat one or more affirmations with your attention fully focused on your intent as expressed by the affirmation.

Cluster 1

- I am bonding with my body and my body is bonding with me.
- I am valuing the physical intelligence of my body.
- I am feeling strong and grounded.
- I am accepting myself the way I am.

Cluster 2

- I am an emotionally grounded person.
- I am expressing my sexuality in healthy ways.
- I am showing awareness of other's emotions.
- I am finding joy in simple things.
- I am showing abundance of everything in my life.

Cluster 3

- I am using my power for the good of others.
- I am making the positive change work for me.
- I am feeling the flow of radiant energy within me.
- I am helping others to find joy and fulfillment.
- I am making the small things work for me.

Cluster 4

- I am giving and receiving unconditional love.
- I am healing myself with the power of love.
- I am enriching my relationships every minute of the day.
- I am surrendering to forces larger than my ego-self.
- I am seeking balance in my life and work.

Cluster 5

- I am pouring creativity into everything I'm doing.

- I am speaking clearly and purposefully.
- I am saying my truth without hurting others.
- I am relishing the richness of each and every moment.
- I am dissolving my ego-identity with every little breath.

Cluster 6

- I am drawing liberally from the reservoir of inner wisdom.
- I am finding truth in every little corner of my being.
- I am seeing clearly what my intuitive mind is revealing to me.
- I am moving past shallower things that provide no satisfaction.
- I am realizing my vision with each passing moment.

Cluster 7

- I am making deeper connections every minute of the day.
- I am seeking oneness with every particle of my being.
- I am experiencing the union of mind, body, heart, soul, and spirit.
- I am achieving higher degrees of self-knowledge with each passing day.
- I am living because I have understood the reality of dying.

The Self-Inquiry Process (SIP)

The objective of this practice is to integrate body, mind, heart, and soul while experiencing the upward flow of integration, from the most ordinary and mundane quests of our daily life to the highest yearnings of our heart and soul.

There are 49 reflective questions, divided into 7 lists. While some of these questions are easy to answer, others are not. As we proceed on this self-inquiry process, questions become more abstract with no clear answer. Questions start flowing like water in a river. Your mind in its pristine calmness witnesses the ebb and flow of the current, holding on to nothing in particular in a state of total non-attachment. You are thinking: Perhaps the best answer to some of these questions is deep silence.

It is recommended that after each session you should take time to write your thoughts in your learning journal.

List 1

1. What is your favorite food? Why do you like this food?
2. Are you afraid? What are you afraid of? Where is the fear located?
3. What kind of work you do? Do you like it? Why do you like it?
4. Do you sometime feel that you are running out of cash? Why is money important to you?
5. When you think of your parents what thoughts come to your mind?
6. What are some of the things that you are grateful for? How do you express your gratitude?
7. Can you describe what you think is the meaning of your life?

List 2

1. Can you describe your sex life in one word? Why did you choose that word?
2. What kind of emotions do you experience on a daily basis? What's most satisfying, what's most disturbing?
3. How do you feel when others make demands on you? Can you say no? If not, why not?
4. Is there pain in your lower back? What kind of pain is that?

5. Do people call you a moody person? How do you react to that kind of description?
6. Do you carry any guilt feelings? What's this guilt about?
7. How many glasses of water do you drink in a day? Why not more or less?

List 3

1. Do you like to have your way in every situation? Why or why not?
2. Have you been called an arrogant person in your life? How do you react to this description?
3. Are you driven to achieving high results? If so, why? If not, why not?
4. How do you see yourself as a person? How would you like to be described?
5. Are you ashamed of anything you have done or said in your life? Why is it difficult to overcome this feeling?
6. Is there fire in your belly? How would you describe it? Do you think it is too intense?
7. What is the scariest thing you have ever done in your life?

List 4

1. Do you feel you are getting as much love as you are giving? Less, more, or the same? What explains the variation, if any?
2. How would you describe your real self?
3. Do you listen to your heart? What does it say?
4. What makes you sad? How do you express your sadness?
5. Do you forgive easily? Why?
6. Have you found the peace of mind you have been looking for?

7. Are you ready to give and receive unconditional love? If not, why not?

List 5

1. Do you like the way you sound? What do you compare your sound to?
2. Name the voice that you hear in your tranquil moments? What does that voice say to you?
3. Can you keep a secret? If not, why not?
4. What thoughts come to your mind when you listen to others?
5. What is your definition of truth?
6. Do you keep a journal? What have you learned from your own writing?
7. Do you communicate non-verbally? Do you worry about any alignment issues between your verbal and non-verbal communication?

List 6

1. What are your dreams like? What is the one dream that repeats itself?
2. What is one spiritual truth you value the most?
3. What role intuition has played in your life?
4. What is your vision? How far away are you from realizing your vision?
5. How do you define beauty?
6. What is your favorite season? Why?
7. What is your favorite archetypal image—Lost Child, Great Mother, Great Father, Great Warrior? What does this image say to you?

List 7

1. When you hear words like self-realization, nirvana, enlightenment, what comes to your mind?

2. If you were having an out of body experience, how would you feel? Describe it in as much detail as possible.
3. Do you feel like giving up everything and becoming a renunciate? What drives that feeling?
4. What does the word God or Spirit mean to you?
5. Do people tell you that you are slightly out of touch with day-to-day realities? How do you react?
6. Can you visualize the day you will depart from this earth?
7. If there is life after death, what kind of life you wish to have?

A Few Other Things

Keep the spiritual connection alive and well under all circumstances through rigorous meditation practices and compassion in action. Share your wisdom and insights with others without any reservations. Spend time in mentoring and coaching without expecting any rewards or "thank you" notes.

Allow different intelligences to find expression spontaneously —cognitive intelligence informing one's emotional intelligence, spatial intelligence doing a dance with mathematical intelligence, musical intelligence shaping a new melody in concert with spiritual intelligence. This means leading a life without self-imposed limitations and boundaries, freeing oneself intellectually, emotionally, spatially, and creatively.

Pursue life's most intricate questions, not with a view to obtaining "correct" answers but allowing the spirit of inquiry to become a guiding force. It is only through questions that the way is prepared to finding some answers; accepting that the process is more important than the final outcome. The spirit of inquiry nurtures personal integration and not incessant search for the "right" answers. Always look at the big picture—not at the pieces of the puzzle but the puzzle itself; not partial answers but the universal truth; not the ground but the ground and the sky and the unknown mysteries of the outer space.

A Poetic Interlude

Self-Actualization

When was the last we looked inside and found a mountain?
When was the last we looked inside and found an ocean?
When was the last we looked inside and found a cave?
When was the last we explored the geography of our being?

There are places of wonder and joy and awakening
that we have been so afraid to visit or get to know.
What has stopped us from climbing that high mountain,
going deeper into that blue ocean, and opening the door
to that mythical cave of million artifacts—the jewelry
of our soul, precious possessions that we have carried
from one life to another, from one body to another?
What has stopped us from being our true selves?
What has stopped us from finding something that is
bigger and brighter than our own selves?

We have told friends to experience their lives
fully while we ourselves have measured
life in tiny spoons, half empty most of the time.
Why is that so? Why have we shied away from our own greatness?
Why have we lived our life in shadows
when glittering lights awaited us on the center-stage of life?

Why have we not been fully human
or greater than our potential humanness?
Why have we let go of our self-actualizing moments?

We have told others that life is a process—
a process that culminates in the end-state,
the state of enlightenment and liberation?
Why have we told this half-truth when we knew
that life is a process as well as an end-state
at the same time? The process is also an end-state.
Our Nirvana is right here in this moment. It's here
in these self-actualizing moments that arise

each day with sunrise and blossom like sunflowers.
It is in our self-reflective moments, in our concentration,
in our self-absorption, and in our daily conversations.

Why have we forgotten that there is a self to be actualized?
Why have we forgotten that the self is actualized every day
in our workplace and in the shopping malls, parking lots
and in the way side cafes where we catch up with the news
while we drink our coffee and eat our bagel for breakfast?
It is actualized when we resacralize the ordinary and find
divinity in the most mundane things of our daily life.
It is actualized when we see goddess in every woman and
goodness in every man and we bow to the divinity in every
being.

When was the last we looked inside and found a mountain?
When was the last we looked inside and found an ocean?
When was the last we looked inside and found a cave?
When was the last we explored the geography of our being?
Now is the time. Just this moment. Just now. Here and now.

From *A Moment in the Universe* (2006, pp. 157-158)

7. A SUMMARY OF KEY IDEAS

- Self-actualizing people, according to Maslow, are without one single exception, involved in a cause outside their own skin, in something outside of themselves. They are working at something which fate has called them to somehow and which they work at and which they love.
- Self-actualization never stops; it is an ongoing process but the choices we make hinder or facilitate our progress.
- Peak moments occur when we are ready to be "surprised by joy" and set up conditions so that peak experiences are more likely than conditions that make them less likely.
- By declaring something to be true and already happening, we are making *autosuggestion*—sending a message to our inner self about an outcome that we desire to achieve. Our unconscious makes a note of our intent and works on making our intent a reality while we are busy doing other things.
- Allow different intelligences to find expression spontaneously—cognitive intelligence informing one's emotional intelligence, spatial intelligence doing a dance with mathematical intelligence, musical intelligence shaping a new melody in concert with spiritual intelligence. This means leading a life without self-imposed limitations and boundaries, freeing oneself intellectually, emotionally, spatially, and creatively.

Part II

A Fable About Authentic Development

1 When Micky Met Crocoda

Beyond the sleepy orchids and bougainvillea vines, and away from passion flowers surrounded by butterflies and hummingbirds, and ahead of the kapok trees that were reaching out to the sky, there was a clearing, an open space by the side of the river, where the lone rose-apple tree stood like a lost traveler, waiting and watching. This was Micky's home and his most precious possession. Since vegetation was sparse around his rose-apple tree, Micky had an unobstructed view of his surroundings.

Dressed in partially black and partially brown fur, Micky had long arms and an equally long grasping tail. Like every other bird and animal in this gloriously magical place, he spoke in a language that was well understood across different species that inhabited this forest. He was much smaller than the monkeys found in other parts of the forest, and, unfortunately, he had lost contact with them. He felt lonely most of the time, desperately seeking contact with other animals, but he had had no visitors sometimes for weeks and months.

"Hi, I'm Micky. How are you?" He passionately longed to say these words to one of his own kind, but he also realized the limitation of living in an isolated part of the forest, with few other animals around him to satisfy his affiliative need.

A river flowed in front of the rose-apple tree—not an ordinary river but a large body of rapidly flowing water that hardly dried up even during the driest part of the year. A patch of white sand divided the tree from the river—forming a kind of tiny private beach if Micky ever wished to come down from his perch and take a walk on the ground.

Floods were a common occurrence. Sometimes the rising water of the river frightened Micky. He feared for his safety and that of the tree. There was no other tree like this one anywhere else in the forest. What will he do if the rose-apple tree is washed away in a flood? The very thought of such a catastrophe was nerve wrecking for him. The tree was highly productive; it bore a bountiful harvest beyond Micky's wildest dreams. He never imagined going to sleep on an empty stomach.

On a routine spring morning when the sun had just risen in the eastern skies in all its flaming glory, Micky looked at the clouds, some tiny patches of white fluffy cotton speedily floating overhead. The clouds were reflecting the light that was now spilling over to the rest of the sky.

Micky felt some movement, a sudden splash of water, as if someone was trying to steal water from the river. He looked carefully with a fixed gaze on the front-end of his beach. A large crocodile was slowly crawling into the open space—quite an ugly sight to watch. Micky couldn't recall the last time he had had an unscheduled visit from one of his least favorite species. Crocodiles—gosh, they are so ugly and they smell like rotting meat. What do they eat, for heaven's sake?

The crocodile looked up in the direction where Micky was sitting on the tree.

"Hello, up there. I hope you don't mind my coming here, unannounced, uninvited. Anyway, crocodiles do not abide by any rules of behavior. We go where our instinct takes us, and we do what pleases us in the moment. You don't like my coming here this morning? That's your problem, little monkey." And there was a deep grunting sound aimed at diminishing Micky's authority over his domain.

Before responding Micky looked carefully at the opposition, and what he saw was quite frightening: heavy, cylindrical and plated body with a long snout and equally long tail. This monster could be fifteen to twenty feet long. What am I going to do?

"I know I'm talking to a crocodile. You guys are not known for civility—are you? But I don't like to emulate you and speak to you in an offensive manner. After all, isn't this a lovely morning? Why spoil this vibrant feeling? So, good morning, my uninvited guest, welcome to my quarters. But remember this is a private property. I will permit you to spend very little time on this beach. You can lie motionless like a log or just roll over on your back, or do whatever you like, but once the time is up, I would like to see you out of here, lock stock and barrel. Do you get me?"

"Not so fast, little fellow. No one orders me around here. I do what I like. What will you do if I decide to make this my permanent home? Are you going to come down and evict me? I would love to see that happen." Again there was the same grunting sound. "But let's not get into an argument. I'm not in a fighting mood. I will listen to you, if you agree to satisfy my need. At this time I need food. Yes, I'm hungry, very hungry. I had nothing to eat last night and nothing at all this morning. Oh, my empty stomach is really hurting me. Give me some fruit. Please, I beg of you, my monkey friend. Feed this hungry crocodile. Be a good host!"

"Now we are talking. Look at a vegetarian crocodile for a change. Do you eat grass too?" Micky wasn't sure the croc got the joke.

"I say this is no time for making fun of me. Got me? I am carnivorous by habit and therefore I like meat; but if you, little monkey, are not ready to be my breakfast, I will be happy with apples. But don't test my patience. I know how to jump. I can break this tree. There is nothing worse than a hungry crocodile at your door. You don't want me around here for long, do you? So, feed me and I'll be gone. Now, what are you thinking, little monkey?"

"I think we can do business. To start with, we need to have proper introduction. My name is Micky. My real name is more complex and it can be properly expressed only in a language that is sacred to monkeys. But Micky is my nickname; that's what my parents liked to call me. I love it too—it's simple and straight forward. What about you? Do you have a name or something like a name?"

"Now, wait a minute. You are talking to someone whose ancestry goes back to dinosaurs. I'm a proud representative of Order Crocodilia and my name is Crocoda. I'm very proud of my name."

"Our actions make our names respectable. Anyway, that might be beyond your understanding at this time. Why don't I select some good ripe apples and feed you?"

"Please do it quickly. I can't wait any longer."

Micky started throwing one apple after another, as if he were throwing balls in the air, like a juggler. This went on for quite some time. Finally, Crocoda shouted, "That's enough for the day. I don't need the fruit anymore. Too much sugar! I need some fresh blood to change the taste in my mouth. I'll be back another day."

Having spoken these words, Crocoda turned towards water and disappeared in a matter of minutes.

Micky sat silently, firmly holding on to the tree, while he reflected on his meeting with Crocoda. This was typical of the way he lived his life, moments of experiencing reality followed by deep reflection. Those who failed to reflect, Micky believed, didn't learn much. In other words, they remained plain monkeys. And who wanted to remain a plain monkey when you could become a wise and better monkey?

Micky also paid attention to the gap between "what the animals actually said" and "what they really needed." Yes, no doubt Crocoda used many nasty words, but he also had a genuine need. Once Micky responded positively to his need, Crocoda was no longer an ugly beast. He behaved like a decent animal, almost like a friend, not that Micky wanted to befriend a crocodile.

To Micky's surprise, Crocoda was back the next morning and he was very apologetic of his bad behavior the previous day. He kept a low profile and spoke in a polite manner, hardly raising his voice.

Thanks for being such a sweetheart, Crocoda, Micky almost told him, but you never say such a nice thing to a crocodile. They can be sweet one moment and eat you the very next. How could you ever trust a crocodile? And why should you? But something was different here. Crocoda was in a somber mood. He told stories that Micky had never heard before. Of course, some were funnier than others. Many were awfully boring. In fact, Micky felt that Crocoda's jokes were simply bad jokes. Some of them were so bizarre that Micky didn't feel like laughing; he felt like throwing up.

In the end, Micky decided not to be the judge. He remembered his father teaching him that in this world everything had a place. There are good things and there are bad things, but you can't be the judge of everything which is out there. Who am I, as a monkey, to reject or make fun of the life of a crocodile? I have to live a crocodile's life in order to judge it, Micky told himself.

Gradually, over a couple of weeks, Micky and Crocoda entered into an uneasy relationship. Micky didn't like the fact that Crocoda was now becoming a permanent fixture at his private beach. But this uncanny companionship had its rewards too. Crocoda was like a living and walking newspaper. He knew everything about the river—what was happening upstream or downstream, places that Micky had never visited. He knew what floated under the water. He could describe the types of fish and reptiles that populated the river.

"Micky, believe me. It's a very rough world out there. Here you are sitting on your idyllic tree, with plenty of food around you and the fresh breeze that never stops blowing, enjoying a magnificent view of the world around you. You are so lucky, my friend. Look at me, poor crocodile, a mountain of moving dirt and filth, leading a miserable life. I get up in the morning and ask myself a question: What on earth am I doing here?"

Micky had no reason to disbelieve Crocoda. It's a rough world out there. He knew it. Micky remembered his parents telling him about the importance of having a secure place of one's own. "Find your place in life that is secure and comfortable and then never leave it." This was great advice. But the last thing Micky wanted to do was to engage in a philosophical discussion with Crocoda about the purpose of his life. That will be quite a day: having a metaphysical discourse with a crocodile! But that was precisely what Crocoda was wishing to have.

Micky had felt like saying: Crocoda, go take an experiential workshop, get some bodywork done, beat a drum, do anything but don't bother me with such a question. I have no idea why crocodiles are here in the first place. But the "I can feel your pain" side of Micky was getting at him. He cursed himself for being so condescending, even cynically elitist, showing little respect for poor Crocoda's feelings. A crocodile has a life like you have, dear Micky, and he has every right to ask questions about the larger meaning of existence.

"Crocoda, you ask profound questions. I don't think I have the answer, but if we continue to be friends, and if we continue to have this friendly discussion we shall soon find a way to get the right answer. Not a patchwork of unfinished thoughts, but some real answers. So, why don't we postpone this conversation until a later time?"

Crocoda was back after few days, and he was in a sour mood. He was angry and sad at the same time; a frowning grin coupled with tears in his eyes. Micky was unable to control his laughter. "Crocodile tears ... Now I know they are real. What's wrong with you, Crocoda? Why are you crying?"

"My companion is very ill. She says she's going to die, whatever that means."

"You never told me you had family?"

"What's so great about having a friend who is dying?"

"What's wrong with her?"

"She's seeing a reptile who is also a shaman. He says that she has an internal disorder and if no cure is found, she will be dead very soon. She wails and cries all the time. It is so sad because we have had such a good relationship. She has taken such good care of me all my life. Don't you think it's my turn now to take care of her? But what can I do? I'm a totally stupid, big fat crocodile. I know nothing about friendship, about sickness and wellness, about life and death."

"Don't be too harsh on yourself, Crocoda. Sickness and wellness—these are two sides of the same equation. Nothing stays the same. Everything will be fine. Take good care of her.... You didn't even tell me your friend's name."

"I'm so sorry. I call her Crocodina. Yes, she is my lovely Crocodina. What a beautiful name! She was really cute when we first met. Now she is big and ugly like me. But that was not the case in the beginning. We were such a loving couple. We hunted together. And we made love and we slept and snored in the little pond of water that we owned. Those were quite some days!"

"Those days will surely return. Let me give you some apples, Crocoda. This is my present for your sick friend. Put them in the side of your mouth and don't swallow. She will surely like them, and hopefully she will feel better as a result."

Micky was quite meticulous in selecting fruit for Crocodina; he picked only ripe apples with rose-like stripes in dark and deep colors. As Crocoda left, Micky felt a sense of remorse for him. He had a feeling that apples would not cure his ailing Crocodina. She needed something else, but since he was not a shaman he had no idea what might actually work for her.

When Crocoda crawled into the burrow, Crocodina was half-asleep. She mumbled something. "Where have you been? Are you listening to me? Why do you leave me all alone when you know I'm dying? Are you seeing someone? I'm going to kill her if I ever suspect that you are being unfaithful to me while I'm still alive and breathing. Do you understand me?"

Crocoda didn't wish to enter into an argument. He knew that when you are sick all kind of thoughts can come into your mind. And he knew that arguing with Crocodina in times like these had never been a good experience.

"My dear Crocodina, I was with my friend Micky. He is so wonderful. I wish you could meet him." Crocodina woke up from her sleep with a whimper.

"Micky? Who is he, or is it she? I knew you were out of control. What are you two up to? You want to dance on my dead body with your sexy friend? Huh?"

"Crocodina, my sweet Crocodina, what's wrong with you? Micky is a monkey. He is no croc. He is so small. He lives up on a rose-apple tree. Look, he sent some apples for you." Crocoda opened his mouth and threw on to the ground dozens of apples.

"These are for your enjoyment, sweetheart."

Crocodina looked at the apples with her half-opened eyes. She crawled forward in quick movements and ate all the apples.

"Oh my God, these are so delicious. Where did you get these apples?"

"I told you. My friend Micky lives on this tree and he sent these apples especially for you so that you could recover from your illness. Do you understand me now?"

"I don't care what you're saying. I like these apples and I want to eat this monkey."

"What are you saying? Are you crazy? He is my friend. You can't eat my friend."

"Let me tell you something. I saw the shaman today and he told me that there was no way for me to recover unless I eat the heart of a monkey. Now, are you listening to me? I need your monkey and I need him right now."

"What are you talking about, Crocodina? You can't eat my friend. I can get you another monkey, if I can find one."

"No, I need this one. He is eating these delicious apples every day. His meat will be delicious. I want you to go right now and get this monkey for me."

"Crocodina, are you aware that you are creating a little moral dilemma for me? On the one hand, I see you, my lifelong companion, and on the other I find my new friend. I can't make this decision."

"I don't know what you are babbling about. I want you to go right now, this very moment, and get me this monkey. Am I clear?"

"Yes dear. Let me see what I can do."

Even before he had finished his sentence, Crocoda slipped back into the water and within a couple of minutes he was on his way to see Micky.

Crocoda managed to put up a good appearance and intentionally added some excitement to accompany the words that followed, "Micky, my dear friend, I want to thank you for the gift you sent for my Crocodina. I can't tell you how much she enjoyed eating those apples, and how appreciative she really was of your very kind gesture. You know what she said? Crocoda, there are still some good animals left in this forest. She would like to meet you, and that's why she asked if you would like to join us for supper. She would like to thank you personally. Crocodina promised that she would find some exotic fruit for you. I know Crocodina always has an eye for good things in life."

Micky was having his late afternoon siesta and was in no particular mood to talk with Crocoda; however Crocoda's gracious remarks were music to his ears.

"Crocoda, I'm so happy to hear that Crocodina liked the apples but I'm sorry I can't join you this evening because I'm fasting. I do this as a routine. Too much eating is not good for my body. I sleep better if I occasionally don't eat."

"Micky, I called you my friend. But I must say you're really hurting my feelings by declining my invitation. I know you don't trust me. Why don't you say this openly? Why give excuses? How does it matter to you that your refusal will truly hurt my Crocodina's feelings? What am I going to tell her? Why was I so confident? I should have told her the truth: Micky doesn't accept me as a true friend. End of story."

"Oh Crocoda, don't take it personally. I do trust you. I value our friendship. You know there is no history of friendship between monkeys and crocodiles. By being good friends we are making history around here. But I would really like to be excused. I have never left this tree for anything. It is not that I don't trust you. I trust you, but I am so sorry ... I can't go with you."

Micky could see tears flooding Crocoda's eyes. He was very sad. "Okay, I will go back and tell Crocodina the bitter truth. She won't like it. Why bother? She is dying anyway. Life has been so unfair to her. What is one more shock? One more disappointment couldn't make life much worse than what it already is. I suppose this is the end of our friendship. It was good to know you Micky."

As Crocoda made a move to turn back towards the river, Micky shouted, "Crocoda, stop—I'm coming with you. I can't disappoint you and your partner Crocodina." As soon as he finished saying these words, Micky jumped to the ground looping around a loose branch.

"Crocoda, I forgot to ask you a very a practical question. How are we going to reach your place? You know, I can't swim."

"Oh, that's no problem. Just hop on my back and hold me firmly. I will take you there in no time."

Micky jumped on Crocoda's back. It was not a perfect place for a ride, but Micky knew he could hold on to Crocoda for as long as the big croc swam carefully and slowly.

In the beginning, it looked like a perfect ride. Crocoda was keeping himself afloat. In fact, Micky enjoyed the feeling of being surrounded by so much water. The air was moist and clean. An eerie silence surrounded them. Micky tried to look back. His rose-apple tree was hardly distinguishable from the other trees. The late afternoon haze had overtaken the clear afternoon view he had seen before.

Suddenly, Micky felt that Crocoda was going deeper into the water. Micky got scared and shouted, "Crocoda, you have to be careful. If you go any deeper, I can't hold on to you. I will be washed away."

Micky heard a chuckle. "Washed away—who cares? You are going to be dead in any case. Stupid monkey, I'm not taking you home for supper. You *are* my Crocodina's supper. Her shaman told her to eat a monkey's heart if she were to recover from her illness. So here you are. I'm so sorry. Whoever thought that two of us could be friends? We have nothing in common. You're very stupid if you thought otherwise."

Micky was in a state of shock. He cursed himself for being so naive to put his faith in a crocodile in the first place. But what could he do now? There was hardly any time to think and plan anything new to foil this ugly scheme that would turn him into a meal for a sick female croc.

"Crocoda, did you say my heart? You are so simple my friend. You should have made this clear before we left. You may not know it, but monkeys don't carry their heart with them. My heart is in a hole in the tree. It is safely deposited there. I take it out only on special occasions. I'm afraid we have to turn back."

"Are you sure you are not playing a trick with me? Don't think I'm dumb. I have a four chambered heart. I know all about hearts."

"Why would I think that you are dumb? You are the only friend I have in this world. Look, I could have refused to come with you in the first place."

Crocoda felt reassured. He decided to turn back.

"Okay, Micky, hold on to me really tight while I try to turn back. It is not easy. I have to move against the current. It will take only a couple of seconds. Ready?"

"Yes, I'm ready."

It was a dangerous turn. For the first time Micky was completely under water. It was a cold and frightening experience. He was nearly washed away.

"Yes, we made it."

Micky shouted with joy as Crocoda resurfaced again and started moving in the other direction. It didn't take much time to reach the bank of the river. Micky quickly moved away and climbed the tree as fast as he could. Once he reached his favorite spot, he heaved a sigh of relief.

"Now, Micky, don't keep me waiting here. Get your heart. We are already late. Crocodina is waiting. She gets very upset when I don't get back home on time."

"Crocoda, I think she will have to wait for a very long time because I'm not coming with you. You are untrustworthy. You can't be any one's friend. I put my trust in you and you betrayed me. Now, I would like you to leave this place. You spoiled my afternoon siesta and I don't want you to spoil my evening as well. Please go away. By the way, monkeys do carry both their heart and their brain with them all the time so that no one can deceive them. Bye for now."

Crocoda looked at Micky with eyes of disbelief while cursing himself for his stupidity. He left quietly without making any fuss.

REFLECTION

1. What's in a name? Have you ever reflected on the meaning of your name? Who gave you this name? What feelings the name generates in you? Would you have liked to be called by another name? Why?
2. Do you notice any differences between needs and actions of people that you have known? Do people act in accordance with their needs? Why not?
3. "In the end, Micky decided not to be the judge?" Why not?
4. How do you resist a demand that you think is morally repugnant?
5. What does trust mean to you? Do you think trust once broken can be repaired? How do you repair it?

2 A New Beginning

Micky rose from his sleep early while the dawn was breaking. His mind was still filled with the events of the last week. He could not overcome the sheer burden of the thought that he had been on the verge of being eaten alive by a crocodile. He was not afraid of dying, but to be eaten by a crocodile in one big gulp, with his body reduced to a bit of mush within seconds, was certainly not the best way to die. It was almost virtuous to have that presence of mind, the ability to think quickly that Micky felt really saved his life.

As the sun rose above the branches and the crescendo of birds descending on the river reached its highest pitch, Micky heard another noise, a big thump, and as he looked down, he found Crocoda spread on the beach in careless abandon.

Micky was surprised. This croc is not going to give up, is he? Does he really believe that I could be fooled once again? Micky had been brought up on a worldview where there was respect for life and a caring attitude towards all species. But when you are a crocodile, what do you do? You think of food and nothing else. Anything living that moves has only one meaning to you. It is your dinner. You let it slip away and you end up sleeping hungry.

Maybe I'm too idealistic and naïve, he thought. How could a crocodile change his nature when there is no consciousness? If a croc could not distinguish self from a tree, or sky, how could he have sense of right or wrong? Where is the place for trust or friendship? At a more practical level, Micky was concerned that Crocoda was invading his private space without his consent. He really wished Crocoda to go away and leave him alone forever.

Micky shouted, "Crocoda, I want you to go away. Leave me alone because I want to have nothing to do with you. Do you hear me, Crocoda?"

"Micky, my dear friend, I am so sorry. For the past several days I have been in pain, in real pain because I betrayed you, I betrayed your trust and I want to offer my apologies."

"Crocoda, you don't know what you are talking about. What do you know about friendship, about trust, and about apology for an utterly wrong action? What do you know about right and wrong in any case? These are all words. These are ideas and beliefs that you can't even understand because you don't have the mental ability to decipher the meaning of these words."

"That may be true. I don't have the brains of a smart little monkey. But I know one thing: once I got home I got into a big fight with Crocodina. She was wrong in demanding your heart and your body, though she is still suffering from her disease. My fault was that I didn't have the courage to stand up to her initially. I agree with your second point that I don't understand myself very well. I use words that I'm not sure I understand. I want you to help me Micky to get some awareness of who I really am. I don't understand the purpose of my life. I am a miserable beast who survives on eating worms and water insects, frogs and tadpoles. I float passively in water like a log to hide my true identity. I have no personality or individuality. I am just a miserable creature." Crocoda uttered these words while he was crying loud and clear.

Micky had to quickly reassure Crocoda to restore his self-esteem. "You have to look at the bright side. Crocodile brain is the most developed among all the reptiles. You are capable of intelligent thinking and action, Crocoda. You can learn and change yourself in fundamental ways. There is no reason to lose hope."

Micky was in a bind. He didn't wish to be a counselor, coach or mentor to Crocoda. But there was also the urge to share, to guide a lost beast—a beast that had the potential of being a better beast, or even a decent beast.

Micky paused and thought for several minutes. He pacified the inner conflict raging in his own mind and accepted the challenge of starting a meaningful conversation with someone several steps lower than his own rather mature self.

"Let me say few things just to create a shared framework around which we could work together. Crocoda, you exist at the most primary level. In fact, there is not much difference between you and the mud that is gathered on the side of the river. Your awareness of self is undeveloped. Self and the material world in your case are highly undifferentiated. You cannot fully differentiate between an object outside of you and your inner self. You can't explain to me how this tree is different from you. You live in a world of ignorance—you are ruled by your instincts at the most rudimentary level. Maybe you are like a mythical serpent that eats his own tail, signifying self-containment, someone who is not able to recognize another as a fully autonomous self."

"That's an outrageous statement, Micky. I hate snakes. I don't like the way they crawl. They are cowards. They can't stand-up and fight like a croc. I am proud of being a crocodile. Don't compare me to a snake."

Micky realized he had pressed a wrong button and he was apologetic.

"I didn't mean to say that you are like a snake. I was using a metaphor—a snake eating his own tail means someone who is disconnected with external reality. I'm sorry; I'm being too harsh on you and I'm also going too fast. Metaphors are like abstract comparisons which are hard to understand at this level of your development. Let me give you a more positive assessment of your current state since you have shown evidence of your friendship with Crocodina; you have shown concern about her health and well-being. This means that you are perhaps more self aware than other crocs who live here in this river."

"That's good. That makes me feel good about myself. Go on, Micky. Tell me more about myself."

"And you have a reactive consciousness. You react to things that happen outside of your control or influence. You can't anticipate. You're not proactive. You don't plan things. If you do, the plan unfolds as a series of reactions to forces in the environment. You are even reactive to your own internal states. You search for food only when you're hungry."

"That's so true! But tell me more about reactive consciousness."

"This is difficult for you to understand at this time. But remember two things: causes are prior to effects, and causes have a force of their own. They force us to react. You react to a word like snake but you have no reaction to the word myth because myth is an abstraction. It's not something real, something that has spatial presence. You are incapable of thinking at an abstract level."

Crocoda was silent. Micky was afraid that with his boring talk he had put Crocoda to sleep.

"Are you awake, Crocoda?"

"I'm not only listening, I'm also thinking, though I am severely limited in my thinking capacity."

"Good to hear that! Now, let me get back to the basic question of the purpose of your life. The purpose of your life Crocoda is to survive. Everything that you do has just this focus; all your energy, all your thinking is centered on that single thought. How can I survive? Where can I get food? The endless search for food reduces you to a position where you're virtually all mouth; the world is all food. You also search for space that you can call your own: where can I get some space to doze off while the sun brings warmth to my body? Crocodina may have a bad attitude, but she is your mate. You must go back to her, not only because you love her, but you have a need for sex and reproduction."

"You are right. I need to go back to her. You know crocs are very sexy creatures. We like to have sex and reproduce all the time, but my sex life is in ruins. Not only because Crocodina is sick, but because she has such a bad attitude. I don't think she loves me anymore. Micky, how can I build a better relationship with Crocodina?"

"You can't do much at this level. Relationships are complex. You can't handle complex issues yet. What you can do is to listen to Crocodina and try to meet her basic needs."

Crocoda lowered the volume of his breathing so that he didn't lose any word that Micky was saying.

"You live in a world that is entirely horizontal—very flat. You don't know about the layers below and above your physical world. The same is the case with your inner world. You don't understand that your consciousness can develop and evolve. You can go up as well as down. We all can. This is one of the most frustrating parts of our lives—our ignorance of what we can really become. And if we don't take care of ourselves, how low we can fall—we can really hit the bottom."

"Micky, I think I can only go up from this point. There is nothing lower than the life of a constantly hungry beast."

"I agree with you, Crocoda."

Some birds appeared overhead and their joint chorus of ear-splitting noise momentarily drowned their conversation. Micky was relieved that he gained a few moments to gather his own thoughts.

"What else do I need to know?" Crocoda asked as the noise gradually drifted away.

"I like the way you phrase the question. When we realize that we have a need to learn, we open ourselves to new discoveries. Let me teach you something that is quite fundamental in the evolution of our consciousness. It's the concept of time. Crocoda, as we speak, you have no sense of time. You may use words like today, yesterday or tomorrow, but you have no idea that time is like an arrow and it moves forward, leaving behind a trail that we call past. Our memory consists of nothing except what happened in the past. Yesterday will not return, but the memory of what happened yesterday can stay with us for a long time. It is a good thing to remember our past, but our memory also adversely conditions our thinking. All our likes and dislikes are rooted in our past and they limit our behavior in many ways. A conditioned mind is no good mind."

"I know that time moves with day and night, the passing of seasons, but what is it precisely?"

"Time is unidirectional. It is composed of a series of events. Once an event happens, we can't make it go away. You tried to cheat on me. Remember? It was an event that we would like to undo but we can't. Time is also continuous—one thing happens after another in quick succession. There is no empty space between events. Although time is continuous, we can slice it into small segments. For example, the dialogue we are having now is our first such conversation. It has a recognizable beginning and we will know it when it ends. Time is measurable though it has no physical existence. We can measure it in seconds, minutes, hours, days, weeks, months and years. The most common measure is the present, which is now, the past, time that has gone, and the future, the time that has not arrived yet. But what is interesting about this is the fact that we can know only the present—the past and the future are mental constructs based on our memories and expectations."

"Micky, I wonder from where you have learned all these facts. I know monkeys are clever but they are not known for their wisdom like bears and eagles. Monkeys are good with their bodies; they are flexible and can jump from one treetop to another in no time. But you talk almost like my father who had learned a few things I don't know from where. My father was really wise. So was my mother. I'm sorry but I can't find them anymore. They went somewhere and never returned."

"Maybe they are dead?"

"What do you mean when you say that they are dead?"

"Crocoda, you couldn't move if you were dead. You couldn't see anything. You would not need anything to eat if you were dead. Dead animals have no sensation of hunger. You are like the stone that stands by the side of the river. It is just there and it will stay there until the flow of water changes its location. It has energy, but it is all locked up energy. Something else needs to happen to release this energy."

"Will I die? Will you be dead one day?"

"Yes, death follows life like a shadow. We are all going to die and this might happen any day. Not only other animals could kill us, we can die of natural causes—disease or old age. And when we die, we shall have no awareness. It is going to be a very long sleep."

"Micky, you're really scaring me. Shaman told Crocodina that she was going to die. No one ever told me that I would also die. I thought that if Crocodina died she would be still around—only she would be unable to speak, or something along those lines. But tell me if I were to die now and then turn into a stone, how could I live inside a stone? Where do I go? Where can I go? I have to go somewhere, don't I? It can't just be nothing. Do you understand what I'm trying to say?"

Micky hesitated for a moment. Crocoda was asking a really hard question.

"Crocoda, we are talking of things that are beyond our understanding. It's not easy to talk about death and dying. I don't think there is any way for me to explain what happens after we die. First, I don't know the answer myself. Second, if there is an answer, that would require really advanced thinking, which is not within our reach at this time. You need to learn to understand other things before you can solve the mystery of life and death."

"But Micky I want to learn. I want you to become my teacher. I promise to come here every day before sunrise and wait for you to wake up from your sleep. Then you will talk to me and I will listen. You will share with me your wisdom, the things that you know and I don't. I promise I will be a good student. I will learn to see the world with your eyes. Don't be too concerned about my lack of understanding at this time. Let the occasional outbursts of my beastliness also not bother you. Of course, I can't change myself overnight."

"Crocoda, you learned a lesson today. If you can repeat what you learned then I will feel encouraged that I didn't waste my time. If you can't repeat what you just heard from me then we need to end this thing now because either I didn't teach it very well, or you didn't learn it very well. And if today's learning is too much for you then you will not be able to handle the more complex learning that would occur in the future."

Crocoda didn't exactly expect this test, but he was happy that Micky asked. "Micky, you told me several things. My life is not very different from dead matter. I make distinctions between self and other beings but in a very limited manner. I'm very instinctive. I spend most of my time seeking gratification of my physical needs. I look for pleasure and avoid pain. I'm very reactive. I don't know much about causes and effects. I have little, if any, understanding of the nature of time. Micky, there are few other things that you didn't say but I think they are relevant to my situation."

"What are those things?"

"I experience very strong emotions and mood swings. I can be nice and happy one moment and truly nasty another. I am very attached to my current way of life. Crocodina is not much of a companion for me but I don't have the courage to leave her. I go back to her as a matter of habit. I have no idea of what is good or bad, right or wrong. Who makes these decisions? At least, I can't. I know earth is good. If there was no earth below me, I don't know what I would do. I feel this need for grounding myself and I can't have enough of it."

"Crocoda, this is a great self-assessment. You said it better than I had expected. We also talked about one more thing."

"Yes, You told me about the meaning of death. When we are dead, we are simply dead."

"This is a very good summary. Can I add something that I didn't mention before? The kind of conversation we had this morning is a form of learning—which is important because this is the only way we can change ourselves. And when we change ourselves, we develop ourselves physically and mentally. We become better, we get more skilled, we have better ideas, and our life becomes more meaningful to us."

"Learning or awakening? I feel I was asleep and you woke me up." Micky could sense gratitude in Crocoda's voice.

"This is just the beginning Crocoda. There is surely more to come. But we need time. I don't expect to see you for the next several days. I want you to practice what we have learned today—search for food, eat, sleep, mate and don't think of any big issues yet. The purpose of your life is the same as the current level of your consciousness. You can't do more, but at the same time you shouldn't try to do less."

"Do you have any parting words of advice for me?"

"Sure, maintain a very strong connection with your body at all times. The best way to resolve your issues with Crocodina would be to start from a point of acçeptance. You need to accept her as she is and she needs to do the same. Continue to be passionate about gaining more self awareness. Accept your current reality—the way things are—but prepare yourself for change. I'm going to suggest a few thoughts or affirmations to strengthen your resolve for inner transformation."

"What is an affirmation?"

"Affirmation is a message that we send to our inner self. We can train our intuition, our unconscious, to work for us if we send the right kind of messages. Can you repeat after me?"

"Sure."

"I feel strongly grounded and secure."

Crocoda repeated.

"I give and receive lots of comfort."

Crocoda repeated again.

"One more affirmation will be good. I am discovering the higher purpose of my life."

Crocoda repeated the last affirmation and the previous two many times before he was fully confident that he could repeat these affirmations on his own.

"Micky, can you also teach me how to meditate? I have heard that meditation is very effective in speeding up personal development. Can you teach me how to meditate?"

"It is important for you to learn to breathe. Try to breathe fully and deeply. Clear your mind of all ideas and distractions. At this level of your mental development, I suggest that you do the earth meditation. Lie down on a flat surface and keep your body grounded. Let every part of your body touch the earth; let each part of your body draw energy from the earth; let each part of your body also transmit energy to the center of the earth where the focal point for renewal, rejuvenation, and growth is located. These currents of energy going up and down will make a cyclical movement and you will feel a sense of grounding that you have never felt before. This will be a great starting point for you." As Micky spoke, he saw Crocoda already trying to practice the earth meditation. He was rolling on the wet sand like a gymnast and making some incoherent sounds. Clearly, the physical and spiritual energies were getting mixed-up in a delightful way.

"Oh, thank you Micky. I'm so excited. I need to go. I need to eat. I'm really hungry. See you later!"

Micky looked at Crocoda as he slipped back into the water. He had mixed feelings about this meeting. He was not sure whether he had done the right thing in starting this "friendly" relationship with Crocoda.

"What the heck!" Micky picked up an apple and dug his tiny teeth into it. It had an unusually sweet taste. "Life is good!" He told himself.

As soon as the moon was up in the sky, Micky went down to the beach and did several rollovers on the sand while imitating different types of animal sounds.

REFLECTION

1. What is the relationship between our thinking (consciousness) and action (behavior)? Is it correct to say that our thinking determines our behavior?
2. How do you apologize for an action that has resulted in the breach of trust between you and another person?
3. What role self-esteem plays in personal (authentic) change?
4. "Maybe you are like a mythical serpent that eats its own tail...." What is the significance of a serpent eating its own tail?
5. What is reactive consciousness?
6. Is time unidirectional? Is time continuous? What are some of the other concepts of time?
7. What is the meaning of "acceptance" in a relationship?
8. What is an affirmation? Why do you think affirmation works? Do you think it will work for you?

3 What's That New Feeling

For several weeks Micky didn't see Crocoda. Where is he? The question popped up in his mind many times, but then he let it slide back into his unconscious since Crocoda still evoked mixed feelings bordering on strong negativity. On the one hand, Micky thought of his "friendship" with Crocoda as his way of paying his debt to the community of animals to which he belonged. On the other hand, he had doubts about a crocodile making much progress on the path of inner transformation.

There is only so much you could do with a crocodile! Irrespective of the true worth of this effort, it had some immediate gain in terms of good animal relations. But Micky was not sure whether anyone was really paying any attention.

Micky had intermittent feelings of his extrasensory perception. He knew about things that were happening beyond the range of his immediate vision. He saw a picture of Crocoda returning in a particularly sour mood. Therefore, Micky was not a bit surprised when Crocoda actually reappeared at his beach the same afternoon.

And what a way to come back! Crocoda was in a miserable condition. He was looking famished. His face seemed particularly grim.

"Micky, you told me about death the last time we met. I have a feeling that I'm going to turn myself into a stone, meaning I'm going to die."

Crocoda's voice had no raw energy. He spoke as if he were mumbling something to himself.

"What's wrong? Why are you so sad, Crocoda?"

"You know when we talked the last time, I spoke to you about my father. When I went home I had an urge to see him. I asked Crocodina whether she had any idea where I could find my father. She had no idea whatsoever. Either she didn't know or she didn't care. I know her face would have lightened up if I had asked her about her own father. Anyway, next morning I swam upstream and I went to a pond that is a sacred ground for the crocs in this area. It's sacred because one of our elders Popa lives there. He is really very old, close to 100, although that may be an exaggeration but most of us live for 40 or 50 years at the most. Anyway, Popa is so old that he can't hunt for food on his own, and no one brings food for him. Popa was very happy to see me. I don't remember when I last met him, but it must have been a very long time ago. He asked many questions. I told him about Crocodina. He was sorry to know about her illness. I asked him whether he could suggest a remedy, but he cut me short saying that he didn't know any. Then I got to the real question for which I had gone to see Popa. I asked him about my father. He was very surprised, as if taken aback by my question. Why are you asking this question? I told him that I was searching for my roots, and in this search my father was my first link because he would provide answers to all the other questions that I had in my mind. Popa was angry. It is so stupid, he said. Crocs don't ask such questions. We live for food, security, and reproduction, and nothing more. When you ask other questions—questions that go beyond the basic needs of an animal like us, they are not valid questions. You don't have the permission to ask those questions."

Micky listened attentively as this was turning out to be a very dramatic story. He knew that Crocoda was on to something big, something really big.

"I told Popa that I had awakened myself to my current reality. I can see that every event that takes place is a part of the world in a physical sense. But each event also has an inner side to it. So when I feel sad I have to cry. When I'm troubled by a question I have to look for an answer. That's my subjective reality that presses me to get an answer. I know that crocs live for food and other basic needs, but I don't want to live like that. I want to be a different kind of croc. Popa laughed and asked me the name of the beast that was telling me that I was not to lead the life I was given. I told him about you, Micky. He could hardly control his laughter—a crocodile, a real crocodile, seeking wisdom from a monkey. He laughed aloud, but I kept my cool. I didn't allow myself to be provoked into any stupid argument. If anyone else had made fun of you, Micky, I would have hit him very hard."

"Then what happened?" This was a truly bizarre tale, but Micky was getting hooked into it.

"Popa told me that when crocs die they don't turn themselves into stones. They become spirits. They continue to roam around, but no one can see them. I asked him how I could talk with my father's spirit. He told me that I could speak to my father's spirit only if I were close to his bones. He mentioned a place upstream where my father had died. He had run into some trouble with a gang of crocs, and they had attacked him as a group and killed him. I went to this place and found no crocs there, but there were many bones strewn around the whole place. It looked like a field where a big battle had taken place and dozens of crocs had died. I sat there and thought about the story you told me about time's direction. What I was seeing had happened in the past. I hoped that my father's spirit would come back and touch me but nothing happened. I saw no spirits, although I stayed there for the entire night."

Crocoda took a breather to gather his emotions. Micky was excited as well as puzzled because he was witnessing the unfolding of a great story.

After a while, Crocoda continued, "Next morning a strange thing happened. I saw a number of crocs in the area. First I thought that I was going to be attacked and killed like my father. But these were nice crocs, so we started to talk. They asked me whether I would like to join their clan. I said yes because I was afraid of rejecting their offer."

"How many were they? Did they have a name for their clan?"

"They were many and they called themselves Crocangers. There were many males and a few females too. In that crowd there was this real beauty. She must have been half my age. I asked her name, but she told me that she would like to remain nameless. I told her that I could live with that. It was love at first sight: my sexual need was at its peak. We had sex every day and night. There were two things going on in my mind at that time: One, I was being unfaithful to Crocodina and I thought that was bad, and when I say bad I still do not know who makes those kinds of judgments. Two, I realized perhaps for the first time in my life that sex was not only a physical act. It was an exchange of energy between two beings, and it was greatly uplifting. My spirit soared while I had sex with my nameless friend. How do you explain it?"

"It is quite simple. Sex is a sacred act. It brings new life into being. It is raw spiritual energy. It is a pity that most of the time animals think that they are just having a good time when they have sex."

"You are right. In the beginning I just wanted to keep it a simple affair. You know what I mean. But as the nameless became my partner things began to change. She suggested that we bring a new perspective to love-making. I agreed thinking that she knew more than me. As we experimented with new ways of making love, the sexual act itself became something sacred. Micky, you can't imagine what a difference it made."

"What else happened?" Micky pushed, urging Crocoda to talk about something other than sex.

"We went on a hunt together and killed some deer, but I never stopped thinking of my father. Many days passed. I was happy because we always had good food, but I was suddenly taken over by this sadness for which I had no explanation. When I returned home several days later, Crocodina refused to talk with me. I really wanted to mate with her. It was not a need for sex. I had had enough of that with my nameless friend. I was reaching out to her and showing her some affection. But she rejected me. I felt very lonely and stopped eating altogether. Every night I looked at the sky, wondering about what I saw. What was going on? I was in a state of awe. As I found no answer to my questions I started to grow weak and weary. What should I do? Where should I go now? Micky, you need to help me, please."

Micky realized that Crocoda was ready for the next step.

"Crocoda, I'm very pleased with what you have discovered about yourself and your father during the past few days. Whoever thought that a crocodile could have feelings for his ancestors? But you are different; you are becoming a different kind of a crocodile and I want to support you in this endeavor. Let me share with you some other secrets: A time comes in our lives when we think that food alone is not sufficient for our survival. We need something more than food, more than a place to live, more than sex. Or to put it another way, these are necessary but not sufficient conditions. We start to look at the sky and wonder what's going on out there. Who is running this show? Who is really in charge?"

Micky stopped for a while to catch his breath.

"Our parents are very important to us because they give us life, and take care of us when we are young. So we need to recognize them and give them our respect. They are our ancestors and there is traditional wisdom that says: honor your elders. They may be dead but they should not be forgotten. In order to show respect to our elders we can perform rituals. When we celebrate the memory of our ancestors we actually celebrate the unending dance of life. We are born and we die. Our children are born and one day they die too and so the cycle of life and death goes on. Look at these trees; look at the water that flows in this river. Where do you think it is headed? Nowhere, to tell you the truth. It stays here. This is the magic of life. Things disappear one moment and they reappear the next one. This is the sacred game of life. In the same manner, one day we shall disappear from the scene. And then we shall be back to see and live for another day. I may not come back as a monkey, and you may not come back as a crocodile. There are hundreds of shapes life can take on. Life itself rolls on."

Crocoda was listening to Micky in what appeared to be a meditative mood—silent yet fully attentive.

"Micky, what you say is so true. Time is like an arrow, but this arrow does not travel straight. It moves forward making little circles. That is why we have greenery at one time and bare trees another time, why we have rains one time and extremely dry weather a few months later. Nothing stays the same, but what comes back is part of the play of nature that we have already seen."

"Crocoda, in the larger scheme of things we are not that important. What is important is to make a difference in our life today. Go back to the place where the bones of your father reside and say some prayers. Ask Popa; he will tell you what prayers to say. Get back also to your clan—you call them Crocangers, don't you? That's your community. You have to seek oneness with them. They will give you strength, and they will satisfy your social needs. Accept the reality of magic. We can't make sense of everything. Anything that is foreign to our senses is magic—it's a play, it's a trick, but it is real. We don't know the trickster or the magician, but the magic never stops. I don't want to create a wrong impression here. Magic is real, but not everything is magical. There are other things for which we can find known causes. Understanding these causes and their effects is important."

Micky looked at Crocoda and paused for a few seconds and then continued, "The world of nature is our home, but we take it for granted. We don't pay much attention to its sheer beauty. Stop all activity at least once a day to look at the clouds, flowers that bloom in wilderness, the flight of birds and the songs they sing in their togetherness. Look at the sunrise and the sunset and try to notice similarities and differences. Go back to Popa as often as you can. He will tell you stories. Talk to him and ask him questions. Never forget the acts of compassion that have benefited you and the kindness of others that has served you well. Go and talk to the shaman that Crocodina is seeing. Shamans have great wisdom to which we have no easy access."

Micky knew that he had said many things in one long breath and it was time to be silent so that Crocoda could respond.

"Micky, why did you stop? Tell me more about the things you know. You seem to know a lot."

"It's not my knowing that matters to you. It's what you are experiencing that is of greater importance. Are you passionate about life, about living?"

"As I told you, the past few weeks have been bad, but I am getting a new feeling. I feel that I can do things that would truly make a difference for me. Never before have I felt this power within me—the power of making a decision for myself. I made a decision to see Popa. I went to his place and talked to him. I sought membership within my community of crocs. I think it was a good experience. Do you think I should spend more time with them?"

"That would be wonderful! Living and working in a community enhances one's learning. These connections make us grow into better animals."

"It is good that you say this because once I was in their company I thought that I was physically part of them. I had lost the sense of being a living and walking crocodile, someone who was different from others. I was, however, bothered about losing my identity."

"We all go through this. It will take time for you to develop that strong sense of identity that will separate you from other animals. But as you mature, you build a stronger sense of boundaries between yourself and the others. It comes automatically."

"Micky, one other question. I thought that I understood this time thing but I really don't. What you call past always looks to me like the present. I don't seem to understand the loss of time. Why can't I experience my past or my future in one gulp? Why do I have to think back or imagine things that might occur in the future?"

"There is no easy way to understand this complex issue. If you are living in the present, that's great. Why do you need anything else? We'll see when the future arrives. In fact, it will never arrive because you will always be living in the present."

"And you must know that this death business is very frustrating to me. I just don't get it. You said that we turn into stones when we die. Popa said that we turn into spirits. Whom do I believe?"

"Both of us are right, or perhaps both of us are wrong. We have to believe what our ancestors told us. They knew much more than we can ourselves comprehend. Isn't that right?"

Crocoda was silent as if in deep contemplation.

Micky wanted to end the meeting with Crocoda and asked, "Did you learn anything meaningful today?"

"Many things, both simple and complex: Show respect to your elders. Spirits do exist though we can't see them. Bonding with your own community or clan is important. Sex is important, but essentially it's a sacred act. This world is a magical place, though not everything around us is magical. Some things have known causes, and known causes must be explored and understood. We should recognize and reciprocate the good that others do to us. We need to enjoy the beauty and splendor of nature because this is our home and it's tremendously beautiful."

Crocoda paused for a few moments.

"My homework includes a few things. I should continue to discover the meaning of my life. Also I should try to suppress my negative feelings and develop a more positive attitude towards life."

"Crocoda, that's so wonderful. We are getting somewhere. Let me give you three new affirmations. Here is the first one: I feel good about myself. And the second: I make my own decisions. And the last: I deserve the love and care that I'm getting."

Crocoda repeated these affirmations several times and asked for a new meditation.

Micky thought for a moment and said, "Crocoda, you have made some progress. The last time we met, grounding was your most important need. Your spirit has now elevated itself from the ground of your being. You are at the water level. Water provides sustenance. Liquids inside your body keep you alive and healthy. Water is also a symbol of change and movement. Before you do this meditation, which is more like deep self-reflection, clean yourself of all dirt. Drink sufficient water to quench your thirst. The core of your meditation is to think of all the things in your life that have changed. Food was a major part of your life, but now it is a smaller part. You had no clarity around the purpose of your life, but now you have some clarity. Our life is a series of movements. Movements occur within a space that introduces us to the idea of polarities, meaning we see one thing here and another thing there, one idea here and another idea there. We want only one thing or idea that we like. But we can't make up our minds. Once we understand the polarities that we are struggling with, we develop the capacity to look at our life issues more meaningfully. Therefore, this water meditation will be about change, movement and polarities. Let all these ideas come to your mind. Just watch them from a distance as if somebody else was doing this thinking inside your body. Is this clear?"

Crocoda hesitated to convey his agreement. "Not exactly. You said many things and you used concepts that I'm not familiar with. However, I will try my best to stay focused on how my life is changing."

"That will be good enough for the time being."

Crocoda left quietly as if burdened with the new knowledge, new instructions to carry the change process to its next step.

Night had fallen. The silence that surrounded Micky was frightening. The forest that was hiding so much life had suddenly turned mute, as if the show of life had retired for rehearsing the very next act; behind the curtain the stage was being set for another show. Nothing was moving. Nothing was still. Everything was in a state of silent flow. Everything moved in the direction of a distant light—an unseen bright spot that was attracting every living creature, every flying object, and each particle of matter for a loving embrace, an embrace that transforms, elevates, evolves, and purifies everything.

Micky thought about his meeting with Crocoda. He could not believe what he was doing—coaching and mentoring a crocodile. Wow!

"My parents would be really proud of me." That was a great thought to hold in his mind while he retired for the night.

REFLECTION

1. Do you think about your death? What happens after death?
2. "I told Popa that I had awakened to my current reality." What is current reality? How do you describe your own current reality?
3. Do you like to work with a group of people? How do you retain your own identity while you are part of a group?
4. "Our parents are very important to us...." What are your personal memories of your parents? What are some of the things that you think you learned from them?
5. "What is important is to make a difference in our life today." In what specific ways are you making a difference in your life?
6. "I should continue to discover the meaning of my life. Also I should try to suppress my negative feelings and develop a more positive attitude towards life."
7. Have you been coaching and mentoring others? Why not?

4 Power Speaks

Several weeks passed. One morning Micky was still asleep when he heard a big rattling sound—like an explosion, a cloudburst, or an earthquake. He looked down and found what seemed to be an army of crocs invading his private space. Some of them were shaking the tree to get the apples and others were laughing wildly, having good time. They were singing a chorus—

We're the Crocangers
The best and the powerful
We rule this world
If you have a problem
Come face us or just shut up
We shall have our way
Ha, ha, ho, ho, bang, bang
We're the Crocangers!

Micky could not believe his ears. After he overcame his initial fear of an untimely demise, he shouted, "Are you there, Crocoda?"

A voice rose from the crowd, "Hi Micky, I'm very much here, though you can't see me. These are all my friends. We are Crocangers and we kick butt."

"Are you out of your mind? I don't care who these crocs are. I want them out of my property right now. Is that clear?"

"And if we don't obey this order, what are you going to do? Call the cops? My friends respond to only one thing—brute force; nothing else matters. But, Micky, you are a friend. I don't want to have a fight with you. I'm going to ask these folks to take it easy and disappear so that the two of us can have some meaningful conversation."

"Better do it now!"

"Okay, I heard you. Please give me a few minutes." Crocoda said few things to his friends in what appeared to be a coded language and they started to slide into the water in quick succession in an orderly fashion.

When it was quiet once again, Micky burst into anger.

"Now, what the heck was that? Why did you bring these creatures here? Do you have respect for anything? You accepted me as your teacher; is this any way to reward your teacher? Did you want to frighten me to death?"

Micky was on fire. His tongue was clearly outpacing his thoughts.

"Calm down, I say calm down, take it easy; it's all over. They're all gone. And now the two of us can talk as we did in the past."

"No talking with you because you do dreadful things. You have no idea what friendship means. You're a risky venture. I don't want to talk with you."

"All right, I wish to offer my apologies to my dear friend Micky who is slightly freaked out at this time but who is otherwise a decent and caring monkey."

"Cut to the chase, Crocoda. What's your point?"

"The point is that I have made a discovery: Power is everything. Let me repeat: Power is everything. Crocs are power-driven animals. We can kill virtually anything that comes our way, but until recently I had no idea that physical power was also a concept. It's a projection. It is the ability to put the fear of God in the heart of your opponent. It is flattening the enemy without lifting any part of your body."

"I don't understand what you're talking about!"

"Okay, let me start all over again. In this world there is an ongoing battle between the haves and have-nots. You have the apples and I don't. How can I get your apples? Very easy, I have to use my muscle power. I will tell you, 'Give me the apples, otherwise…' and I know you'll get the message. Should I be ashamed of telling you what I need? No way. I'm powerful; you're not and that decides it. No shame in using what God has given you. I am within my right to gratify all my needs. I have to overcome all resistance wherever it comes from. And above all, I don't have to worry about consequences. Might is right. Yes, might is right."

Micky made a creaky sound to gesture that he wanted to say something. Crocoda was in no mood to accommodate him, but Micky persisted and found an opening.

"If you stop talking and let me think about it then I will get the essence of what you are telling me. Life is a jungle. We know it because we live in one. The fittest tend to survive because they are tough and they overcome forces that can kill the weak. If the only language that you speak is power language, you don't ever say sorry. There is no guilt because having guilt makes you lose your power. Nothing stands between you and the object of your desire. Power is exercised in the present moment. So there is no tomorrow. It is now or never. I get this. It makes sense, but how did you get it, Crocoda? Does it mean that you have become a thinking animal, or what?"

"No, I am not a thinking anything. I'm just an animal. But things come your way, you get enlightened. It's life. As you know, I was spending a great deal of my time in the company of Crocangers. We were just a happy-go-lucky bunch. We killed; we ate and rested like logs by the side of the pond. Then, one day one of us said something that caught everyone's attention. He said: 'We have the power to get what we want.' And all of us started to question the croc who said it. 'What do you mean? What is power?' And slowly it dawned on us that power is a feeling. It is a feeling of fullness, being on top of the world. You can get whatever you wish for because you have the power. You control everyone and let no one control or intimidate you. Power is magic but it is also beyond magic. You don't wait for things to happen; you make them happen. Power is action. It is unilateral control."

"This means that if you have power and know it, then you go around throwing your weight like a wild croc."

"No, you go around throwing your weight like a wild elephant."

"An elephant is a much nicer animal. Anyway, let me ask you a question. Of the two statements 'We have the power' or 'I have the power' which one would you choose?"

"I would say the latter. Anyone can feel empowered as part of a group, but the real thing is to feel the power within your own veins. It's the feeling that I have become something important. I can change the world the way I like it without any guilt or remorse. If I have that I-feeling then I can let my ego do the talking for me."

"This is a big leap forward for you, Crocoda. You have become a proud animal, though highly egocentric, not caring for the consequences of your actions, but a power being with an I-consciousness. Am I right?"

"Yep!"

"If I have no power over you, how can I influence your behavior?"

"You have to appeal to my self-interest. Show me the carrot, sorry an apple. I mean you can try to bribe me. Power likes flattery. If you tell me the truth about myself I will kick your butt. It's that simple."

"If that doesn't work?"

"Then you have a real problem. Of course, I may do anything for you in the name of our friendship, but otherwise you are nobody. I don't have to pay any attention. You're inconsequential. I can count you out. Ooh! That's called playing the power game."

"You have become a pretty smart fellow, Crocoda. At the same time, you have lost the ability to look at your self objectively."

"I know only one thing: I'm right and you are wrong. Ha, ha."

"I am glad that you are using the words right and wrong which I'm sure mean nothing to you. But wait for some time; you will start to question yourself. You will get an urge to find out the difference between right and wrong, and, therefore, lay the foundation of your future development. What else is going on? Do you have some concerns?"

"Micky, are you a mind reader or what? I was trying to hide several things by talking about power. But of course, you won't let me get away with the other stuff that also weighs heavily on my mind."

"What stuff?"

"Little things, but you may see more in it than I do. I still continue to have mixed feelings about myself. Sometime I feel very good, and at other times I feel very bad. I have no self-confidence. For example, I want to go back to Crocodina and tell her that I am finally out of her life, but I can't muster the courage to do that. I know my tongue is sealed in her presence and my brain doesn't work. I can't utter a few straight words. Where is my sense of power in that situation? And she is the most unreasonable and powerless creature on earth. On the outside I feel power but inside I am hollow with feelings of guilt and shame. There is some good news about this power thing, but you should know I'm still stuck deep in the mud of my own making and I don't see a clear path to success."

"Crocoda, I do not share your disillusionment. You have made a great discovery yet you have some issues, something normal for a creature going through major transformation. The great thing is that you have no hesitation in acknowledging your problems."

"One other thing that I consider positive is that I am developing some capacity for self-reflection. While I'm spending most of my energy in coping with my outer reality, there is a streak of energy that is following an inward path. I may be starting a journey to self-understanding."

"Yes, you are right. You have shown evidence of self-analysis because you are raising fundamental questions about your inner fears. You are not in denial anymore."

"What's your advice, Micky? What should I do differently now?"

"Crocoda, you have to learn to use power in subtle ways; that is, you have to be more self assertive without the appearance of being obsessed with power. The appropriate use of power also requires accepting responsibility. You have to accept responsibility for the consequences of your actions. You cannot use blame as a self-protective mechanism. Learn to integrate the outer and inner energy currents for the good of the self and of others. This will liberate you from the feelings of guilt and shame."

"Are you going to give me some new affirmations?"

"I have a big storehouse of affirmations. Here is my choice of three for helping you negotiate the intricacies of your current situation. Number one: I use my power with humility and compassion. This should directly address your obsession with your new found power. Number two: I project my self-esteem in all my actions. You did say that you're still struggling with self-esteem issues. And number three: My life is making a positive difference. You can make this statement only if your actions are contributing to some common good. You can't say it if you continue to be a beastly creature."

As usual, Crocoda practiced his affirmations and waited as usual for a new meditation.

"The purpose of this meditation is to take advantage of the fire that is burning inside your body. This fire is the raw energy that you experience, and it shows up as a sense of being in control. Fire is also a converter of energy. When the wood is burnt it turns itself into charcoal which is another form of energy. For this meditation, close your eyes and keep an image of a burning flame in front of your eyes. Feel the heat of this flame. See how much light this flame is emitting. See how this fire is burning up your baser desires, your ugly motivations, your lies, and your machinations. Everything that should not be part of your new self is cleansed by this flame. Everything that is no longer needed is turned into ash. Every time you complete this meditation, you will feel that you are a totally new animal. Slowly you will burn the threads that unconsciously tie you to your older tendencies. Good luck!"

Crocoda understood and left after a short goodbye.

Micky felt relieved to see Crocoda slip into the river. He looked at the trees. The morning fog was lifting. The forest was coming back to life and the struggle for survival was beginning anew for another day.

"Only the fittest will survive!" Micky murmured these words as if he had discovered Nature's biggest secret.

REFLECTION

1. "Power is everything." Do you agree? Why not?
2. "If I have no power over you. How can I influence your behavior?" How can you influence others without formal authority?
3. How can you gain confidence to convey bad news to someone who is very close to you?
4. "The appropriate use of power also requires accepting responsibility. You have to accept responsibility for the consequences of your actions."
5. Are you conscious of the fire in your belly? What is this fire about? Is this fire energizing you? Why not?

5 Believe It Or Not

Two months passed, but there was no news of Crocoda. Micky was afraid that, given his new lifestyle and the bad company, the croc might have hurt himself or done something completely stupid to land himself in a worse mess. Anyway, life was too short to think about wild crocs, Micky assured himself and instead focused on matters of immediate concern like removing dead branches of his rose-apple tree.

One afternoon Micky heard a murmuring sound under his tree. It was Crocoda, spread out under the rose-apple tree in a kind of saintly composure.

"Crocoda, when did you come?"

"Oh, I have been resting under your tree for days. You have not paid any attention to me."

"Why didn't you call me to get my attention?"

"You know, during these past few weeks I have been paying attention only to myself and to nothing else. What is inside is more important than what is outside."

"Is that a new kind of philosophy that you have learned or what? And what was that murmur about?"

"It's a mantra that I have to repeat 121 times every day."

"What mantra? What are you talking about?"

"It's a mantra that my shaman gave me."

"Have you been seeing a shaman?"

"Her name is Badi Mai."

"Where did you find her?"

"I did not find her; she found me. Don't they say: a teacher appears when you are ready?"

"I thought I was your teacher, Crocoda."

"Yes, you are my teacher as well as my friend. She is my spiritual guru. She is so old and so wise, she has changed my life."

"It would seem so. The last time I saw you, you were a different kind of creature. You were riding the high horse of power."

"If I see a horse I will eat it."

"Never mind, it was just a metaphor. What happened?"

"You know, power takes you only so far. When you have everything it feels like you have nothing. I would kill and conquer and I would still be very unhappy. I would lie awake at night and look at the stars and I would ask myself questions about the meaning of it all. Who am I? Why do I exist? What's the purpose of my life? What is the Force behind everything? What is right and what is not? What is good and what is not?"

"I'm very glad Crocoda that you got to a place where I thought you would never go. It's truly fascinating. Tell me more. What did Badi Mai tell you?"

"Huh, she said many things. She opened my mind to new realities. This world is not just standing there on its own feet. There is a Force that holds it together. Micky, do you have any idea what God is?"

Micky didn't wish to get into a metaphysical discussion, but he did want to answer the question. "God is a big fat monkey and the world stands on the head of this giant monkey."

"You're wrong my friend. God is a big crocodile that holds this world in balance on his giant nose."

"Monkey or crocodile—what's the difference? Are we not talking about something that is so far removed from us that it doesn't matter whether it is one or the other?"

"You are wrong again my friend. God is with us at all times. He watches our every action. He is listening to the conversation that we are having right now. He keeps a perfect record of our good deeds as well as the bad ones. He punishes as well as rewards."

"God is not a neurotic being, Crocoda. He has better things to do than to eavesdrop on our conversation."

"I think our roles are reversed now. I am the teacher who knows the answers to these fundamental questions and you are an ignorant student, because you talk like one. But don't worry, God is caring and loving. He is compassionate and takes care of believers as well as non-believers. You will be redeemed."

"Crocoda, if you are my soul doctor then I think my future is doomed."

"Don't say such harsh words. God is merciful. He will forgive you if you stop talking like a non-believer."

"What should I believe in?"

"You have to believe in my God."

"Are we having a fight about definitions? Okay, God is a big croc. What next?"

"Thanks for being so generous. I forgot to tell you about a great discovery. I'm a born-again crocodile. I always had this suspicion that I'm someone very special. Now Badi Mai has confirmed it. I died and was born again as a croc. I will die and then be born again as a croc. Isn't that wonderful? No need to guess. I know what I'm going to be."

Micky wanted to change the topic. He asked, "What happened to your other friends. I mean Crocangers?"

"I'm trying my best to save each one of them by converting them to my faith. But not everyone is ready. Some need more time. I am very patient. Imagine if everyone believed in God in whom I have my faith; then there would be peace in the world. I wouldn't have any fights any more."

"You think peace in the world is that simple?"

"One other thing. If they embraced my faith I would want them to recite the same mantra that I recite 121 times a day."

"And if they don't comply with this demand?"

"Then, I will break open their skulls."

"Wow! I thought once you turned God-loving you became non-violent. Am I missing something?"

"You have to not only believe in God, you have to spread God's message too. And that can take persuasion as well as force."

"And is that the right thing to do?"

"My faith tells me what is right or wrong."

"You mean there is nothing beyond your faith?"

"What else could there be? Look at the other benefits. When you believe in one cosmic authority there is safety, security, order and predictability. Life becomes a serious business. We can dream of having a shared future."

"But you do give the control to an external authority?"

"That authority is both inside and outside. Before I became a believer my ego was like a wild elephant, but now it is tamed. Before I do anything important I ask Badi Mai's approval and acceptance. It feels so good."

"Are you concerned that your spiritual leader could become an authoritarian figure?"

"She does not make rules; she only interprets them."

"How can you be so certain?"

"I am certain because I have faith in her goodness."

"Well, Crocoda, this has been a most illuminating conversation. I wish you all success in your new life as a missionary and a believer. I'm sorry if my comments hurt your spiritual sensibilities. To me Nature is Mother, my Goddess. She is within me and outside everywhere, in the air that I breathe and in the fruit that I eat. She does not ask anything of me and I don't have much to give. We have a healthy and nurturing relationship and I'm quite happy about it."

"I'm sorry, Micky. I think you are doomed. If you don't believe in my God you are a non-believer. You will rot in hell, perhaps. But if you change your mind, please let me know. I can bring Badi Mai here and she can convert you in a minute."

"Convert me into what?"

"To my religion. Sorry I didn't mention it at the very outset."

Micky fell silent, almost speechless. He felt he had nothing more to say. This was not the conversation Micky felt like having at this time. If we are not able to challenge our beliefs, then we are bowing to an inner authority that could be as cruel as the external authority. But Micky himself was faced with an inner conflict. How could he tell Crocoda that unquestioned belief was a dangerous thing when he himself was acting out of an unquestioned belief that critical thinking was better than unconditional acceptance? Micky felt that his inner conversation sounded like a value judgment, a sense of superiority that was stimulating for his own ego-self. If Crocoda was inspired by his belief and his devotion to the words of a spiritual guru, there was nothing wrong with it. Developing faith in an entity, or in a doctrine, was part of the transformational process. Micky knew this well, but in this moment of conflicting ideologies he was forgetting this essential truth and acting like a critical parent.

Micky wished Crocoda well and said good-bye. As the cool breeze touched his nostrils, he stretched and yawned and curled upon a branch. With his eyelids becoming heavy with dreams that were ready to be unbundled, he looked at the darkness enveloping the whole forest. There were many big things weighing on his mind—the nature of God and how belief in God shapes animal thinking. But at the most practical level, he had no other concern other than having a good night's sleep. He closed his eyes and within minutes went into rather deep and restful sleep.

Micky woke up late at night and looked at the full moon that was traversing some stray clouds. It was a beautiful night. The thoughts of his conversation with Crocoda returned and he wondered how religion could have such a strong impact on animal behavior. On the one hand, it opens the animal mind to God. On the other, it makes the Truth look much smaller. It closes avenues for independent thinking and spiritual discovery. "God is within you," Micky's father used to tell him. "You have to find him inside. Spirit is within you, you have to find her there." These early childhood messages were imprinted in Micky's mind.

Micky also realized how careless he had become lately about his meditation. He had not done any serious meditation for days. Being Crocoda's teacher had certainly inflated his ego. He was spending more time thinking about Crocoda's salvation than his own.

"Micky, are you awake?" Crocoda's sleepy voice had the soft touch of the late night breeze.

"How did you know that I was awake? Did I stop snoring?"

"No, you never snore but I do. I just feel that my intuition is becoming stronger. I can see things that I never saw before. I can hear voices that I never heard before."

"It's because you're paying attention now."

"It is such a good feeling ... Micky I may have said things that you found annoying."

"Like what?"

"Like God being a croc. This is my talk for Crocangers who are completely ignorant of their spiritual side, but you are not one of them. You're self-aware; you know it all. I don't have to convert you to my belief system. That was just a bad joke."

"I see some qualitative improvement in your jokes."

"Badi Mai may have limited my vision in some respects, but she has also opened my heart. I feel I'm connected with the unknown in a direct way. I find great peace of mind in reciting the mantra. It is true that the desire to build a close relationship with God has also made me overzealous. I am pushing my faith as much as I'm following it. But that is my personal weakness."

"How is Crocodina?"

"I have no idea. I saw her one day, said a prayer for her well-being and kissed her goodbye forever. She is history; I still wish her well but this was a time for me to move on."

"You know Crocoda every relationship, in the beginning, is a symbol of love and beauty, but, when we reach a breaking point, the same relationship becomes a symbol of darkness and death. You reached a point when this had to end and I appreciate your courage in making this breakup a moment for prayer and reflection."

"I feel there is more love and compassion inside my body now than at any time in the past. This love is not a hidden desire for physical gratification. I left that desire behind. I love everything that I see. I am developing faith in the goodness of other animals. I don't think power should ever be used to satisfy one's selfish needs. The legitimate use of power is to further the interest of the whole community."

"Crocoda, you may still face the challenge of understanding the true nature of spirituality; it's not the same thing as uninformed following of a doctrine."

"That is a good point, and I don't know the difference yet."

"You should do something that is in the interest of all members of your community. Community service is a great purifier. If you feel love within your heart, don't keep it bottled up; you have to release it and mingle it with your creativity. Let your heart express unconditional love."

"What is unconditional love?"

"It is love that is free of all preconditions, so to say. It is love that does not expect anything in return. It is love that radiates warmth, care and healing."

"Do you think I'm capable of giving this kind of love?"

"Yes, if you recognize the power of strong relationships; if you accept the logic that you can get only what you're willing to give. Let your heart be open and strong. There is nothing more that you will ever need to do."

"Thank you Micky once again for your support. I will be going away this morning to practice what I have learned tonight. Give me some new affirmations."

"Since you are at a point where your heart is defining your beliefs, I am giving you three new affirmations, but all three of them are about your heart. They will keep your heart open to new realities and others will gradually start seeing you as a loving and caring creature."

"That's great. Please go ahead. I am ready to practice."

"First affirmation: I am one with my heart and my heart is one with me. Second: My heart is a great healer. And the third: My heart is the container from which love pours forth undiminished."

"These are beautiful affirmations. I will start my practice now."

As Crocoda started rehearsing his affirmations, Micky looked at the sky to find that the moon had disappeared. There were dark clouds, wet and heavy. As a few drops of rain fell on his forehead, Micky went into a meditative mood. He wanted Crocoda to learn the heart meditation that Micky's father had taught him.

"Crocoda, heart is the center of love. Therefore, any meditation centered on heart has to be a meditation about love. Love is the central organizing principle of this creation. The Creator created this universe in an unbounded act of love and compassion. We survive when we are young because of the love and care of our parents. Communities of animals and birds survive because they are able to establish supportive networks. For this meditation, close your eyes and breathe easily and deeply. Focus all your attention on your heart. Listen to the sound that it generates. This is not a sound that is produced by two objects colliding. This is an unstruck sound. This is a sound that transcends any known physical cause. It is a sound that was produced for the first time when this universe was created. It is a sound of birth and celebration of life on this planet. Our hearts started to beat and to produce this sound even before we were born. And they will continue this nonstop rhythmical odyssey until the moment we die. What is that energy, that inner drive that keeps it going? It is the energy of Spirit within us. It is the energy to do good deeds. That is why when we think bad thoughts we drain this energy; we shrink the size of this organ. When we love others genuinely, there is a surge of energy that expands the heart, and the vibrations that we emit create an aura of peace around us. Imagine the impact if all of us are able to do it together. We will change this forest; we will change this world. We may not succeed in ceasing all conflicts and mindless violence, but we will surely create a better world than what we have today. There will be wholeness in place of that disjointed array of elements that are creating all this confusion and chaos. We will redraw our ego-centered boundaries to include others who were excluded. When we think materially we create separation. When we see things move, we feel that they are drifting away from us. When we view ourselves as power beings, we tend to look down upon others. When we think through the heart, we create relationships, unity, oneness and balance. We become healers in place of oppressors. So, Crocoda, while you are deeply in touch with your heart, fill yourself with love and compassion and listen intently to the sound of your heart. Do it as long as you can. You will never be the same beast ever again."

Crocoda didn't say a word. More light rain drops fell and Micky felt sleepy once again. The sunrise was still hours away. Everything seemed to be covered with a blanket of silence, as if peace had suddenly returned to this forest. Behind the forbidding clouds, a light was struggling to dispel the magic of this murky night.

REFLECTION

1. "What is inside is more important than what is outside." Is it true in light of your own experience?
2. If you consider yourself to be person of faith, reflect on the ways your faith has impacted your life. What do you find?
3. Consider arguments for and against accepting someone as a spiritual guru. Does having a spiritual guru reduces one's freedom of choice?
4. "Community service is a great purifier. If you feel love within your heart, don't keep it bottled up; you have to release it and mingle it with your creativity."
5. What is unconditional love? Is unconditional love possible?
6. "When we view ourselves as power beings, we tend to look down upon others. When we think through the heart, we create relationships, unity, oneness and balance. We become healers in place of oppressors."

6 A Visionary Entrepreneur

It was the stormiest summer Micky could recall in years. It rained every day and there were ferocious thunderstorms the likes of which he had not seen before. Several branches of the apple tree were broken and most of the fruit was lost. Micky was afraid that the tree itself might fall to the ground, rendering him homeless. He could not imagine living on a tree deep inside the forest where there was darkness even during the day. There were too many hazards, including the danger of being eaten alive by roaming predators. There was also no reliable food supply like the rose-apple tree.

These were lonely and desolate days and Micky could not wait for this dreadful rainy season to end.

But where was Crocoda? Generally, when Micky remembered Crocoda the latter made an appearance soon thereafter. This time there was no croc in sight except a baby croc that Micky spotted one afternoon. It appeared as if the baby was separated from the rest of the family and was looking for shelter. Although Micky felt compassion for the baby, he had to assert his right to protect his domain.

"Hey, where do you think you are headed? This is private property. All intruders are immediately asked to leave. I mean they are expelled, which means they are thrown back into the river, or whatever."

The baby croc looked up and tried to spot Micky hiding behind one of the branches of the tree that was still intact.

"My salutations esteemed sir. In fact, I was just looking for you." The baby croc spoke in a squeaky voice.

"Looking for me? A baby croc looking for me? Why?"

"If I may say so, sir, I am not exactly a baby. Appearances are sometimes deceptive. I'm not too old either, just the right age to be running my own messenger service."

"Crocodile messenger service...that's quite an idea! Okay, what's the message?"

"There is a message for you, sir, from Miss Tip-tip, special assistant to President Crocoda of Forest Community Enterprises."

"Say it aloud."

"President Crocoda would like you to come to his riverside community business center for a special meeting and, if you don't mind, I can give you a comfortable ride!"

"Oh, no. I am not falling into that trap again. Crocoda tried to cheat on me once and I have learned my lesson. No more sweet invitations. Now please be kind enough to leave my property immediately. I have nothing more to say to you."

"You do not have to be consistently rude to me, sir. Will you please permit me to make an observation?"

"Please do."

"Because you are living in this isolated place, you are not mindful, sir, of the many wonderful changes that have taken place in the social ecology of this forest. A full-fledged market system has emerged where all kinds of goods are being bought and sold. Promises are being honored. When I say you will be safe in my company I truly mean it."

"If what you are telling me is true, I am very pleased to hear this. But at present I am in a very fragile state—physically and psychologically. I cannot think of riding a baby croc to cross this river. It is not only a question of trust, but also of physical energy and stamina needed for a venture of this kind. I would very much like to see my old friend Crocoda but my choice of venue is here rather than over there. The known place is always better than the unknown."

"Very well, sir. President Crocoda has several openings tomorrow. What time would best work for you?"

"It makes no difference. I'm free all the time. Don't forget I'm just a little monkey stuck on this broken tree. I'm not a celebrity. Time and comfort are irrelevant. Why not say the very first thing tomorrow morning?"

"All right, sir. That should work. I should be conveying this message to Miss Tip-tip before it's too late. I would like to apologize for the inconvenience and my unsolicited entry into your private quarters. Bye for now!"

"Please leave me alone!"

Micky spent a restless night. This was the first rainless night in several days. The view of the sky was clear and majestic. He looked at the stars and wondered about what had happened to Crocoda. Not very long ago he was an ugly and ferocious beast with no idea of anything. He was essentially a food body without any thoughts. Now he asks serious questions about life and death. He runs his own business. He has become an entrepreneur. He is taking risks. From where has this awakening come? How can this rising wave of consciousness make so much difference in the life of a beast? These were extremely puzzling questions and Micky spent the whole night reflecting on them.

Crocoda was on time for the meeting next morning. He was a different kind of beast now. His skin was radiant and bright. There was little dirt around on his body. His vision looked sharper and he crawled at a stable and dignified pace.

"How do you do my old friend? I'm really glad to see you again."

"To put it rather mildly, I am very displeased with you, Micky. You still think I'm a scumbag who would not honor his promise. If I planned for you to come to my office there had to be a plan on my part to turn you into my favorite meal of the day. How could I think of anything other than food? I have news for you my friend. I am not the same old beast. I have changed in fundamental ways. And I can't live with those who can't manage personal change. Let me give you one example. I told you how much I loved Crocodina. I really cared for her, but did she really care about me? The answer is: not at all. She always badmouthed me, my family, my mother in particular, blamed me for all her ailments, making me feel guilty as if I were the sole cause of her misery. She was extremely selfish. She thought of her comfort above everything else. As she refused to change and grow, I sought separation from her. I think that was a painful yet necessary decision. I do miss her. You know it is so painful to forget those who were part of our lives for so long. Crocs are as emotional about relationships as everyone else. But we have to move on and live our lives the way we like. One good thing that I can say about myself is that eventually I learned to live by a set of values, values based on trust and integrity, and I'm one heck of a happier animal than the one you used to know."

"I find it extremely gratifying, Crocoda, what you have achieved within such a short time. I am however very curious to know about your latest venture. Are you really running a business? I find it difficult to see you in the role of an entrepreneur. I thought you were on the road to becoming a missionary, going to distant lands and preaching the word of God, converting other animals to your faith. What happened?"

"Well, there was a positive side. My interest in organized faith helped me find clarity on many fundamental issues. What is God? What is reality? What is the purpose of life? I don't claim perfect understandings of these matters as these are very complex questions, but I got some idea. This was very satisfying. On the negative side, I felt that I was limiting my freedom to think liberally on my own and make my own choices. To make matters worse I found Badi Mai was not only interpreting rules, she was making some of her own to suit her convenience. She was also becoming extremely authoritarian. I am still a person of faith in the sense that there is God who is the great provider and protector, but I have reclaimed my life. My thinking is no longer reactive. I absorb all new ideas but examine them for their validity. I am not passively seeking anyone's approval. I don't accept orders or opinions without questioning basic assumptions. I just wanted to change the way crocs live. We can't change how we look physically or perform mentally but we can improve our material conditions. Like every other species we have the right to seek the so-called good life. When everything around us is changing we can't stay unchanged. Remember what happened to dinosaurs, our great and mighty ancestors? They plainly refused to change and adapt to new life conditions. A crocodile's learning ability is limited, but I'm certain we can learn some elementary crafts like building better traps to kill animals that we eat, and learn the techniques to store extra food during times of scarcity. We can learn to beautify our surroundings. The possibilities are endless."

"You talk like a visionary. Where did you learn this new language, these new concepts of efficiency and beauty?"

"I would say some inner urge, some form of rational motivation that came with this spiraling awareness. You know more and you can do more when you are more aware. Ignorance really kills creativity and limits our choices."

"Wow! Crocoda, you have truly become my teacher. What else are you going to teach me?"

"I know I will be a lousy teacher if I try to become one. I'm good in straight talk—just shooting from the hip. What I have found is that personal success may not be attained at the cost of others. You can be better than others and yet it is not good to boast about one's achievements. If you succeed in life there is a very high reward for success. We know winner takes all. Even if you are not a winner but are reasonably successful, you can possess a great deal of positive social recognition."

"So where do we go from here? Or more precisely, where do you go from here, President Crocoda?" Micky was being unconsciously sarcastic. Crocoda, on the other hand, was serious about comprehending the next stop on his transformational journey.

Micky himself answered the question he had asked. "You have reached a new height of self-awareness, Crocoda. I call the present state of awareness the place of clear communication and creativity. You got the voice and you have unleashed your creativity. You could not have accomplished what you have done for your community without voicing your concerns and sharing your ideas. You have become a leader and no leader is born without the power of speech and creative thinking. Now you have something that your followers value because they don't have it. They see you as breaking new ground, showing a new path, and making a difference in their lives with the power of new ideas."

"All this sounds very nice, but what does it actually mean? Micky, I want you to be more specific. I know what I have done, but I can't make any sense of it. How can I conceptualize this change?"

"Crocoda, once you centered your attention on your heart, you found a path that motivated you and excited you. This simple fact triggered several emotional reactions in your body and mind. This unleashed ideas that were shackled in the cage of your egocentric mind. Instead of thinking of self, your own needs and wants, your conflicts with the self, you created a new dynamic in which you were not in the center of things although you were a key player. Everything that you planned was a projection of the loving energy in your heart, of doing well and helping in the creation of a new community."

"This makes more sense to me. I can also now think in terms of images, symbols and metaphors. To me this is abstract thinking, a thinking in which the thought appears in a different garb. Thought is not just a jumble of words; it's a picture in my mind. It's a picture that speaks to me, and when I share this picture with others, it speaks to them too. I feel empowered, but it is a very different kind of power. There is no feeling of domination. I feel one with others; only a bit better in some respects, first among equals or something like that. I have a feeling that my inner boundaries are either diminishing or becoming so porous that I am gaining this unity consciousness: I'm in everything and everything is in me."

"The important thing is that you are not only thinking these new thoughts, you are communicating them with clarity, understanding, and empathy, and that is truly remarkable."

"One other thing that I have discovered is that I have found a sense of purification within me. I feel that someone has flushed out all those ideas, those base desires that were such an essential part of my life. I had lived with that dirt—that unwanted baggage for a long time. And here I am today feeling light, healthy, fragrant like a flower, and free of any disease."

"Crocoda, you have not only purified yourself; you have become the purifier. The subtle vibrations that you feel within yourself are intimations of a higher calling. Your consciousness is rising to a higher ground. It is therefore clearer and more transparent. The vibrations that you are emitting are reaching a longer distance, and they are meeting less resistance. Your affirmations have more impact now. Your words sound right to others. Your ideas generate more interest."

"So what are my new affirmations? What is my new meditation?"

"You don't need any of that stuff. Practice what you already know."

"Don't hold back Micky. I know there is something you have to teach that you are holding back."

"You are in a situation, Crocoda, where every word that you speak sounds to me like an affirmation, where your whole life is becoming a living meditation."

"I understand that...but there is more to it than that. I need help. I can't grow on my own."

"Let me do a guided meditation... Close your eyes and breathe deeply. Imagine that we have a secret place in our body where we are hiding something extremely precious. This treasure has a name. It is called Truth. We do not know what it looks like, but we have felt its power all our lives. When we were in the dark tunnel of doubt, its power showed us the way. When we were beset by anxieties of right and wrong, its brilliance helped us make the right choice. When we were caught in the battle of polarities, its guidance brought us closer to the best option. On the other hand, we have faced problems because we have not discovered Truth. When we desired wisdom we received only information and we couldn't tell the difference. When we wanted experience, we got opinions and we didn't know the difference. How can we become authentic in our thinking and speech when we are still searching for Truth? Let us go deeper within ourselves, beyond our ideas of guilt and shame, beyond the shadows of fear and trepidation and try to find the secret door to this cave. As we get closer to Truth, we also get closer to Spirit because Truth and Spirit are not different."

As this meditation proceeded, Crocoda felt that he was entering zones of his being that he didn't even know existed.

Micky asked him to practice deep listening.

Crocoda listened to his breathing, his heartbeat, the flow of water in the river, a bird song coming from deep within the forest. In that listening there was the power of wordless understanding, a language that only heart knows, a song that is sung only when you are one with Spirit.

Suddenly a thundering sound came from both the ground and the sky.

Crocoda's concentration was broken. "Micky, I think I lost it. I was so close and now it is all gone."

"This means that we are being too ambitious. We are not yet ready to discover Truth. We have to wait and practice more what we have learned so far. We shall get there one day but it is going to take time."

"When are you going to be ready for the river cruise with me?"

"When we meet the next time, perhaps."

"I take your word for it."

"It will be a long and beautiful cruise and I look forward to it."

As Crocoda left, Micky's eyes followed him for a long time. Crocoda was no longer an ugly beast. He was a friend and his physical ugliness didn't matter one bit.

As he slept that night Micky had a wonderful dream of a vast blue ocean. Micky saw himself having beautiful silver-colored wings and he was flying over the water against the backdrop of the red glow of the setting sun. Micky continued to fly until he merged with the red glow of the sun and became the light itself.

Micky reflected for many days on the larger meaning of this dream. The more he thought about it the more he remembered the last teaching that he had received from his father. Although those words were spoken some years ago, and Micky was then too young to fully comprehend the significance of what he was told, they had stayed fresh in his memory. There was a power in those words that time could not erase.

Micky's father had been ailing for some time. His mother had told him that his father was about to die and that he should learn to accept the fact of his father's mortality.

As his father lay on his back breathing with great difficulty, he looked despairingly at Micky and said. "Micky, my dear son, what I am going to say today is so important yet so difficult for you to understand that the very purpose of this conversation seems to be a waste of time. But I will say it nonetheless. Maybe a small part of it will register in your unconscious and you will learn more as you grow up. Listen carefully. Micky, you are not just an animal. Of course, you look like a monkey when you see your reflection in the water. But you have a soul that makes you immortal. Your ability to evolve is not strictly the function of your own potential; it's truly the potential of the soul within you. And what is this soul? It is immortal, it is never born and therefore it never dies. Your soul is not a thing by itself; it is a mirror image of Spirit. This means that you are connected all the time with something much bigger than yourself. There never was a time when you didn't exist, and there will never be a time when you will cease to exist. Of course, you will die a physical death as I am going to die now, but you will be born again as long as the desire to be born is deeply engraved in your heart. On the other hand, you have an opportunity to break free of this cycle of life and death if you erase the barriers of ignorance that separate your soul from Spirit. When you realize yourself, you realize the power of Spirit within. Your soul is transformed by that touch of immense luminosity and then you become one with Spirit. Do not search for Spirit in the outer world. It resides within you, always inviting you for a blissful union. And through this union you will achieve perfect realization. This is the only reality. Nothing else is real...."

Micky's father closed his eyes to regain some energy and spoke once again.

"There are two ways to achieve the goal that I just described. One, you can prepare yourself for union with Spirit through rigorous meditation practice and leading your life according to the highest spiritual values. The second is to demolish all mental structures of consciousness by cleaning up your mind, by going beyond rationality to a place where the differences between right and wrong cease to exist, by sacrificing all distinctions based on logic, which means by realizing Spirit on the ground of emptiness, where nothing exists, where nothing matters anymore. Neither way is superior to the other. I like the first way, but you can follow the last one too. I leave it to you to decide when you grow up. But a life not lived in pursuit of Spirit is a life wasted in pursuing transitory pleasures. What is not permanent is not real."

Slowly the voice sank. With eyes closed Micky's father struggled for a while and then fell silent for good.

REFLECTION

1. "I am not passively seeking anyone's approval. I don't accept orders or opinions without questioning basic assumptions." What's wrong with a person who seeks approval?
2. "You got the voice and you have unleashed your creativity. You could not have accomplished what you have done for your community without voicing your concerns and sharing your ideas. You have become a leader and no leader is born without the power of speech and creative thinking." If creative thinking is a prerequisite for becoming a leader, how do you rate yourself? What are you doing to enhance your creativity?
3. "As we get closer to Truth, we also get closer to Spirit because Truth and Spirit are not different."
4. "Your ability to evolve is not strictly the function of your own potential; it's truly the potential of the soul within you. And what is this soul? It is immortal, it is never born and therefore it never dies. Your soul is not a thing by itself; it is a mirror image of Spirit."
5. In Micky's dream, his father talks about two ways of seeking self-realization. What is the difference between these two ways?

7 Finding An Inner Mountain

The dream and the subsequent remembrance of his father's last words continued to resonate in Micky's consciousness. He wondered about the immense power of Spirit that his father talked about. Where is this Spirit? Whenever he tried to go deep within himself he could see only his own small ego self, but not Spirit, although he had spoken to Crocoda about its existence with great confidence. Where is the hiding place for Spirit? Micky knew that Spirit is not something concrete, something that could be felt like an organ inside his body. It is just a presence, something that watches from a safe distance, an observer, a witness. Maybe it is like the breath, or it is the breath.

Micky felt sad that his father had died when he was so young. If his father had lived longer, Micky would surely have received more guidance to get in touch with Spirit.

For several days Micky meditated on the words: "What is not permanent is not real." If this was true, then it followed that the world in which Micky was living was unreal. How could that be true? This world is real, this river is real, and so is this tree. Could it be that the world exists but it is not real? Could it be that the "real" in this context meant something that is unchanging, that is God, and that is beyond cause and effect? That's not the nature of this world. It changes all the time. There is virtually nothing here that stays the same. Therefore, existence does not guarantee realness of anything. But alternately, if existence is viewed through the eye of Spirit it becomes Essence, the inner core of reality, that which is eternal, that which was never born, that which would never die. The world is real in the same way as a dream looks real in the dream state. With this insight, the difference between what is real and unreal slowly sank into Micky's consciousness.

Micky also saw some metaphoric significance in his dream. What does it mean to merge with the red glow of a setting sun? For Micky this meant the death of his physical body and the start of a new life. What kind of life that would be, he was not sure. Will he be born again, or will this be the end of his biological journey?

Why worry so much about life and death? I have lived a useful life, he told himself, and now it is time to move on. Of course, underneath this thought, there were several worldly concerns. Who would take care of the rose-apple tree? And what would happen to the private beach? Will another animal come and make this apple tree his home? Will that animal take care of the tree in the same way as I have done? These worldly attachments were pulling Micky away from his spiritual goal—to become fully detached, to give up thoughts of this life, to remain centered on the discriminative awareness that was slowly taking root. The inner conflict was rising like a tide—advancing then receding, but leaving behind seeds of concern, of apathy, of meaninglessness. What did I achieve, any way, in this life that was given to me as a gift by my parents? I have worried about hunger. I have lived with the fear of losing this shelter. I have spent sleepless nights worrying about my physical security. What has all this added up to?

The long summer ended slowly, limping at its core, resisting its inevitable demise. The weather had stabilized. There were still infrequent showers, but the worst of the rainy season was over. Fall arrived, unnoticed, silently slipping through crevices. Trees were changing their colors, feasting the eyes of the beholder with a splash of subdued crimson, shiny gold, and bristling blue.

Micky waited for Crocoda to show up before it was too late. As his longing for a new manifestation, a new context, and a new challenge grew in intensity, he told himself, I will move on if he comes; I will move on even if he doesn't come. I can't wait for him too long.

Crocoda finally arrived one afternoon, a bright sunny day, a little warmer than usual but the warmth of the sunlight was making the body drowsy, limiting the span of attention. A new species of birds that were on their migratory route had settled on the nearby trees for rest and relaxation, but they kept up an earsplitting screech. Crocoda was in a somber mood. He had lost some weight. Without saying a word he looked at the apple tree trying to locate Micky. The little monkey was sitting there on his favorite branch waving and saying hello, but somehow this didn't register with Crocoda. He continued to look at the tree and the emptiness beyond.

Micky had to break the ice. "Crocoda, I knew you would come before the weather became milder. Remember, this is the time when we can go on our river cruise; if the water gets too cold, it would not be a good cruise for me."

"I am so happy to be here, my friend. But I'm not going to speak with you if you stay up on this tree and I stay on this sandy ground. If you want to have a conversation, a real dialogue, please come down, come close to me, look into my eyes and say that you trust me. Only then can we have a communion. Otherwise, it is very artificial. We are just protecting our respective boundaries."

Micky thought for a minute. It was now or never. If I don't reach out this very minute it is the end of the story. But on the other hand, if I do go down I might be dead meat in a second. He heard a voice from within: So what if you die. You would have died for a cause—the cause of trust and friendship. The world doesn't keep a record of such sacrifices, but isn't your own conscience the best record keeper? Do what you think is right.

Micky hung on to a branch and carefully lowered himself to a safe distance from where he could easily jump to the ground. He stood there facing a huge monster, eye to eye, feeling the hot breath of a massive body of flesh, at a safe distance from Crocoda's long snout and sharp teeth, which were just one gulp away; just one movement would have eliminated him from the face of the earth. He felt good. He had never looked into Crocoda's eyes before. These were sad eyes. These were the eyes of someone who had lived a lonely life. There was no animal fury and raw passion there. These were eyes that were searching for something real and not finding it. These were eyes that had grown old looking at the deeper meaning of things.

"I am here Crocoda, right in front of your eyes. You can't tell me now that I don't trust you. At this time, you are like any other harmless creature. You can't harm me because within the tough exterior you have the heart of a honeybee. There may be some poison within, but outside it is pure sweetness."

"I don't carry any poison anymore. There is no bitterness inside me either. I have learned to love everything. I love you, I love your tree, and I love this river. A person who loves can never hurt."

"How is your business doing?"

"I am no longer running the business. I gave it up. There is a new generation of crocs who can do the same thing and they can do it better than me perhaps. I have moved on to accomplishing a higher purpose."

"What is that higher purpose?"

"I don't have a name for it. I am not a shaman, and I can't identify changes in the state of my mind. I am a simple croc in search of truth and meaning. But I know one thing; I'm not the same animal whom you saw a few months ago."

"What has changed?"

"I may have to say this several times before I get it absolutely right. But let me try. I am more of an inner being than at any other time in my life. What it means is that I'm very deeply connected with my innermost self. I feel I'm part of a larger community. My community is not only the crocs, but also every other animal and bird in this forest. My community includes bushes, trees and all kinds of vegetation. I exclude nothing. I feel that all of us, whether we crawl on the ground, live on the trees, or fly in the air have equal access to the resources that Nature has provided for us. By sharing what we have we grow bigger and stronger. By dividing and excluding we become weaker and poorer. Greed is no good; greed is a disease of the soul. We need to make all decisions by taking everyone into confidence, through consensus, by listening to different viewpoints and honoring them. We need to incorporate spiritual values into our daily life. We need to change in order for this world to survive."

"Crocoda, I fully share and appreciate the sentiments that you have just expressed. But what made you think differently? What triggered this change?" Crocoda hesitated for few moments as if he were searching for the right words.

"A short answer may not be the best one in this case, and I can't articulate it very well. Sometimes abstract ideas slip through my mind. They fall into cracks and my mind goes blank, but let me try. I would say that material success has its own pitfalls. Every time you succeed, your loneliness increases. Material prosperity for some does not guarantee prosperity for all of us. The limitless possibilities I was so obsessed with have a tendency to become mirages, illusions that you try to grab but miss every time. As a result, I was less free and less satisfied. On the other hand, when I simply nourished sound relationships they provided me with greater satisfaction. They led to greater interpersonal harmony and acceptance. I have learned that there is great enrichment—personal as well as social—when the community accepts your work and honors you for what you have achieved."

"What happened to your commitment to entrepreneurship, the urge to make a success of the business model you were pursuing?"

"You know, business models only take you so far. I call it the golden point. Beyond it, reason or logarithms don't explain anything. It's as if one moment you have all the answers and the next one you have none. It's a total blackout. That is quite frustrating. And it's scary."

"What would explain the unexplainable?"

"I don't know, frankly. But I know two brains are better than one. When you are part of a community or a network, when there is diversity, when you can hear many voices at the same time, then you are closer to the truth than otherwise."

"But isn't there a risk that groups or the communities would kill individual initiative? Community can become authoritarian and suppress all forms of dissent. Groups within communities are pretty good at creating oppressive hierarchies."

"I agree there is a real risk of community becoming more powerful and the individual animal reduced to just a number or a label. That is why I suggest that communities have to pay attention to how they organize themselves, and how they manage their decision-making and communication processes."

"What about equality of the sexes?"

"I'm all for it. I treated Crocodina fairly when I separated from her. All animals need to follow my example."

"What about right and wrong? Who is the judge?"

"I'm not going to be the judge, nor do I want any other authority figure to take that role. Every individual animal should decide what's right or wrong consistent with their moral intuition."

"Should there be any authority at all?"

"No, I think authorities and hierarchies are oppressive. They have no role in the new ecological society that I want to help shape. Don't forget that we are highly interdependent as a community—elephants, tigers, monkeys, crocs, birds, everybody. It's just one big family. When one part of the community is hurt every one is hurt."

"Crocoda, as an animal are you more compassionate than before?

"Yes, I am."

"How can you kill for food if you are more compassionate now? When you kill you take some life for your personal satisfaction, correct?"

"I know that's a trick question. Yes, I'm more compassionate now because I kill only to satisfy my hunger, not for sport. I do it with respect and integrity accepting the act of killing as a law of Nature. But remember, both of us are food bodies. If I kill someone for food I give the same right to another animal to do the same to me. I'm ready to be eaten any day. I know I will make a horrible tasting dinner, but if someone has really bad gastronomic sensibilities, I can't quarrel with that, and I would wish that being to enjoy every bit of me."

"Will that feeling of compassion resolve every problem we can think of?"

"Love can surmount any problem."

"Are you afraid of dying?"

"I'm not afraid of any of the unknowns. Death is a big unknown."

"Do you have ego?"

"I think I killed it but I could be wrong. Still sometimes I sound very judgmental—I'm right and you're wrong kind of thing. But by and large I speak from the heart and that has made a big positive difference."

"Who controls you now?"

"I think all my buttons are inside except that I still believe in higher reality, which you call Spirit."

"Crocoda, do you realize how far you have advanced in your thinking since our first encounter under this very rose-apple tree?"

"Before we go there, I want to say another thing. I have developed a very strong intuition. Sometimes I feel that I have a third eye and I see through it. I am seeing a lot. I can see even in the dark. I also see lots of colors. The world was black and white before and now I see it in color. What magnificent views I have missed in my life!"

"You are the light element seeing through the third eye. It is really the last level before you are fully enlightened."

"What does it mean?"

"It means that you have attained an intelligence that is not only residing in your body, it extends in all directions. Your intuition is connecting you with the unknown—something you can't see, something that exists in a different domain. You have gained the ability to self-reflect. You are seeing patterns in place of a jumble of facts and symbols. You are seeing archetypes—original forms from which we draw meaning."

"I also dream a lot, and my dreams are more vivid than ever before. And I know when I'm dreaming and what I'm dreaming. I also get dreamless sleep and I know when it happens. And I know nothing happens in dreamless sleep. I am having this ever-present consciousness that really bothers me. Sometime I feel I'm losing my mind; I'm going crazy."

"We seek this craziness with passion, don't we?"

"Micky, you were saying something when I interrupted you...."

"Yes, I was just wondering how far you have traveled within a short time. Well, all of us go through different levels of consciousness, but I have seen you grow and change before my very eyes. You have moved through different levels within a matter of months."

"I don't know what you are talking about. What are these levels? Where do I stand now?"

"You were at the ground level of consciousness when I first met you. Your thinking was limited to food, water, warmth, sex, etc. Nothing else mattered even a bit... Please remember that there is no value judgment when I describe you in this manner. I'm describing you and your behavior as I saw you. You lived for yourself though you showed some concern for Crocodina and her failing health."

"Sounds familiar. That's the level of consciousness in which most crocs live. Give them food and they ask for nothing else. Such blessed ignorance!"

"When the second level of consciousness opened up you started to search for your roots, your lineage, and your father's spirit. You were seeking the blessings of your elders. You put some faith in magic as if your father's bones would speak to you. You were very emotional in certain ways."

"That was a big turning point. No croc had ever cared about his ancestry. When I stood next to my father's bones I was transformed in a deep way. I realized that I was part of a chain of creatures that are born; they live and die. I felt that I was fully connected at that moment with what came before me. I got this faint idea that I was going somewhere."

"When the third level unfolded, you discovered your ego, the sense of power, the confidence to shape things according to your own will."

"I remember that phase. It was good as long it lasted. We kicked a lot of butt. Crocangers—my dear friends, we were great company and we were so happy together."

"Then we came to the fourth level, which works like a midway house, where currents from upstream and downstream intermingle. You almost turned yourself into a monk. You discovered—or at least attempted to discover—a lot of love and compassion within yourself. It found expression within the confines of a creed which is normal for those at that level. You acknowledged the existence of a higher power and tried to clarify your connection with the Unknown. You thought you had been born with a mission. You acquired a sense of direction. You had a living spiritual mentor and a creed that promised salvation."

"That was a great achievement and my relationship with Badi Mai—God bless her soul—was a breakthrough. I was truly transformed. I may have been overzealous but it was good for my soul. There was realization perhaps for the first time that I was something more than my body. I still don't get it fully. How could there be something more important than the body? But there I was fully committed to the rightness of my cause."

"As the fifth level dawned I saw you as a creative entrepreneur and a social activist. This is when you created a community business. You committed yourself to a rational way of thinking. You were highly motivated to make a difference by using specific methods and techniques."

"Yes, that was good work. I trained a new generation of crocs to think differently, to make use of their creative abilities, to achieve excellence in ordinary things."

"And now I see you, sitting here in front of me having reached the boundary of the next level of consciousness. You care deeply for others, you have committed yourself to strengthening the bonds between species, you have become highly sensitive, participative, relational, empathetic, and I just can't find the words to describe you."

"Wow! You think that I have really become that?"

"Yes and one more thing that you don't realize: You stand at a high peak from where you can see the whole climb, everything below you, the mountain and the valleys beyond. When you look down at the entire climb, you like some things more than others. My advice to you would be that you resist this temptation. There is some good at every level. No single structure of consciousness was wholly good or bad. Even at the ground level you were engaged in a useful activity. Satisfying basic needs is important. Because the good that's once gained can never be lost, you have within you the ability to use all these insights as the occasion demands."

"Micky, you said I'm standing at a high peak. Is this the highest peak?"

"The next level represents the highest peak, the real summit. I am planning to go there, or at least that's my aspiration, but I'm afraid you are not as yet fully prepared for this climb."

"Micky, don't even think of going there without me. You can't do that. I will go with you ... You can't leave me behind. We are in this together, aren't we?"

"Crocoda, we are talking about a climb that can take no time—a second—or it can take several lifetimes. My parents taught me how to meditate, to reflect deeply on matters of life and death. I have done that for years. Now I am starting to get a picture of a summit covered in mist. I am starting to see a path. The climb for me is still steep; I don't know whether I will ever make it."

"Sometimes I don't understand a word you say. Where is the mountain that you are talking about? I am sure it is somewhere downstream. If you come with me we can find it."

"No Crocoda, the mountain that I am talking about is within us. The height that we have to climb is within us. It is nowhere outside; it's all within."

"You have lost me again. I had no idea that there were mountains inside our bodies."

"Well, I was not talking about a real mountain. I was talking about inner realization of Spirit. It is as difficult as climbing the steepest mountain that nature ever shaped into existence."

"Well, let's go and discover this inner mountain. I mean our long-awaited river cruise ... we can have fun and you can tell me more about our inner geography."

"Crocoda, we can go for the cruise but we can't talk about things that are untalkable. I was hinting about awareness beyond all awareness. We shall never get there. Our current awareness, in fact, is our final destination. For our animal existence this is the summit of our psychological and spiritual development. We should not even think of what lies beyond this awareness."

"But I really want to know what comes after this. Let us just talk about it. You say it is untalkable. Nothing is untalkable in this world. We may not have the right vocabulary but we can still talk about it without showing any desire within our hearts to actually go there. So why don't you hop on my back and we go downstream enjoying the beauty of nature while we are having a conversation about this untalkable awareness: an awareness that has no name, no number, where no animal has ever gone. There could be no stupidity in our well-intentioned idealism!"

With some hesitation, but without saying a word, Micky jumped on Crocoda's back and off they went in the direction that the water flowed.

REFLECTION

1. "What is not permanent is not real."
2. What does it mean to merge with the red glow of a setting sun?
3. "If you want to have a conversation, a real dialogue, please come down, come close to me, look into my eyes and say that you trust me." What else do you think is required for building trust?
4. "Material prosperity for some does not guarantee prosperity for all of us. The limitless possibilities I was so obsessed with have a tendency to become mirages, illusions that you try to grab but miss every time." Under what conditions can we create material prosperity that is good for all?
5. "Community can become authoritarian and suppress all forms of dissent. Groups within communities are pretty good at creating oppressive hierarchies." What is the best defense against a community becoming oppressive?
6. "You stand at a high peak from where you can see the whole climb, everything below you, the mountain and the valleys beyond. When you look down at the entire climb, you like some things more than others. My advice to you would be that you resist this temptation. There is some good at every level. No single structure of consciousness was wholly good or bad. Even at the ground level you were engaged in a useful activity. Satisfying basic needs is important. Because the good that's once gained can never be lost, you have within you the ability to use all these insights as the occasion demands."

8 A Cruise To Remember

Crocoda was floating very carefully. The flow of water was unusually even. As they moved away from the rose-apple tree, the ecology of the forest started to change. There were trees and bushes that Micky had not seen before. There were birds and animals that looked unfamiliar. As a comfortable ride on a clear sunny day, with light easterly wind blowing, the experience exceeded Micky's expectation.

"Are you comfortable, Micky?"

"I'm just fine. What about yourself?"

"I am feeling great too. I never thought it would happen. I mean this ride...once the trust is lost it is very hard to regain."

"You're right. Trust lost once is very hard to regain."

"I have a question for you, Micky."

"Shoot."

"Are you also at the same level of self-awareness where I am? I hate to imagine that both of us could be at the same level. It won't hurt my self-esteem if that were not to be the case."

"It is very hard to say. I hate to boast about myself. I see a challenge in front of us and I think we can meet this challenge working together."

"How is the seventh level of consciousness different from the sixth?"

"Different in many fundamental ways I must say. When you are at the sixth you look at life from your own perspective and reject a number of things that are not in accord with your worldview. Anyone at the seventh accepts life in all its hues and colors. You identify with everything because everything is Spirit. Everything has a purpose and usefulness. Everything is interconnected with everything else. Life is a flow; it is like a river in which many things flow. You may not like some things, you may like some things more, but you accept everything. The world is made up of wholes and parts; everything is both a whole and a part. You see common threads in multiplicities of aspirations. You don't generally make judgments of what is right or wrong. Everything in this world is partially true. So we need quite a bit of flexibility and adaptability to lead a life of fulfilment and contentment. In order to solve the problems that we face as a community of animals we need different competencies—basically skills that we draw from those who are at lower rungs of the ladder. For example, I would not be enjoying this wonderful swim without your ability to float in water. You gave me something that I could not do on my own."

"Your compliment is respectfully acknowledged my friend! Micky, you have everything that any animal could aspire to. So why are you looking for another peak?"

"The point is not to have something more; it is about giving up what I have. I want to rise above everything that changes moment to moment; I am seeking Oneness with Spirit."

"I think you lost me, Micky. You can share what you have but you don't give it up. That's not a good idea."

"There are some things that don't make logical sense."

"I'm a very practical animal. I don't want to give up what I have earned with great effort. It is time that you accept me as your teacher."

"I have already learned a lot from you, Crocoda, for which I'm truly grateful."

"Micky, you are trying to be kind and generous. Your father gave you access to some kind of sacred knowledge. I had no meaningful contact with my father. Therefore, you know more than I do and logically you remain my teacher."

"It's true my parents were wise and they were very generous in giving me the gift of true knowledge. They taught me one great lesson, which was greater than just whispering a secret into my ears. They taught me to rely on my own direct experience. I have sat on the branches of the rose-apple tree for years and I have reflected on many questions of life and death, right and wrong, our relationship with Spirit—and that has made me a better animal."

"You talk about Spirit. Where can we find her?"

"Spirit is within us and Spirit is everywhere."

"You mean Spirit lives inside my body. That's pretty scary."

"It is true, Crocoda. Spirit lives within us, but the term 'within us' does not simply mean our body. We also have a soul."

"I can't imagine that Spirit, which also means God, lives inside my dirty body or inside my soul if I really have one!"

"Spirit not only lives within us; we are nothing but Spirit and we don't know it. This is the most difficult and subtlest part of our self-awareness."

"I don't comprehend these abstract ideas very well. Give me an example so that I can follow what you are trying to tell me."

"Let me use a simple technique called subject-object discrimination."

"What discrimination?"

"Subject-object discrimination. The large oak tree over there is the object of your experience because you can see it. You are the one who is seeing it; therefore you are the experiencer. Are you that tree? Obviously not. Similarly, when you are happy or when you are sad you are not those feelings. You are the experiencer of those feelings. Those feelings come and go, but you continue to exist independent of those feelings."

"Not true; sad feelings hurt me and I get very depressed."

"This occurs because you identify yourself with your feelings and your body. Your body is a medium of your experience. It is not the experiencer. It is an object and not a subject. Your body changes, it falls sick, and it dies. Since essentially you are a soul you will never change and never die. If you can become an observer or a witness of your own self, you will discover that your essence is the same as that of Spirit, which is no different from God. God is not a big fat monkey or a giant crocodile. God is awareness; God is Consciousness. God is Supreme Reality that lives in everything. Crocoda, you are that awareness that is God."

"If it is so simple, why don't we understand God?"

"Because we identify ourselves with our bodies. We care only about our mind, our thoughts, and the illusions that it gives rise to. We can't detach ourselves from the things we love. On the other hand, if we get to know ourselves as Spirit—that's who we really are—all the pain, all the fears will disappear in a split second. Your body will die one day, but you will continue to live. Maybe you will get a new body, a different kind of body; it doesn't matter because that body will also die one day. The good news is that you will live forever. Your essence exists outside the boundaries of time and space. This is the secret my father shared with me while he breathed his last. And I have kept this secret with me all these years and now I am sharing it with you."

"Micky, I knew that you were holding on to something big. Thanks for giving me this piece of wisdom, but I don't feel any divine presence inside me. And keeping track of what is an object and what is a subject is giving me a real headache. I don't think I can ever remember it."

"Crocoda, you simply have to remember the principle. Just one more time.... Something that is not Spirit has a beginning and an end. Bodies are born, bodies die. Body is therefore different from Spirit. Something that is not Spirit exists within time and space. You were a child once but you are not a child anymore. Something that is not Spirit has qualities and characteristics. Someone's body is beautiful or ugly; day is bright or gloomy, and so forth. Something that is not Spirit exists in past, present and future. Something that is not Spirit appears differently in three body states: waking, dreaming, and dreamless sleep. Spirit, on the other hand, is always present; Spirit is spaceless; Spirit is not located in one place, it's everywhere; Spirit is the witness of everything. Did this help?"

"I think so. My headache went down a bit, but I have one more question...."

"Go on...."

"Is Spirit same as mind?"

"Oh, not at all. Our mind is at the root of most of our problems. Our mind can think only of what it knows. Our thoughts make up our mind. It is the source of many illusions and delusions. Awareness that we seek is beyond mind. It is in the moment. It has no memory. It has no record. It is like opening ourselves to what is rising moment to moment."

"But animals that are at lower levels of being also believe in God or something close to God. How do you explain it?"

"It is a belief rooted in fear. It has no spiritual grounding. The guiding principle is: Be afraid of something that you don't understand."

"I was not afraid but I was ignorant and ignorance is worse than fear because it stops you from moving forward."

"You are right Crocoda; mind obscures our vision. It stops us from seeing beyond the physical reality of things."

"What happened to my mind?"

"It is still there, but it is in a subordinate relationship to higher levels of awareness that you have discovered and nurtured over time."

"That means I have more than one mind?"

"No, you have only one mind, but your awareness has changed over time to keep pace with your spiritual evolution. When you became obsessed with power, the physical mind gave up its sovereignty and became a subject of ego-mind. The ego-mind itself was subdued by the spiritual mind that believed in only one truth and because of its fanatical rigidity it almost closed all options for your future growth. But you escaped that calamity by opening yourself up to reason, creativity and imagination. The rational mind helped you do good work for your community. But reason has its limitations too. Your spiraling consciousness freed you from the magical spell of the rational mind, and I think you are at a level where your mind could be described as ecological or egalitarian. Your mind was changing at the same time you were reaching higher levels of awareness, but anything that changes or evolves is not Spirit. This much is clear."

Crocoda felt that his mind—ecological or whatever—was exhausted as if it had run out of its electric charge. The sheer power of abstract knowledge that he was exposed to within a short time made his mind shut down. He was physically tired too and needed some rest.

"Micky, I think I need some rest. It is getting dark too. I'm hungry and my physical mind is calling me to get my attention. Why don't we find a place near that opening on our left? I can smell some fruit trees for you behind those bushes. Maybe I can find something to eat too."

"That makes perfect sense to me." Micky responded with a big yawn.

REFLECTION

1. "...once the trust is lost it is very hard to regain." How do you regain the trust that is lost?
2. What distinguishes consciousness at the highest level from that at the lower levels?
3. "Something that is not Spirit has a beginning and an end. Bodies are born, bodies die. Body is therefore different from Spirit. Something that is not Spirit exists within time and space. You were a child once but you are not a child anymore. Something that is not Spirit has qualities and characteristics. Someone's body is beautiful or ugly; day is bright or gloomy, and so forth. Something that is not Spirit exists in past, present and future. Something that is not Spirit appears differently in three body states: waking, dreaming, and dreamless sleep. Spirit, on the other hand, is always present; Spirit is spaceless; Spirit is not located in one place, it's everywhere; Spirit is the witness of everything."
4. What is subject-object discrimination? Find some examples from your daily life to illustrate the concept.
5. "...mind obscures our vision. It stops us from seeing beyond the physical reality of things."

9 Mutilating Skepticism

Crocoda's guess was correct. There was a big cluster of wild berries very close to the river. When Micky looked at the sheer abundance of ripe berries, he felt his hunger had taken hold of his senses. He couldn't think of anything else. His mind went blank. Crocoda found the remains of a previous kill. Once their stomachs were full, Micky gathered some dried underbrush and started a fire. Fire-making in the wild was another thing that Micky's father had taught him. They lounged around the fire and resumed their conversation. They had not gone very far when they heard a voice coming from one of the trees.

"I see something very strange here. A crocodile and a monkey having a good time! Never seen something like this before and I'm not sure whether what I'm seeing is real or I am just dreaming."

"Will you please identify yourself? We can explain a thing or two that might be bothering you." Micky said these words while his eyes unsuccessfully surveyed the darkness for the source of this voice.

"I'm a parrot. My name is Tota-rama and I'm sitting on one of the branches where I can see both of you but you can't see me."

"That's not fair. Don't we have a right to privacy? Why can't you come down and join us? What is holding you up there?" Crocoda was visibly annoyed with this unsolicited intervention.

Micky decided to interject because he thought that Crocoda was rather quick and harsh in his reaction. "I would like to apologize on behalf of my friend, Crocoda, who is apparently tired, but I can assure you that he is an extremely gracious and warm hearted animal unlike the general impression about the likes of his species. He didn't mean to say that your intervention was less than welcome. We would very much want to learn from you because parrots are known for their wisdom.... Sorry, I didn't introduce myself. My name is Micky. We are so glad to hear a friendly voice in this part of the forest where we hardly know anyone. Please come and join us."

"I appreciate your kindness but sorry I have to decline your invitation. It's not that I'm afraid of Crocoda. I just won't be very comfortable. I'm a tiny talking bird.... I feel very lonely. There was a time not very long ago when there were hundreds of parrots in this part of the forest. Then we were struck by some disease. Dozens died and the rest decided to migrate. I decided not to leave. So here I am watching animals come and go, but I have never seen what I am seeing now—a friendship that cuts across boundaries of two very different species. So if you don't mind may I continue to sit here and listen to your conversation?"

"It suits us perfectly. Make yourself a part of our extended circle of friends and please join the conversation."

"What are you two up to? Where are you coming from and where are you going? Please don't answer if you think it is impolite for me to ask this question."

"No, no, this is a perfectly legitimate question. The two of us are on a journey of self-discovery. We are looking for answers to life's most perplexing questions."

"That's quite interesting...what have you found so far?"

Micky looked at Crocoda expecting him to answer. "Hey, don't look at me. I have no clue what we are looking for and why we're here. Micky, you are the teacher and you'd better answer this question." Crocoda was in no mood to talk.

"We haven't found anything miraculous yet, but we are on our way and we hope to find something worthwhile as we move along."

"That's quite an evasive answer. I presume you're uncomfortable answering my question which is fine with me."

"Oh, no Tota-rama, please do not take it wrongly. I have some personal beliefs that I acquired from my father. He told me that I have to find Spirit that resides within me. I like to use the word Spirit, others prefer to say God. They are one and the same. We have this source of eternal bliss within us, and we can't find it without making an effort. This world exists, my father told me, but it is unreal. Only Spirit is real. Our self-realization frees us forever from this world of suffering. Crocoda is not fully convinced of this argument, but he is willing to give me the benefit of the doubt."

"This is very interesting; however, what you say about the world and God is so different from what I have learned from my teacher—may God bless his soul! My master was an enlightened yogi. He meditated under a tree and by the time he attained enlightenment his body had dried up; it had become like the lifeless branches of the tree under which he meditated."

"Would you like to elaborate please? We need to know if our beliefs are false by any measure."

"No belief is absolutely true or false. There are different ways to reach the same destination. All paths converge at some point, I believe."

"I hope they do! I am very curious to know what you learned from your teacher, if you don't mind."

"Well, my teacher taught me that God is real and this world which is a creation of this Being is also real. We should not sacrifice one for the other. We are a divine creation, but we are not divine by any means. Our soul is perhaps the only thing that is somewhat closer to God. But our soul is not Spirit as you describe it. We have to lead the life we are given. We cannot close our eyes and treat this world as unreal. It does not mean that you cannot aspire to reach Spirit. You can do it through prayer and meditation and detachment, but eventually God will decide whether or not you get liberation. Even as a liberated soul you will stay close to God but you can never become an integral part of the Divine. No way. I'm so sorry if I disappointed the two of you, but I can't tell a lie. My teacher prohibited me from telling a lie."

Micky looked into the darkness and saw his world come crashing down. How could this be true? My father was quite certain about what he told me. My mother confirmed those thoughts in no uncertain terms. What Tota-rama is saying could not be true. He is just tricking us. Maybe he is an angel sent here by God to test our faith. Micky tried to suppress his feelings and asked Crocoda, "What do you think, Crocoda?"

"I think I am totally confused. Micky you were saying one thing and now Tota-rama is saying another. I can't reconcile these two viewpoints. My mind does not work at night. I am going to doze off and would let the two of you sort this mess out. Good night my parrot friend and Micky of course." It was not long before Crocoda went into deep slumber and started snoring.

Tota-rama took a dive and landed several feet from where Crocoda and Micky were seated. He slowly but majestically walked to a spot facing Micky. He looked at Micky with eyes that were still struggling to resolve this monkey's strange partnership with a crocodile.

Even in the darkness broken sporadically by a flickering flame Micky was able to see the parrot's beautiful red and green feathers.

"Tota-rama, I think you were quite clear in terms of your exposition, but maybe my own understanding of these matters is not very good. So may I request you to repeat what you already told us, but this time with greater clarity and more depth?"

"I think I was too quick in saying what I said. Let me go through this time at a much slower pace.... God of course is ultimate reality. There is no power higher than God. He is self-existent and as such does not depend on any one or anything else. On the contrary, everything that exists in this world is divine creation and consequently depends on God for sustenance. In a relationship of dependence of one on the other, the one who is independent is logically at a higher level than the one who is dependent. They are not co-equal by any means. So logically the higher being cannot live inside a lower being. Doesn't it make intuitive sense to you?"

Tota-rama paused and waited for Micky to gesture his agreement, but Micky said nothing.

"Even when the world is in a state of dissolution, God exists separately from disembodied souls. An animal or a bird is made up of two components: first, there is a soul that lives in freedom or bondage depending on its actions. God relates to us through our souls. The second component is our body which is pure matter. God has a rather distant relationship with matter. Souls are endowed with free will and therefore they get liberated only through divine grace. Two things need to happen before grace can be had: passion for detachment, meaning getting oneself detached from the worldly pleasures obtained through our senses, and a loving relationship with God, unending, at all times, pure, and everlasting."

Tota-rama stopped to regain his breath. Micky was silent but attentive. He had not missed a word or syllable.

"This is my belief based on what my teacher told me. I would never spend anytime searching for Spirit or God within myself. This would be a futile search. You can't find someone inside who is not there in the first place. I have looked for God outside, in the pristine water that flows in this river, in the flowers that bloom, in the clouds that pass overhead, in the rain that keeps everything green and healthy, and I have found that God has endless shapes but in every shape He is beautiful. My life is dedicated to seeing God in everything. That is my detachment and that is my devotion."

Tota-rama fluttered his feathers, rose up and was lost into the surrounding darkness without saying a proper good-bye. Micky felt completely drained. He could not think or move. He fell to the ground as he had never done before. With his head resting on sand he looked at the stars. If God is not within me, He is definitely somewhere out there, behind these shiny stars, where darkness meets light. Micky felt blinded by the very thought of ever encountering this transcendental light. He didn't know when he fell asleep.

REFLECTION

1. "No belief is absolutely true or false. There are different ways to reach the same destination. All paths converge at some point."
2. "Well, my teacher taught me that God is real and this world which is a creation of this Being is also real. We should not sacrifice one for the other. We are a divine creation, but we are not divine by any means. Our soul is perhaps the only thing that is somewhat closer to God. But our soul is not Spirit as you describe it. We have to lead the life we are given. We cannot close our eyes and treat this world as unreal. It does not mean that you cannot aspire to reach Spirit. You can do it through prayer and meditation and detachment, but eventually God will decide whether or not you get liberation. Even as a liberated soul you will stay close to God but you can never become an integral part of the Divine. No way. I'm so sorry if I disappointed the two of you, but I can't tell a lie. My teacher prohibited me from telling a lie." How is this viewpoint described by Tota-rama different from Micky's?

10 Getting Nowhere

Next morning they rose from sleep before sunrise. Micky didn't want to miss his sumptuous breakfast; therefore, he moved between the trees picking the best fruit. Crocoda didn't want to eat anything. They had a little argument as to whether they should go downstream or return to their old dwellings. Crocoda wanted to get back.

"This is not the same river any more. There is different kind of vegetation. Different kind of fish. The river is much broader and shallower. I don't know where we are headed. Do you know anything about it?" Crocoda looked worried.

"I think we are headed in the direction of an ocean where this river will merge into a very large body of water."

"What's an ocean?"

"Consider it to be a very large pond, very deep and very broad."

"I can't swim in deep water."

"Imagine you don't have to do anything. Let the one who has brought us here take care of us!"

What Micky said was less meant for Crocoda than a reassuring statement for his own self. They were indeed headed towards the ocean. The movement of birds, the smells, the sounds, everything pointed to one conclusion: the ocean was near.

There were many things crowding Micky's mind. He was still uneasy about his conversation with Tota-rama. If there was any truth in Tota-rama's views, it meant that Micky had wasted his life chasing a shadow. But at this point in his life how could he let disillusionment overtake him? Many thoughts came to his mind that revealed contradictions in Tota-rama's arguments.

If there is nothing real except God, meaning everything is His creation, how could God not be there in every tiny particle, in every living creature? What's creation without the Creator?

If God made this universe with materials that he borrowed from someone else, then that "being" would naturally be at a higher level than God which is impossible. There is no other being higher than God.

How could any creation stand apart from its creator? How could creation not be imbued with Creator's Spirit? This world has to be a manifestation of God, a manifestation of His nature. Otherwise, it is worth nothing.

Maybe there is more than one God. There is a higher God who is beyond everything and can't be described in words. He is truly untalkable. The lower God, on the other hand, creates and sustains this world. Both Gods are one but we can't notice any difference. Maybe Tota-rama was talking about the higher God while I was thinking of the lower God. Maybe both of us are right. Maybe both of us are wrong.

This confusion was killing Micky and he wanted to get away from these disturbing thoughts.

To change his mental state he started to think about his own dream. Was he really growing silver wings? Was he eventually going to fly deep into the ocean?

Micky noticed that Crocoda was somewhat disoriented. Maybe he was upset about being forced to travel downstream against his wishes.

"Do you have any questions for me Crocoda?" Micky tried to get his attention.

"No questions, not at all."

"Why don't you ask me questions like what is happiness and where can we find it?"

"Why should I do that? What is the value of your answer to a question that I don't understand?"

"Don't you care about happiness? Don't you think happiness is important?"

"I do."

"Then ask me the question."

"All right, what is happiness and where can we find it?"

"Okay, here's my answer and please listen very carefully. Not knowing what happiness is, we always try to find it in wrong places. We try to find happiness in things. But we know that no 'thing' is permanent. Things give us happiness one time but not another time. The first apple is so tasty but not the tenth or the twentieth one. We also try to find happiness in attachments. Remember one time you found happiness in being with Crocodina, in her company, but then things soured between the two of you and she started to make you unhappy. Eventually, you reclaimed your happiness by separating from her. There is no enduring happiness either in things or in attachments. The real happiness is in being one with Spirit. When you submerge yourself in Spirit and you are not identified with any of the objects of perception, you will be in a state of permanent bliss. You will always be free. No sorrow will reach you. No worldly excitement will touch you. Things will change around you, but you will be unchanged...."

Micky uttered these well-rehearsed words as a cleansing act; he wanted to clear his head of all thoughts that Tota-rama had put there. Crocoda listened intently and kept quiet.

"Crocoda, you are not talking any more. Are you okay? Are you angry with me?"

"You know I have been thinking about what you told me yesterday. If Spirit is real and everything else is unreal, why have I spent all my life pursuing the unreal? Was I blind? Was I stupid?"

Micky was glad that Crocoda asked this question. What it meant was that Crocoda remembered the conversation that the two of them had had earlier yesterday, but he had no memory of Tota-rama's argument later in the evening.

"You are not blind or stupid. You have done what other normal animals do. It takes time to get this realization. It is so simple, yet so elusive. We want to be self-realized, forgetting that we are already self-realized. There is nothing that we have to do except to recognize the fact that Spirit we seek outside is within us all and we are that Spirit. The whole logic of self-realization is counterintuitive. That's why we don't get it easily."

"Wait a minute...you mean to say that the world is so unreal that we should not spend anytime bothering about it? There is no need for us to work? There is no place for achievement motivation? The river in which we are floating is a figment of our imagination? You don't need anyone in your life except yourself? You sit all alone on a tree and be happy? Are you saying this?"

"No, I'm not saying that. There is no incompatibility between living in this world and pursuing self-realization or Spirit. There is enough scope in life for achievement motivation, creativity, and pursuit of excellence. We have to work and we have to take care of our families and our young ones. If you stop swimming now both of us will probably drown. But we should not get attached to our work or achievements. When we do that we invite a whole host of problems and we also move away from Spirit. The world is 'unreal' in the sense that nothing is permanent. Therefore, attaching ourselves to an ever changing reality will not give us any lasting joy or satisfaction."

Micky didn't know whether his words carried any meaning for Crocoda. Maybe this stuff is just too dense. Why on earth am I playing with the sensibilities of an animal that has come a long way, but cannot become a saint or a philosopher overnight? These thoughts are too subtle even for highly evolved apes.

Micky felt a mounting frustration about the inner conflict that had subsided but had not completely disappeared.

If I'm not sure of myself then how can I find liberation? Tears came rolling down Micky's cheeks. The dying face of his father appeared before his mind's eye.

"O dear father, how much I miss you! I need you now ... come wherever you are and show me the path. I will be lost without your guidance."

Micky felt that someone somewhere listened to his request and made a note of it.

REFLECTION

1. "If there is nothing real except God, meaning everything is His creation, how could God not be there in every tiny particle, in every living creature? What's creation without the Creator?"
2. "Not knowing what happiness is we always try to find it in wrong places. We try to find happiness in things. But we know that no 'thing' is permanent. Things give us happiness one time but not another time." How do you define happiness? Where do you find it? Have you found it?
3. "We want to be self-realized, forgetting that we are already self-realized. There is nothing that we have to do except to recognize the fact that Spirit we seek outside is within us all and we are that Spirit. The whole logic of self-realization is counterintuitive. That's why we don't get it easily."
4. "There is no incompatibility between living in this world and pursuing self-realization or Spirit."

11 A Teacher Appears

They floated slowly and cautiously for several hours. By midday Crocoda was exhausted; he felt a sudden loss of energy. He could not swim any more. He took a sharp turn toward a fallen red oak tree on the banks of the river. Micky jumped on one of the easily accessible branches. It was a large tree with bristle-tipped leaves still looking healthy. Micky reached the highest part of the tree to get a clear view of his surroundings. Upstream there was forest, downstream there were wide open grasslands. Beyond the rising fog that blocked the view, there probably was the ocean. Micky had never seen an ocean, but he had heard a story from his mother in which the ocean was compared to a bottomless pit—things fall into it and they are lost forever. These images of a large body of water, that was deep and dark, evoked fear and concern, but Micky was so certain of his dream that he knew that he would not get drowned; he would get the wings that he saw in the dream and would simply fly away.

Micky sat upright on a branch keeping his feet firmly planted. He tasted a few seeds, but they were bitter. He was tired too and wished for a quick nap. He closed his eyes.

Something moved. He felt as if someone had come and had taken a place in front of him. A few moments elapsed and then Micky heard a voice that was close like a whisper, but deep as if originating from some place in the outer space.

"Traveler, I understand the pain in your heart. I know you need clarity of purpose. You are hearing so many conflicting voices. These voices are simply compounding the confusion. You have to put your trust in me because I have witnessed the Truth."

Micky was overcome by emotion and started to cry like a baby. Once he stabilized himself he looked in the direction where the voice came from. What he saw with his teary eyes was an owl, sitting on the branch immediately facing him.

"You can hurt me if you want to. I am ready to die because my life is worthless in any case."

"I don't want to hurt you. I want to teach you something important. My name is Ullu-Lala. What's your name?"

"My name is Micky."

"I was an enlightened saint once but through sheer ignorance—traces of which are still present in my body—I became too proud, too arrogant about my own spiritual might. I even challenged gods once. Therefore, I was cursed to live the life of an owl. Owls are often misunderstood because we lead a secretive life. We are invisible during the daylight. We are quiet in flight and sometimes we make weird calls which leads to many superstitions. Imagine: I never touched meat when I was an enlightened saint, but now I am forced to eat insects, lizards, and small mammals. But one thing I have not lost is spiritual wisdom. All owls are wise, but I am especially blessed to advise you because of my karma in the previous lives. I must say that we owls have a special relationship with monkeys because we have a face like you guys—the face that has the shape of a heart. You are the first monkey I have seen in this part of the forest. Micky, do you want me to help you?"

"I need your help, Ullu-Lala. Please do guide me to find the right path."

"Micky, listen carefully. There is a body of wisdom that has been passed from one soul to another, from one generation to another, for hundreds of years. In fact, these beliefs are the work of Spirit itself—they reside deep within us as Nature's gift yet they are not self-evident. Our own ignorance often hides them, keeps them away from our consciousness. My thinking might be biased to some extent because my truth is strictly my own; it's not universal in any way. But you must know that I speak with great sincerity and integrity. Are you ready for me, Micky?"

"Please go ahead, Ullu-Lala, I am ready.... I will listen to every word that you speak with full attention."

"I want to tell you something important about inner transformation which is quite different from the way we look at change in our daily life."

Ullu-Lala stopped speaking for a few seconds as if something was stuck in his throat. He cleared it and started to speak once again.

"Change is generally perceived as a movement from one point to another. All our life, we try to change or reposition ourselves to cope with changing external circumstances. Spiritual change is in essence 'changeless change' because in order to realize Self, we do not have to do anything special, or to go anywhere. Self-realization can occur right here within a second."

"Why is this spiritual change needed? I hope you don't mind my asking a question"

"Change itself is nothing but a realization that what we always believed to be real is real only in a relative sense. We have to live in the world but we have to do it with dynamic detachment. By becoming one with Spirit, we are not negating the world. We cannot negate the world because it is also Spirit at the cosmic level. What we negate is the grand illusion of our own separation from Spirit; the illusion that our affections, our possessions, and our attachments are the only reality that we need to care about."

"Is this a fundamental shift of perception?"

"Definitely, this is a fundamental shift of perception. Instead of looking outward our gaze shifts inward. We like things that we can feel, see, or touch. We adore possessions that give us comfort. We value relationships that make us feel secure. But what is hidden beneath the surface is the center of our gravity. What is hidden within us is Spirit, something that we search outside all our life and never find."

"When I look at the world it seems real at times but at other times it seems so unreal. How could the world be real and unreal at the same time?"

"The world in which you live exists, but it is not real. If a stone hits you, you are going to be hurt. In that sense, the world is real. But it is not real because it changes all the time and it is subject to the laws of time, space, and causality that make it relative and dualistic. Beyond the fleeting images of this material reality, we find Spirit, which is eternal, limitless, and totally unaffected by fluctuations in the physical world."

"From what you say it follows that true happiness lies in finding out our center of gravity and seeking oneness with Spirit. Am I right?"

"You are correct. In order for us to realize our true happiness, our true potential, we have to go much deeper, way beyond the superficial questions of meaning and purpose of life that we frequently ask ourselves. We have to come face to face with the realization that what we call our narrow self is nothing other than Spirit. It could never be anything else because the whole existence is nothing but Spirit."

"If I was born with Spirit within me, what has blocked my spiritual progress? I should have been Self-realized by now. Shouldn't I?"

"Your path and everyone's path is blocked by egoistic tendencies, such as selfishness, anger, jealousy, fear, and arrogance. When these tendencies are present they are the biggest barriers to any kind of positive personal change. They make the Spirit turn away from us."

"I know I have a soul. Is my soul different from Spirit?"

"We casually talk about soul. But we fail to realize that our soul and Spirit are one and the same. Of course, there is a part of us that is doing the worldly stuff. There is a part of us that dreams when we sleep. There is yet another part of us that relaxes in a dreamless sleep. All these parts are familiar to us. But we never stop to think: how could we ever do this if there was no all-pervading Consciousness that was illuminating every little detail of our life? This Consciousness is eternal Spirit."

"But why can't we stay in ignorance? Apparently, it is not hurting us. Why pursue self-realization?"

"Our ignorance is not the function of any lack of information. It is the work of the grand illusion that makes everything in the world look so real. Our nests are real, so are our forests. Our struggle to satisfy our basic needs is a real struggle. Nothing comes to us easily. How could we ever doubt the reality and the brutal presence of these phenomena? Yet behind this phenomenal world of multiplicities, there is reality and that reality never changes. It does not have to. Spirit is not born; therefore, it never dies. It is a witness of our waking, dreaming, and sleeping states; it is the only light in the universe that energizes all life and matter. It is pure joy and bliss because no sorrow ever reaches it."

"How can I get to know Spirit? How can I seek oneness with Spirit?"

"There are three ways in which we get to know Spirit. First, Spirit is nothing but Nature in disguise. You can look at the rising sun and see the face of Spirit. You can look at rivers, lakes, mountains, and blooming fields of flowers, Spirit is everywhere. If you believe in this view you are intimate with Spirit by celebrating the beauty and grandeur, and sanctity of Nature. To worship Nature is to worship Spirit. We can be very spiritual and God fearing while using our gross energies—singing and dancing, celebrating and laughing, eating the sweet and sour fruit of every tree in the forest."

"Is there another view?"

"There is a second view of Spirit that is based on the idea of separation, sin and isolation. Our birth is an act of separation from Spirit and it is an act of moving away from Spirit—physically and spiritually. This could be a punishment for sins done in a previous incarnation or thoughts and actions that we harbored in violation of the essence of Spirit. Given this condition, we are really far from any thought of intimacy with Spirit. Our life then becomes an effort to move toward, or rise up to the level of Spirit. Through the power of our individual Consciousness we steer ourselves to the Universal Consciousness. This struggle can take one lifetime or it can take up to several lifetimes. The intimacy is achieved if at all through numerous sessions of intense prayer and meditation. We use our subtle energies to get a vision of Spirit and center our thoughts and passions on our goal. Is success assured at the end of this long road? No one can say."

There was a silent pause—a silence filled with thoughts that Micky had not known before.

"And what is the third view?"

"There is a third view that says that we were never separate from Spirit at any time. We are that Pure Consciousness that Spirit is made of. We are the witness who is seeing and hearing everything. We are that ever-present reality that has no end and no beginning. We were present before this universe was created, and we shall be present once the universe ceases to exist. Spirit by definition is immortal and eternal. The question of intimacy in this scenario is irrelevant. How could you not be intimate with your own self? It is a provocative question because in our state of perpetual ignorance we identify ourselves only with the body and the material objects around us."

"Is there any connection, Ullu-Lala, here with our dualistic thinking? We are always holding this tension between good and evil. If Spirit lives within our heart, what accounts for the evil, treachery, oppression, terror, violence, injustice, disease, and suffering that is our daily life?"

"We exist in a world of relativity and duality; Spirit does not. As long as we believe in the existence of relativity, there will always be polarizing forces, stretching us in different directions. Once we shift our attention from this world of evil and injustice, all dualities and multiplicities will begin to disperse. If evil, injustice, and violence are bad, who imposed these limitations and constraints on us? It is hard to imagine that we are born with these limitations and innate tendencies. Mostly we do it to ourselves in a conscious manner. Spirit and evil do not coexist as light and darkness cannot coexist. Only when we are truly touched by Spirit, the spell of evil and injustice is shattered. In Spirit's presence there is no duality."

"What about our body? Spirit is immortal; body is mortal. Spirit is real; body is unreal and so forth. At the same time, we need to build a healthy and enriching relationship with our body. How can we do this?"

"While our body is our most precious asset, in reality we live in three bodies. Our primary attention is fixed on the gross body that needs continuous care and nourishment; it feels pleasure and pain, and experiences joy and happiness. The subtle body comes next and it consists of subtle elements like breathing, mind, and intelligence. This body plays an important part because we achieve extraordinary results by using our mental and intellectual capacities. The third manifestation of our body is causal body that is closest to Self and we get to experience its blissful state in moments of deep sleep. We also identify these three body states with three energies—gross, subtle, and causal. Self is a witness of these three bodies but cannot be identified with any one of them. Authentic change does not require separation from our body or any of its manifestations. Our body is sacred because it is the abode of Self; it is only in this body and through this body that we can attain enlightenment. Therefore, any lack of care or unnecessary hardship caused to the body is counter-productive in achieving the overall goal of self-realization. Yet at the same time our total identification with our body is wrong. We have a body, but we are not our bodies. Total identification with body is limiting and false."

"Do I need to renounce everything before I reach the goal of self-realization?"

"Renunciation is needed but not in the sense the word is commonly understood. There is no need to go to high forests (we are already in one), no need to give up your loved ones, and no need to give up your favorite tree. The renunciation that is needed is a spiritual one in which we inculcate within ourselves the power to discriminate between the real and the unreal and, in some sense, give up the unreal. We need to be clear what this giving up entails. Self does not need anything from us. What we give up is purely a personal matter for us. We should give up excessive attachment to things. What is excessive, you might ask. This is the function of the power of our discrimination. As we cultivate and nurture this capacity, even little attachment might look excessive. We have to make this decision on a daily basis. In the end the answer may be how far are we mentally and psychologically detached from the concerns of the moment?"

"What about karma? Is there payback for actions of our previous life?"

"One important reason why we start our lives at different spatial points away from Spirit is that we bring different karma with us when we are born. Karma is the sum and substance of our past actions that have an impact on our present life. Karma simply means action—an action that produces results or consequences. Every thing that we do in this life has consequences—some known, others unknown. Actions and their consequences get accumulated and get attached to our personal consciousness that we carry from one body to another."

"How do we get to select another body?"

"We are born as a body that is in fact crafted by us. Our karma and our innate tendencies work to shape us in a certain way."

"If karma decides who we really are, where is the place for free will?"

"There is much that we can do. Any progress that we make to reach the goal of self-realization in this life eradicates proportionately some residue of our past lives. A fully self-realized person has no karmic baggage because he has moved away from the world of causality."

"Can we say that authentic change can be accelerated by the effort that we make to nurture spiritual qualities?"

"It is good to have certain qualities of mind and heart, but self-realization is much more than summing-up of certain qualities."

"Is living in the present moment an opportunity for us to actually live in Spirit?"

"Present moment is the only moment that we can live in. Past is history and the future is just a projection. The valid question is not whether we are living in the present moment, but what are we thinking and doing in the present moment? If we are just paying attention to things around us, that is of little use. On the other hand, if we are living in Pure Consciousness it is a different matter. Any moment lived away from Spirit is not helpful for reaching the goal of self-realization. We should live not only in the present moment, but in a meditative state where on the one hand we pay attention to the drudgery of our daily life and on the other stay fully absorbed in Spirit."

"Ullu-Lala, I am going back to one of the lessons my father taught me, that is, there has to be motivation for achieving anything in life. Where does the motivation to unite with Spirit come from?"

"Authentic change and inner transformation may follow some steps, levels, stages, or it may not. There is no one true path. Every path leads to the summit if one has the right motivation. Self-realization is an ever-present state. But we don't know it. The day we break these mental barriers and remove layers of ignorance that surround our real nature we shall be self-realized in a second. "

"I think I have run out of questions. There is only one more question: What can I do now to seek oneness with Spirit? Is there a magic formula?"

"There is no magic formula, but just remember a few things."

There was a thundering noise that drowned Ullu-Lala's words. He stopped speaking for a few seconds and resumed when it was quiet again.

"Spirit manifests in endless ways. We often fight over its name and form. This is sheer ignorance. Spirit is love. When Spirit created this universe, it was an act of sublime love. Spirit created beings and creatures and sent them away, but it didn't send them away all alone, to languish and to suffer on their own. It gave them free will, but ensured that every living creature had an equal chance to return to itself in a state of perfection. That is the role of the witness within us."

There was a complete silence for few moments. Micky heard his own breathing, something he had never heard before. Ullu-Lala spoke again.

"I have to leave you, Micky, at this point. I have given you all the knowledge I had...about life and death, about matters temporal and eternal. You are free to pursue the path of wisdom that you think is best for you. We shall see each other another time, in another form. The beautiful thing about this creation is that nothing really goes away; everything stays here in one form or another—from one creation to another, from one period to another. Suns die and are born again, planets come and go, but we stay here. This universe is really like a small forest. Call me by any name and I will respond. Good bye, Micky."

Ullu-Lala moved away, receding slowly but surely. His deep melodious voice submerged itself in the rustling of the wind, in the noise that was arising from far corners of the forest.

Micky was all alone, in mind, body and spirit. And he didn't know what to do. He closed his eyes and went deep within, to the inner reaches of his consciousness. Everything came to a standstill. The past, the present and the future all merged into one massive emptiness. The world as he had known it ceased to exist for him.

For the next seven days Micky didn't move. The fallen tree had become his temporary abode. Slowly, he began to see oneness where he had seen dualities or pluralities before.

In this formless void Micky saw forms he had never imagined before. Form and formless were one, a circle and a point around which everything revolved.

Micky saw himself gazing at the whole universe. It was not like he was looking at an object. In that act of seeing Micky had become the universe. There was no separation, no distance, no desire, no craving for anything; it was a state of contentment, fullness beyond measure.

He died moment by moment to be reincarnated at a higher level of consciousness. Death brought renewal and a sense of immortality.

He was alone, but this loneliness was not isolation. There was fullness and vigor in this aloneness, a connectedness that knew no boundaries.

Time had come to a still point; a still point that signaled a rebirth, a beginning of total egolessness and timelessness.

Without seeking anything he felt richness beyond measure, not deficient in anything, not wanting anything more, a state beyond all things, all possessions, all states of body and mind.

REFLECTION

1. "Change is generally perceived as a movement from one point to another. All our life, we try to change or reposition ourselves to cope with changing external circumstances. Spiritual change is in essence 'changeless change' because in order to realize Self we do not have to do anything special, or to go anywhere. Self-realization can occur right here within a second."
2. "The world in which [we] live exists.... But it is not real because it changes all the time and it is subject to the laws of time, space, and causality that make it relative and dualistic. Beyond the fleeting images of this material reality, we find Spirit, which is eternal, limitless, and totally unaffected by fluctuations in the physical world."
3. "We exist in a world of relativity and duality; Spirit does not. As long as we believe in the existence of relativity, there will always be polarizing forces, stretching us in different directions. Once we shift our attention from this world of evil and injustice, all dualities and multiplicities will begin to disperse. If evil, injustice, and violence are bad, who imposed these limitations and constraints on us? It is hard to imagine that we are born with these limitations and innate tendencies. Mostly we do it to ourselves in a conscious manner. Spirit and evil do not coexist as light and darkness cannot coexist. Only when we are truly touched by Spirit, the spell of evil and injustice is shattered. In Spirit's presence there is no duality."
4. "Present moment is the only moment that we can live in. Past is history and the future is just a projection. The valid question is not whether we are living in the present moment, but what are we thinking and doing in the present moment? If we are just paying attention to things around us, that is of little use. On the other hand, if we are living in Pure Consciousness it is a different matter. Any moment lived away from Spirit is

not helpful for reaching the goal of self-realization. We should live not only in the present moment, but in a meditative state where on the one hand we pay attention to the drudgery of our daily life and on the other stay fully absorbed in Spirit."

5. "Authentic change and inner transformation may follow some steps, levels, stages, or it may not. There is no one true path. Every path leads to the summit if one has the right motivation. Self-realization is an ever-present state. But we don't know it. The day we break these mental barriers and remove layers of ignorance that surround our real nature we shall be Self-realized in a second."
6. "Spirit manifests in endless ways. We often fight over its name and form. This is sheer ignorance. Spirit is love. When Spirit created this universe, it was an act of sublime love. Spirit created beings and creatures and sent them away, but it didn't send them away all alone, to languish and to suffer on their own. It gave them free will, but ensured that every living creature had an equal chance to return to itself in a state of perfection. That is the role of the witness within us."

12 Spirit Is All There Is

On the eighth day Micky got down from the tree and asked Crocoda whether he wanted to go home. Crocoda looked weak as he had not eaten anything for all these days.

"Micky, I don't have the energy to swim against the current. Let us go to the ocean. Let's go where all the water is going."

"I'm afraid we might die. You can't swim in deep water. Can you?"

"If death means nothing to you, why should I be afraid of death?"

They spent the entire day floating in shallow waters. Micky thought that the ocean was near but it took a very long time to get there.

As the day's shadows lengthened and the darkness started to embrace everything around them, Micky got a first clear view of the ocean. He looked at the sky. The sun was setting right in front of his eyes. It felt as if someone had thrown innumerable buckets of color over the sky. Micky shouted in unrestrained ecstasy: "Yes, we have arrived..."

Crocoda didn't say a word.

"Crocoda, listen to the song that the sea gulls are singing. Listen to the music that is embedded in this water. Smell the breeze; it has a different texture. Have you ever seen such wide-open spaces? There are no trees around here. There are no stones either. It's just water and the two of us...."

They moved in the direction of the sun...slowly like a boat getting into the heart of the ocean. All the sounds overhead and under water were like prayers, thousands of prayer bells ringing in unison, saying the same words....

You cannot see That
Which is the Witness of vision

You cannot hear That
Which is the hearer of the hearing
You cannot think That
Which is the thinker of thought
You cannot know That
Which is the knower of knowledge
This is your Self or Spirit
That is within all
Everything else but This is perishable*

They were deep inside the ocean; they were seen one moment and gone the next one. No one saw them flying into the red glow of the dying sun. But one thing was certain. They had become part of the radiance of Spirit—the light, the sounds, and the vibrations under water; there was nothing to separate them from the rest of the ocean.

They had returned to a very special place—a place that was untouched by sorrow, a place of absolute bliss, a place that had no boundaries, and a place that was inside every particle in the whole living universe.

---

* *Brihadaranyaka Upanishad*

REFLECTION

1. *You cannot see That*
   Which is the Witness of vision
   You cannot hear That
   Which is the hearer of the hearing
   You cannot think That
   Which is the thinker of thought
   You cannot know That
   Which is the knower of knowledge
   This is your Self or Spirit
   That is within all
   Everything else but This is perishable
2. "They had returned to a very special place—a place that was untouched by sorrow, a place of absolute bliss, a place that had no boundaries, and a place that was inside every particle in the whole living universe."

Appendix

Personal & Organizational Development Tools

Activities & Exercises

1
Life-Cycle Learning

Experiencing, Reflecting, Actualizing

Background

If we have to lead a meaningful life, we have to enhance our life-long learning abilities. We can create greater joy and satisfaction in every little thing that we do if we are open to experiencing life in all its hues and colors. The diagram below shows three stages of life cycle, which in reality are three very distinctive phases of sense-making and internalizing life lessons. If we can pay attention to each one of them, we can easily enrich the quality of our life.

Process

Every movement around this self-reinforcing loop is a journey from unconscious to conscious living. Every rotation around this cycle provides a new learning opportunity.

- Experiencing (as against "experience") is always in the present moment. Its perspective is free from all conditioning, desires, biases, and prejudices.

- Reflecting occurs after each action, or at the end of each day, or any other convenient time. It is a way of finding meaning, purpose and lessons, if any.
- Actualizing is the process of internalizing our "experiencing"—nurturing a permanent sense of truth and wisdom.

Each subsequent round takes us closer to a higher level of consciousness. Work around this cycle yields immediate positive results; greater satisfaction with relationships, greater effectiveness in the workplace, greater ability to guide and help others, and a stress-free existence.

Experiencing involves...

- Performing actions from an inner sense of purpose and duty as their own rewards (engaging in desire-less action).
- Listening with deep intensity.
- Living as if every moment matters.
- Walking as if every step is part of a sacred journey.
- Staying centered in the most troubled moments of life.
- Taking moderate risks to try out new things.
- Caring for the environment and biodiversity.
- Caring for physical-self (body) and its needs.
- Supporting charity and sharing the fruits of one's labor with others.
- Being a global citizen and a champion of the planet.

Reflecting means...

- Finding time to reflect in the midst of one's busy life.
- Taking nature walks alone or in the company of a loved one.
- Doing breathing and mindfulness exercises.
- Listening to music.
- Reading and writing poetry.
- Maintaining a journal.

Actualizing requires...

- Demonstrating oneness with soul or spirit in word, deed, and action.
- Internalizing meaning of one's actions.
- Using the wisdom gained to continuously search for truth.
- Mentoring self and others to lead a virtuous life.

Process

Select a medium size (easy to carry) notebook to be used as a Learning Journal. This journal will contain a record of your learnings and reflections as you are going through the authentic change process. Make it a point to spend about 15 minutes each day for your reflective writing. As this is your private journal, you can write anything. Writing leads to clarity. It helps you become more creative, and above all it creates a firm commitment for change.

As a starter, write down your responses to the following 5 questions. This is an open-ended self-reflection. There are no right or wrong answers. Whatever comes to your mind is the right answer:

1. What have you learned during the past one-month, the last six months or the past one-year that has made a difference in your life?
2. Draw a line that represents your entire life up to this point. What events (no more than 5) that stand out in terms of your personal development? Who were the key people who played a role in making those events so important for you?
3. Based on your answer to question 2 write a note of gratitude to all those people whose names you had written in response to that question.
4. If your current life looks like the face of a clock or a pie, what are its 4-5 major segments? What is the relative size of each segment pertaining to work,

family, friends, community, religion or spirituality, and recreation (including time for vacations) based on the actual time spent? How would you like to rearrange these pie segments based on how you want to change your life priorities?

5. What is one thing that you want to accomplish in your life? What is your dream? What are you most passionate about? Write 2-3 pages of text as thoughts flow into your mind. The quality of writing does not matter. We are not aiming for neatness or clarity. Just write down what comes to your mind. Close the book after doing this. Let these ideas and thoughts settle down in your mind. Do not write anything else in the journal for a day.

2
The Hero's Journey

Background

Joseph Campbell, the great mythologist, in his book *The Hero with a Thousand Faces* (1949) identified a story that shows up in all cultures, and that's the story of Hero's Journey. Hero is a male or a female character, supernatural in qualities of body, mind, heart, and spirit, who ventures to go into the deep forest to fight a dragon or some other destructive force that is guarding something which is very precious for the Hero to attain. He or she wins the battle and brings home the "jewel."

This is how Joseph Campbell poetically describes this journey:

> The heroic life is living the *individual* adventure.
>
> To refuse the call means stagnation.
>
> You enter the forest at the darkest point, where there is no path.
>
> Where there is a way or path, it is someone else's path.
>
> If you follow someone else's way, you are not going to realize your potential.
>
> The very cave you are afraid to enter turns out to be the source of what you are looking for. The damned thing in the cave that was so dreaded has become the center.
>
> The goal is to bring the jewel back to the world, to join the two things together.
>
> The goal of the hero trip down to the jewel point is to find those levels in the psyche that open, open, open, and finally open to the mystery of your self being Buddha consciousness or the Christ.
>
> That's the journey.
>
> It is all about finding that still point in your mind where commitment drops away.
>
> (Osborn 1991, pp. 22-24)

At the core this myth is an exceptional story of renewal and change. Authentic development requires us to undertake such a journey. It requires us to kill our demons. It gives us the jewel if we are victorious in terms of managing and sustaining the change effort.

Process

Robert Dilts, the founder of NLP University and a gifted teacher, has adapted the Hero's Journey for learning purposes. For this exercise, find some empty space inside your home. As you go through 8 stages of this journey you will be moving few steps at a time to indicate progress in your journey:

1. Stand in the original position. Breathe deeply a few times and be very relaxed. Standing in this position you hear your "calling." Your calling is your challenge of change, whatever you aspire in life. For example, you may focus on your life mission or something equally important.
2. Standing in the same spot accept the calling. This acceptance is important because unless you internalize the calling and show your commitment, you cannot make much progress.
3. Now, move a few steps. With this movement you cross a "threshold." This is the point where safety and security ends. Beyond this point, you're very vulnerable. There are dangers all around and you have to be very alert.
4. Move one more step and search for a guardian or a mentor. You need help. You need someone who has already traversed this path. The guardian protects you and teaches you how you will carry on this fight.
5. Move another step or two. Now, you are facing the dragon or the demon (the challenge). You engage in a battle with a view to overpowering the demon.
6. You don't kill the demon, but transform it into a special skill or capacity. The point is to turn the demon into a friend rather than a foe.

7. Move the final step or two. You enter the cave where the jewel is kept. You grab the prize. You have completed the task for which you were called.
8. Having won the battle you come back to the original position from where you started. This is called "finding your way back home." Once the hero is back, he or she does not simply sit around. Having realized your own vision, you help other people fulfill their dream.

This story contains several archetypes of authentic development. First of all, there is a dragon, which is the challenge of development itself. Second, there is the innocent—the person who wants to develop. You are innocent because you don't know that dragon exists. The process of development is an unchartered territory with grave risks and opportunities. Third, there is the orphan (the change seeker) because you have to fight the dragon who is much more powerful than you. You are afraid of being hurt. Fourth, there is the martyr if the dragon prevails. Fifth, there is the wanderer—you try to approach the cave in such a way that you avoid the dragon. Sixth, there is the warrior because eventually you end up challenging the dragon. Last, there is the sorcerer because you transform the dragon into a resource.

3

Synergy: The Invisible Difference

Background

Abraham Maslow defined synergy as a point of resolution of the dichotomy between selfishness and altruism.

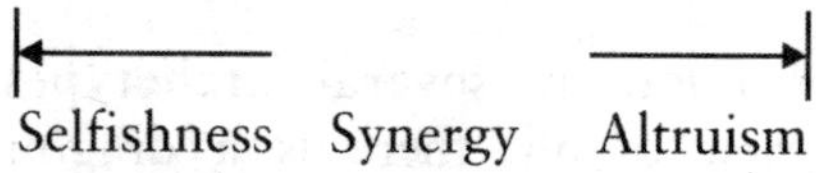

As we look at this drawing, we find greater "selfishness" on our left-side and greater "altruism" on our right side. Synergy is the point of resolution between these two opposing forces. The balance is critical in the sense that I can't move left or right of the center without disturbing the fine balance between my needs and those of the others. The "resolution point" is the point where others approve of my selfishness and I openly acknowledge my willingness to work for the well-being of others.

Maslow's favorite synergy example was that of Blackfoot Indians who honored as part of their long held tradition the richest person in their tribe at the annual Sun Dance festival but with richness defined as the quality of maximum giving. Thus, the richest person was the one who gave the most to others.

Members of synergistic teams use this resolution point to satisfy their needs as individuals while at the same time reaching out to others to create high quality outcomes. They are effective in balancing organizational demands for higher productivity and individual aspirations for greater self-actualization. The only thing that tends to disturb this balance is the presence of fear and anxiety in the workplace. Nothing drives individuals to the left side (selfishness part of the continuum) more quickly than the fear of losing their jobs.

Process

Synergy Related Exercises

Exercise 1

Take a walk. Listen to the different sounds around you. Look at the colors of trees. Look at any peculiarity of people you see around. Smell the air. Be aware of your feelings. Just take a note, but do not be critical of self, other people, or objects. As you continue to walk, be open to all kinds of sounds, colors, smells, and feelings without any judgment of good or bad. Be a silent observer. Nurture that feeling of "a leaf in the wind" as you build new connections with the environment around you. Let loose your sense of identity. Do not censor any thoughts that arise spontaneously. Do not resist thoughts that seem to come from outside. Let them find a temporary home within you. After the walk, take a few minutes to do some reflection, write down any new insights or some exciting discoveries in your journal.

Do this exercise every day for one week and notice how others perceive you. You will feel unusual warmth around you. Notice how your openness creates more opportunities for you to experience synergy in your interactions with others.

Exercise 2

Engage in a work-related conversation. Make a strong inner resolve to say a few things about the subject matter under discussion that represents your true feelings—feelings that you have harbored for a long time but have shied away from expressing them in the past. For example, you may say:

- "Sorry, I can't carry this workload any longer. I need some help."
- "I don't think we are getting expected return from this project. We need to evaluate our options."
- "Our business environment is sending us signals that we are not paying attention to..."

- "I'm not clear about our long-term strategy. Can someone explain it to me?"
- "There are interpersonal issues in our team that we need to address. Can we have team retreat where we can discuss these issues?"
- "Lack of diversity in our group is a concern to me."

Speaking your mind on issues that are dear to you will send a signal to others about your fears and concerns. It will also reinforce the perception that you speak up on vital issues. You talk about things that you deeply care about. Such openness promotes synergy as people move out of their shells to talk about the important issues.

Exercise 3

Look at a painting. Think of the ways in which you would have painted the picture differently. What other colors you would have considered? What other objects or human figures you would have added? What would you have deleted altogether?

Stand a couple of feet away from the new "painting" that you have just created. Go on making further changes until the time you are fully satisfied. Think about what this reshaping really means to you. Take a note of your creative ability and ask yourself how you are using this skill in your day-to-day life.

Exercise 4

Make a habit to ask reshaping or reframing questions. These questions take the form of "glass half full"—looking at the positive outcomes. Remember the lines from a famous *haiku*—

My barn having burned to the ground,
I can now see the moon.

Here are some practical examples:

- "Your point regarding work-family imbalance is quite valid, but this is the first time in years that we have exceeded our quarterly targets."

- "When team members take time off for training it does create work problems, but look at the new learning that they are bringing into our teamwork."
- "It's true that we are spending a lot of money on external consultants, but look at the great skills that they are transferring to our staff."
- "Your point regarding the new database being very slow is correct, but this is the first time that we can get all the information and all of us are sharing this one system."

Exercise 5

While taking a walk, notice similarities between objects and how things live in a state of unity and harmony. How one thing blends into another and produces a new layer of reality—individual houses form into a suburban habitat, trees become part of a forest, a road meanders and becomes part of a much larger highway system. Blending is a "chunking up" process whereby our perception shifts to a higher level. Blending works the same way in the world of ideas; we move from lower layers to the upper layers; from minor details to the big picture. Bring the lessons from the world of nature to your day-to-day reality. Some examples:

- "You were talking about the problems in the procurement system. Another colleague earlier mentioned about suppliers not getting paid on time. This makes me think that we need to align our procurement and financial management systems."
- "Our managers resist attending training courses and learning in general. But as someone just mentioned they are also not showing much of a leadership. Most of them recycle old ideas. This makes me wonder how efficient our screening system is for promotion to managerial cadre."
- "We are showing greater cultural sensitivity in our international operations, but the number of complaints by foreign workers at the hands of our resident staff

has increased over time. This makes me think that we need to revisit our values and offer training in diversity skills on a scale not tried before."

Exercise 6

Listen to a conversation that two people are having. Try to capture the essence of what they are saying. You intervene in the manner of providing a synergistic twist to the conversation, a form of blending in action. Here is an example.

Person A: We are spending too much money in developing new products, which may not sell very well.

Person B: There are opportunities in the market that we have not really exploited.

You Say: Development costs need to be assessed in relation to customer needs. If customers need those products, then we are well positioned to exploit market opportunities.

Exercise 7

While talking to others, try to restate your favorite positions in a different set of words. Use more feelings where there were none before. Use more body language, gestures to convey your understanding of issues. You will feel the difference in the impact it will have on others.

Exercise 8

Add a short preface to whatever you are about to say.

- You won't believe what happened the other day...
- I am going to say this only one time...
- I have been reflecting on this issue and have come to the conclusion...
- There are ordinary solutions to problems and there are great ones and I'm going to share a great one...
- I have been trying to find a direction how we move from point A to point B and this is what I think...

4
Emotional Intelligence (EQ)

Background

Carl Jung was right when he wrote, "...emotion is the moment when steel meets flint and a spark is struck forth, for emotion is the chief source of consciousness. There is no change from darkness to light or from inertia to movement without emotion." No one except a few academic researchers talked about emotional intelligence before 1990s. Emotional Intelligence as a form of expression was unknown in the business context. But it changed with the publication of former *New York Times* writer Daniel Goleman's book *Emotional Intelligence* in 1995. Goleman made a strong case for paying attention to EQ besides IQ that had been accepted as the principal measure of assessing one's intelligence. Previously, Harvard psychologist Howard Gardner had published research during 1980s about "multiple intelligences"—meaning that there is more than one form of intelligence. He came up with 8 broad categories of intelligence:

Linguistic intelligence: The grasp of written or spoken words.

Logical-Mathematical intelligence: Numbers, logic, and abstract concepts.

Spatial Intelligence: Vision and spatial judgments (looking at shapes in a space).

Bodily-Kinesthetic Intelligence: Muscular coordination and movement; body-mind coordination.

Musical Intelligence: Creating music or listening to music and enjoying it.

Interpersonal Intelligence: Capacity for effective interactions with others.

Intrapersonal Intelligence: This has to do with emotional self-awareness (EQ); knowing oneself; knowing our desires and motivations.

Naturalist Intelligence: Connecting with nature and natural phenomena; letting nature become part of our life; working for sustainability of the global environment.

Besides Goleman and Gardner, there are three other pioneers who need to be mentioned. These are Reuven Bar-On (who coined the term "emotional quotient"), John Mayer and Peter Salovey. Goleman's approach has been specifically applied to leadership development issues by his associates Richard Boyatzis and Annie McKee in their books *Primal Leadership: Realizing the Power of Emotional intelligence* (2002) and *Resonant Leadership* (2005). Bar-On approach outlined earlier is better suited for individual coaching and self-awareness. For business and leadership development, Goleman-Boyatzis-McKee approach is more solid and has found greater acceptance in the business world. Goleman and his associates work around 4 domains and 19 competencies of emotional intelligence, as shown in the following table.

Personal Competencies

DOMAIN 1. *Self-Awareness*

Emotional Self-awareness: Reading one's emotions accurately.

Accurate Self-assessment: Making correct assessment of one's strengths and weaknesses.

Self-confidence: Having a good sense of one's self-worth and self-esteem. No over-confidence or under confidence.

DOMAIN 2. *Self-Management*

Emotional Self-control: Keeping one's negative emotions under control.

Transparency: Being open and frank in one's dealings with others.

Adaptability: Being flexible and changing with the need of times.

Achievement: Pursuing a standard of excellence.

Initiative: Exploring and seizing new opportunities.

Optimism: Seeing the glass as half full.

Social Competencies

DOMAIN 3. *Social-Awareness*

Empathy: Putting your self into the shoes of others.

Organizational Awareness: Knowing what's going on in the organization, including power dynamic, informal networks, and future challenges.

Service: Providing high quality service to organizational clients.

DOMAIN 4. *Relationship Management*

Inspirational Leadership: Guiding and motivating others with a compelling vision.

Influence: Creating impact without having formal authority.

Developing Others: Bolstering others' abilities through coaching, mentoring, feedback and guidance.

Change Catalyst: Initiating, managing, and leading in a new direction.

Conflict Management: Resolving disagreements to the satisfaction of all parties.

Building Bonds: Cultivating and maintaining a stable web of relations.

Teamwork and Collaboration: Fostering cooperation and teamwork.

Source: Adapted from *Resonant Leadership* (2005, p. 29)

Process

The following instrument (see the next page) based on Goleman framework above, is a quick and cost-free way of measuring your EQ. This instrument is aimed at serving only a limited purpose of self-awareness and is not a substitute for a more comprehensive developmental feedback. The four comprehensive instruments in use at this time are:

A Self-Rating EQ Instrument

Please read each statement and circle the appropriate number	*Strongly Disagree*	*Disagree*	*Neutral*	*Agree*	*Strongly Agree*
1. I know when I'm sad and I know when I'm happy.	1	2	3	4	5
2. I am good at knowing and acknowledging my strengths and weaknesses.	1	2	3	4	5
3. I'm neither over confident nor under-confident.	1	2	3	4	5
4. I can easily put myself into the shoes of others.	1	2	3	4	5
5. I understand the core business of my organization and its current and future priorities.	1	2	3	4	5
6. I know my client's needs and do my best to meet them.	1	2	3	4	5
7. I am comfortable in managing negative emotions like sadness or anger.	1	2	3	4	5
8. I am always transparent and authentic.	1	2	3	4	5
9. I adapt myself easily to changing circumstances.	1	2	3	4	5
10. I am always striving to set a new standard of excellence in whatever I do.	1	2	3	4	5
11. I am always ready to make use of new opportunities.	1	2	3	4	5
12. I persistently pursue the goal that I have set before me.	1	2	3	4	5
13. I am very good at inspiring and guiding others.	1	2	3	4	5
14. I am effective in persuading others to my viewpoint.	1	2	3	4	5
15. I help other people grow and develop.	1	2	3	4	5
16. I am rarely satisfied with the status quo and want to change things for the better.	1	2	3	4	5
17. I am really good at managing conflict.	1	2	3	4	5
18. I develop strong and nurturing relationships with others.	1	2	3	4	5
19. I like working with teams and groups.	1	2	3	4	5
20. My emotional life provides me with support and sustenance for future growth.	1	2	3	4	5

Goleman and Boyatzis' ECI 360

Bar-On EQ-i® and EQ-360™

Mayer, Salovey, and Caruso's MSCEIT™

Orioli and Cooper's EQ Map®

There is no such thing as a perfect instrument. All the above instruments have relative strengths and limitations. Other things being equal, a 360-degree instrument is much more valuable than a simple self-assessment. But a self-assessment could be a good starting point. Therefore, go ahead and assess yourself. Try to look upon yourself more objectively and critically. Whatever response comes to you the first time is perhaps the right answer.

Scoring

Scores between 75-100 indicate high levels of EQ, which need to be sustained with continuous effort.

Scores between 50-74 indicate a medium range that may not be adequate for success in today's globalized world.

Scores below 50 indicate the need for serious attention to your deficit of emotional competencies.

Please remember that we can't change our IQ but EQ can be developed through appropriate changes in our behaviors, thinking styles, and adoption of reflective practices like writing a journal.

5

Personal Mastery

Background

Peter Senge identified "personal mastery" as one among the five disciplines outlined in his landmark book *The Fifth Discipline: The Art & Practice of The Learning Organization* (1990). Personal mastery (not in the sense of gaining dominance over others) is important for business organizations because they "learn only through individuals who learn. Individual learning does not guarantee organizational learning. But without it no organizational learning occurs." The concept is centered around growth and learning, but beyond the skills and competencies that people routinely acquire while doing a job. This involves some form of spiritual development. When personal mastery becomes a discipline it means two things. First, it continually clarifies what is important to us. Second, we continually learn so that we see our current situation more clearly (Senge uses the term "current reality"). Those who pursue the path of personal mastery share some common characteristics:

- They have a sense of purpose that lies behind their vision and goals.
- They look upon their vision as an inner "calling."
- They see their current situation as an ally—accepting what is good and helpful and not simply focus on barriers and obstacles.
- They are deeply inquisitive. They ask lots of questions.
- They feel connected to life itself and others while retaining their uniqueness.
- They look upon themselves as part of a larger process.
- They never really arrive; meaning personal mastery is a process rather than an end-state. The journey is actually the reward.

If personal mastery is such a wonderful thing, why would organizations not invest in it or why would they oppose it? According to Senge, there are several reasons for this: First, this is looked upon as a "soft" skill having no substantive or quantifiable value. Second, there is lot of cynicism in organizations around the human potential movement and there is an inbuilt resistance to some of these ideas. Third, some people view ideas like personal mastery as dangerous and disruptive of the status quo. Although there is lot of merit in these points, we saw during the 1990s tremendous change in the way organizations view learning. In fact, *Fifth Discipline* itself contributed in a big way in bringing about this change.

Process

There is a powerful exercise designed by Rick Ross that can help us in sustaining self-awareness, which is so essential for personal mastery. The exercise called "Moments of Awareness" (or Ma) involves deep self-reflection in which we ask ourselves three questions. These questions are:

1. What is happening right now?
   What am I doing right now?
   What am I feeling right now?
   What am I thinking right now?
2. What do I want right now?
3. What am I doing right now to prevent myself from getting what I want?

Make a choice at this moment by saying, "I choose...." Take a deep breath and move on.

For complete text of the exercise, please see *The Fifth Discipline Fieldbook* (1994, pp. 21´-217).

6

Creating Personal Vision

Background

Our life vision is closely related to our purpose, mission, or goals, but it is also different and we need to be very clear about these distinctions. Purpose or mission is a very broad and inclusive statement about why we are here on this planet. But this statement, by its very nature, is somewhat abstract. The following statements are all valid statements of purpose, though they touch upon only one aspect of our being.

I want to be a good citizen of my country.

I want to represent the best values in my culture.

I want to help those who need help.

I want to save the planet from mindless destruction.

I want to offer unconditional love to all sentient beings.

I want to enrich my spirit and work for spiritual enlightenment.

These are very powerful statements, but they are perhaps too abstract for daily use. Purpose is a statement of broad direction but it is not a vision. On the other hand, goals are always very specific and quantifiable. For example, I can say that my goal is to be fluent in spoken Spanish within the next two years. Or I will have an x amount in the bank as my savings within the next 5 years. Again goals are useful but they are not a substitute for vision.

Vision, as the word itself makes it clear, is a picture of the desired future—the future that's just a dream at this time. What we have is the "current reality"—my worries; my concerns; my strengths and limitations. How do I move from the current reality to the vision? Here Peter Senge (1990) introduces the concept of "creative tension." There is always a gap between vision and reality, but this gap is also a source of energy. That's why the gap is called "creative tension". Senge gives the example of a stretched rubber band: "When stretched, the rubber band creates tension, representing the tension between vision and current reality. What does tension seek? It seeks resolution or release. There are only two possible ways for the tension to resolve itself; pull reality toward the vision or pull the vision toward reality. Which occurs will depend on whether we hold steady to the vision." (p. 150)

Process

This is a four-step process for creating a vision.

1. Create a picture in which you can see yourself at some future time (normally 2-5 years) in a certain situation. If my vision is to be a performing artist, I can see myself performing on stage. If my dream is to be writer, I can see my book displayed in stores with my picture on it. If I want to become a senior manager, I can see myself in a big corner office. The visual itself has to be clear and colorful. Seeing yourself in black and white is not as effective as seeing yourself in color. You can enrich your picture by adding sound, a frame, or 3-D effects. Once the picture is complete, you should keep it alive in your mind at all time.
2. Make an assessment of your current situation: What is working well and what is not? Who are your allies? What obstacles do you see on the way? What exactly is driving you to the vision? What are your resources—mental, intellectual, emotional, and financial in relation to your dream? What do you want to have more of or less of?
3. What are your core values? What drives you in the moment? What makes you get out of the bed in the morning? What are you passionate about? We need to zero in on only 2-3 values, though we may have a long list of values that we cherish.
4. Integrate the three elements into a single whole—**the vision, the current reality, and the core values.** Make changes or adjustments if there are elements that

would not mesh with the whole structure. You can lower your vision so that it becomes more easily realizable. Or, you can enhance the resource inputs so that you can speed up the process. Once you are satisfied with the integrated picture, write down the most essential details in your journal. From this point on, everything you do must bear a relationship to your vision. But we must remember that visions are not cast in stone. Your vision can change too with change in circumstances. Revisit the whole picture every few months and make appropriate realignments.

7

Force-Field Analysis

Background

Force-Field Analysis is a simple technique for identifying the opposing forces that exist in any situation. The process of identification of forces in two categories is itself a step toward understanding the situation. For achieving the desired result, we have to strengthen the supporting forces and weaken the restraining forces. Visually, we can represent two opposing set of forces on two sides of a single line (which represents the equilibrium).

We can illustrate the technique by a simple example. Let us say that you are looking at the possibility of rotation assignment in your organization. You will draw a line in the center of a plain sheet of paper and you will write down forces that support your aspiration for a new job. Below the line, you will write down forces that are more like hindrances in the realization of your dream. What we may end up may be something like this.

Forces Supporting Positive Change

Unutilized or under utilized potential in the current job.
Specific IT related capabilities, which are in high demand.
Supportive manager in the targeted job.
Strong personal commitment to change.
Strong family support.
Clarity of vision and sense of direction.

Forces Restraining Positive Change

There are some unresolved issues in the current job.
The current manager may not support reassignment.
Many strong candidates targeting the same job.

Organizational record is not very strong in supporting internal reassignments.

Process

Look at your own situation. What is the most important issue you are facing that involves change. Write down a clear statement. Then do brainstorming highlighting both supportive and restraining factors. For all the items that are restraining you must build a clear action plan. For example:

There are some unresolved issues in the current job
Identify issues
Prepare a time line to resolve each issue
Seek help if needed

The current manager may not support reassignment
Talk to the manager and get his or her input
Do not make prejudgments
Address concerns
Try to focus conversation on your future development and not any shortcomings you see in the current assignment

Many strong candidates targeting the same job
Reexamine your strengths
Focus on marketing yourself
Focus on factors that uniquely set you apart from the others

Organizational record is not very strong in supporting internal reassignments
Don't be frustrated by generalized assessments
This is not an actionable item

8

Open Space Technology

Background

Open Space is a participatory technique to identify major issues in a complex situation. As people to be affected by the decisions are the people who are participating in the event, it creates commitment to options as well as final solutions. There are **Four Principles** of Open Space:

- Whoever comes are the right people.
- Whatever happens is the only thing that could have happened.
- When it starts it is the right time.
- When it's over, it's over.

In addition to these principles, there is **The Law of Two Feet**—standing up for what you believe, and if you feel you are neither contributing nor learning where you are, use your two feet and go somewhere else.

The facilitator has a very specific role:

- Supporting the presenters in expressing the theme.
- Making the sponsors aware that once the "organization" (the entity that is going through change) has been opened, it doesn't go back to its original position.
- Creating a safe space.
- Coaching the sponsor (s) on staying open to what emerges from the organization—sometimes it can be very unfamiliar and uncomfortable.

Process

Open Space is a very useful technique for initiating large system change like a community trying to resolve an issue (high crime or low scores in schools) or an organization trying to cope with a problem of, say, declining service quality. The change catalyst or the sponsor will get large space like a townhall with adequate supplies of markers, paper sheets, masking tapes, and other supporting logistical items. The announcement goes out to the targeted audience, but no one is forced to show up. People come on their own because they take responsibility for the outcomes. The sponsor allows people to have conversations in an open space but he or she has no controlling role.

Open space concepts can also be used at micro level, involving fewer people, a unit rather than a large organization. The significant point is the philosophical underpinnings of this concept. If people are not passionate about change, no change will happen. Also if they take no responsibility no progress will be made.

For more information on Open Space, please see *Open Space Technology: A User's Guide* (1997).

9

Appreciative Inquiry

Background

Appreciative Inquiry (AI) is the cooperative search for the best in people, their organizations, and the world around them. It involves systematic discovery of what gives a system "life" when it is most effective and capable in economic, ecological, and human terms. According to David Cooperrider, one of its founders, "More than a method or technique, the appreciative mode of inquiry is a means of living with, being with and directly participating in the life of a human system in a way that compels one to inquire into the deeper life-generating essentials and potentials of organizational existence."

Appreciative Inquiry Principles

The Constructionist Principle: Words create worlds and reality is a socially created construct, created through language and conversations.

The Simultaneity Principle: Inquiry creates change—the moment we ask a question, we begin to create change.

The Poetic Principle: What we choose to study makes a difference. It describes and even creates the world, as we know it.

The Anticipatory Principle: Human systems move in the direction of their images of the future and the more positive the image, the more positive the present-day action.

The Positive Principle: Momentum for large-scale change requires large amounts of positive affect and social bonding. This momentum is best generated through positive questions that amplify the positive core.

The Wholeness Principle: Bringing all stakeholders together in large group forums stimulates creativity and builds collective capacity.

The Enactment Principle: To really make a change, we must be the change we wish to see.

The Free Choice Principle: People perform better and are more committed when they have freedom to choose how and what they contribute.

AI Summit

Appreciative Inquiry meeting is called AI Summit; it is the place where participants gather together and go through a four-stage AI cycle. D is the key letter indicating names of the four stages: Discover, Dream, Design, and Destiny.

The facilitator's role covers four aspects:

- To view the organization as living spiritual-social systems, mysteries of creation to be nurtured and affirmed, not as mechanistic or scientific operations with problems to be solved.
- To work in the affirmative, continually seeking to discover what gives life to the organization and its members.
- To be facilitators of possibilities, hopes, and inspired action.
- To continually seek ways to give the process away, to support organization members in making it their own.

In practical terms, it means:

- Introducing AI to the organization.
- Focusing on the "business" and "economic" issues.
- Training groups in AI.
- Supporting the Core Team.
- Facilitating the Summit.
- Assisting the organization to integrate AI into daily practices.

The major tool used by AI facilitators is called "appreciative interview." The uniqueness of this technique is its affirmative focus. The interview uncovers what gives life to an organization, department, or community when at its best, what people value, what they hope and wish for to enhance their organization's social, economic, and environmental vitality.

Process

There are four stages of the AI cycle:

DISCOVERY: The key questions in this phase are: What gives "life" to the organization? What is working? What is worth preserving? What are we doing right? What do others appreciate about us?

DREAM: Dreaming is envisioning the future. What do we want to create? What is our calling? What is our potential? How can we enhance our positive influence? How can we enhance our impact in the world?

DESIGN: How do we co-create or co-construct the organization that we dream of? How do we design strategies, processes and systems, decisions, and collaborations that would support the new organization to come into life?

DESTINY: This is about moving ahead, publicly declaring intended actions and asking for support. Empowering self-selected groups to plan the next actions.

For more information on Appreciative Inquiry, please see *The Power of Appreciative Inquiry* (2003) and *Appreciative Inquiry: A Positive Revolution in Change* (2005).

10

Future Search

Background

Future Search is a meeting format that brings all the right people together with a view to thinking about their shared future. The unique meeting format makes people let go of their stereotypes. New relationships emerge. Surprising projects become possible,

Key Principles

- Have the right people in the room—that is, cross-section of the whole system.
- Create conditions where participants experience the whole "elephant" before acting on any part of it.
- Seek and build upon common ground.
- Think globally before acting locally.
- Have people manage their own future ("getting everybody to improve whole systems").
- Let people take responsibility for learning and action
- Experience and accept polarities.
- Instead of changing the world or each other, change the conditions under which people interact.

Facilitator's Role

- Help people decide if future search will serve their needs.
- Help sponsors gather the necessary information, courage, and resources to proceed.
- Manage tasks and time.
- Keep purpose front and center.
- Encourage self-management and responsibility.

- Allow the uncertainty until people decide what they will and will not do together.
- Help people resolve the struggle between old patterns and new paths.

Process

Future Search Conference typically involves 60 to 80 people. Sixty-four is considered to be an optimal number—eight groups of eight. The purpose of the meeting is to create a joint action towards a desired future.

The process consists of five tasks—

Task 1: Focus on the past using a time line.

Task 2: Focus on the present, external trends; stakeholder response to external trends; focus on the present, owning our actions.

Task 3: Create ideal future scenarios.

Task 4: Identify common ground; confirm common ground; not consensus but what "they" want and how to get there.

Task 5: Action planning based on personal responsibility (not recommendations to others).

The whole process takes 2-3 days to reach fruition.

For more information, please see *Future Search* (2000).

11

The Four-Stage Stress Reduction Meditation

Background

Stress is a fact of life. Most organizations are trying to do more with less, which means there is more work for everyone. Also the advances in information technologies have further blurred the lines between work and the rest of life. Under these circumstances, people have to make a special effort to relax themselves through physical workouts and meditation. The objective of the four-stage meditation is to provide deep physical, mental, emotional, and spiritual relaxation in the midst of highly demanding work environment.

Process

Find a quiet place where you are not likely to be disturbed for at least 15 minutes. Sit comfortably in a chair with your back straight and try to relax your body and mind as much as possible. The exercise is divided into four parts but different parts just flow into each other making it one continuous meditation.

1. *Physical Relaxation**

- Start with the toes of the left foot and slowly move up the foot and leg, feeling the sensations and directing the breath into and out from different regions.
- From the pelvis, we go to the toes of the right foot and move up the right leg back to the pelvis.
- We move up through the torso, through the lower back and abdomen, the upper back and chest, and the shoulders.

*This part is based on instructions provided by Jon Kabat-Zinn.

- Then we go to the fingers of both hands and move up simultaneously in both arms, returning to the shoulders.
- We move through the neck and throat, and the regions of the face, the back of the head, and the top of the head.

2. *Mental Relaxation*

- Gently approaching your mind, take note of all the thoughts that are present at this time. Do not make any judgments. Just notice what those thoughts are. Take the perspective of an observer, someone looking at those thoughts from a distance. These thoughts have a life of their own. They do not simply belong to you. They come and go.
- Imagine thoughts are formed in the same way as clouds are formed and they are floating on the empty spaces of your mind (the boundaryless blue sky). Clouds come and clouds go. You are just an observer making note of all these changes.
- Imagine the most beautiful place you have ever seen. Possibly the place was in the hills or close to an ocean. Recreate the scenery adding color, adding texture, smells and sounds. Let that past experience come alive with full force. As you see this soothing picture, let your mind relax, completely blocking all thoughts or images that may be causing you any anxiety or concern.
- Expand your mind to include the whole universe, seen and unseen. Let there be no barriers or boundaries. Each time you inhale, you are inhaling the beauty and magic of the whole universe.
- What is your mental state like at this time? Pick a name or a symbol that best describes your relaxed mental condition.

3. *Emotional Relaxation*

- Now we get to the emotional state. Be aware of all the emotions that you may be experiencing at this time.
- You want to fill yourself with positive emotions. Instead of consciously trying to censor any negative emotions, add more of positive feelings and emotions.
- Consciously try to strengthen three positive emotions. These are love, compassion, and forgiveness.
- Allow love to take all the space in your heart and mind. Remind yourself of all the people you love and you have loved over the years. Send your love to them one more time and then let them disappear from your consciousness. But stay with the feelings of love that you have generated, love for not any particular person, but for all beings in their collective existence—those who are sick, suffering, and needing love anywhere in the world.
- Now let your heart be filled with compassion knowing that you are a generous human being. Make a commitment one more time to support all causes that deserve your support. With a spirit of sharing, reach out to those who have not yet benefited from your generosity.
- Forgiveness is another positive emotion. It helps us forget old grievances, grudges, and feelings of animosity. Forgive yourself if you feel that is needed. Forgive all the others who may have done wrongs in the past. Let go because you do not want to carry this burden anymore.
- Think of a word or a symbol that accurately describes your emotional state.

4. *Gratitude and Countdown*

- As you come to the conclusion of this meditation, express your gratitude for what life has given you. Express your thanks to people who have played a positive role in your life, especially your teachers and mentors who have given you gifts of knowledge.

- Feel that you have come to a very special place that you can call your home. This place is sacred because it is in this space that you connect with your higher self, with a power that is beyond you.
- Imagine this place to be in the universe that is highly supportive of you, that wants you to be fully relaxed, free from all tensions.
- Start the countdown from 7 to 1 with each descending number gradually bringing you back to the real world. Seven—it is the seat of higher consciousness. Six—it is the center of our intuition, our ability to know the unknown. Five—it is our voice, the words we speak, the joy we provide to others with our spoken words. Four— it is the heart center where love and compassion reside. Three— it is the house that our willpower has built, a symbol of our commitments and agreements. Two— it is our connection with people who continue to play an important part in our life. One— it is the ground, it is the real world to which we return now, fully relaxed and rejuvenated.
- Open your eyes when ready.

12

The Work of a Compassionate Heart

Background

Cultivation of compassion is a challenging task as one has to fight a battle with one's egoic mind, which does not want to care about anything other than itself. This guided meditation places you in a most challenging situation in a difficult humanitarian role. How do you cope with this situation? How do you bring your compassion into the open to work with you? How do you make your inner-self as your best friend in serving these people who need utmost care and love.

Process

Close your eyes and breathe comfortably. In this exercise, you are going to experience the meaning of compassion. Where does it come from? What happens to you when you act compassionately? And what happens when you don't?

Mentally transport yourself to a land that is in a total state of anarchy. There is no law and order. People commit the most heinous crimes against one another. There is death caused by malnutrition and hunger. It seems that God has ceased to exist in that part of the world.

Now imagine that you are working for an international relief agency and it's your duty to take care of the sick and dying children and the old who can't even walk. Why did you take this job? You had other options to make a living. You were moved by a commitment to serve people who are suffering. This urge or desire came from deep within you. You knew that you alone could not put an end to these peoples' suffering. You knew that you were up against forces bigger than yourself. But you decided to take the job and the accompanying risk.

And what do you do? You are nursing a sick child. You are feeding an old man, who is dying, having his last meal. You are nursing a wounded soldier, a perpetrator of violence against his own people. You are caring for a mother who lost every member of her family.

You see yourself in all these roles. Your compassion knows no boundaries. You are compassionate at the risk of your own well-being. To the suffering men and women, you are like an angel of hope.

When you act compassionately, you go outside of your own social boundaries to do things that couldn't be done otherwise. It is compassion, a bundle of divine energy located at the bottom of your heart, that makes you perform acts that are unimaginable in the normal course.

Compassion is about caring. Compassion is about forgiving people for the wrongs they have done. Compassion is about giving people another chance in their life.

You say a silent prayer of thankfulness. To be compassionate is a gift of the divine; it is doing the work of a higher force. It is not just your own doing. It is a prayer, a way of worshipping the creator and the creation. It is both a process and an end. It is both a work and the reward of work. It is the way to honor your own being.

Open your eyes when you are ready.

13

The Power of Prayer

Background

There are hundreds of beautiful prayers coming from different spiritual traditions and belief systems. They all carry the same message of love and harmony for all humanity.

St. Francis Prayer

Lord, make me an instrument of Thy peace
Where there is hatred, let me sow love
Where there is injury, pardon
Where there is doubt, faith
Where there is despair, hope
Where there is darkness, light
And where there is sadness, joy
O Divine Master, grant that I may not so much seek
To be consoled as to console
To be understood as to understand
To be loved, as to love
For it is in giving that we receive
It is in pardoning that we are pardoned
It is in dying to self that we are born to eternal life.

A Hindu Prayer

May my speech be one with my mind, and may my mind be one with my speech.
O thou self-luminous Brahman, remove the veil of ignorance from before me, that I may behold thy light.
Do thou reveal to me the spirit of the scriptures
May the truth of the scriptures be ever present to me
May I seek day and night to realize what I learn from the sages
May I speak the truth of Brahman

May I speak the truth
May it protect me
May it protect my teacher
OM … peace, peace, peace

[from *Aitareya Upanishad*]

A Muslim Prayer

In the name of God, the Compassionate, the Merciful
All praise belongs to God, Lord of all worlds,
The compassionate, the merciful,
Ruler of Judgment Day.
It is You that that we worship,
and to You we appeal for help.
Show us the straight way,
the way of those You have graced,
not of those on whom is Your wrath,
not of those who wander astray.

[*Quran, Surah 1, "The Opening"*]

A Sikh Prayer by Guru Arjun Dev

As long as one divides people between friends and enemies
It is difficult to realize God.
As long as one discriminates between self and others
There is a gap between self and God.
O Benevolent Lord, grant me such understanding
That I serve only true sages
And do not forget You for a moment.
O my fickle mind, why didn't it occur to you
That forsaking the Lord is being like your own worst enemy.
If I do not indulge my ego-mind woe will affect me not.
Such is the wisdom I have gained in the company of sages.
Pay as much attention to worshippers of material wealth
As you do to the waft of the wind.
When my mind is enveloped in million sins
There is hardly anything I can say.

In Nanak's name I seek Thy protection O Lord
Erase all my deeds and shower Thy blessings.

[Translation by Daler Deol]

Process

Choose your favorite prayer from your own or from a different spiritual tradition. Find a fixed time when you will spend a few minutes every day reciting the prayer. A distinction is generally made between a petitionary prayer (when we ask for something in return) and a contemplative prayer. The sample prayers in this section are contemplative prayers. Such prayers are not different from deeper forms of meditation because they concentrate our mind and make us forget our day-to-day worries and concerns.

There is another form of prayer called the intercessory prayer, which is used for the wellness of others who may be going through a medical crisis. A major research study published in March 2006 showed that such prayers do not yield any positive results.

One of the medical doctors who looked at the results of the above study rightly commented: "Perhaps the value of prayer is not to the sick who are prayed for, but rather to those who pray for them. Medical research increasingly demonstrates the health benefits of being in caring, connected relationships. Communities of prayerful faith provide that social support for many."

14

What is Consciousness?

Background

What is consciousness? Notwithstanding the high-sounding conceptual resonance of this word, consciousness is a simple experience of our daily life—the sum and substance of our five sensory experiences like watching a football game, listening to music, eating a hearty meal, making love, or creating something new. It is an inseparable part of our joyful ecstasies and our heart-breaking sufferings. It is an unequivocal part of every sensation that we experience. It is there for us to make sense of everything that we feel, see or hear. It never leaves us alone, not even when we are asleep.

Following Sri Aurobindo, the great 20th century Indian sage and philosopher, we can define six characteristics of consciousness:

1. *It is impersonal and universal.* Consciousness is not simply a reaction of our personality to external forces of nature. It arises out of something that is impersonal and universal; it spreads out even while we are motionless and barely self-aware.

2. *It is a bundle of polarities.* Consciousness is a summation of several polarities. It is on the surface as well as deep within us. It speaks and it is silent. It is visible as well as invisible. It is reactive as well as proactive. It is projected as well as withdrawn. It is active as well as inactive. It is conscious as well as unconscious.

3. *It is a creative and dynamic energy.* More than just awareness, consciousness is dynamic and creative energy. It is the Eternal Force that animates all existence—the macrocosm as well as the microcosm. It touches the minutest part of our life as well as the most significant aspects.

4. *It is below and above our mind.* We limit the scope and power of consciousness by limiting it to our own mental capacities. Consciousness embraces several levels above and below our mental thinking.

5. *It appears in wave-like structures, which are not controlled by us.* We do not create gradations or waves of consciousness. On the other hand, our personality is shaped and determined by these gradations of consciousness.

6. *It is highly diverse in its unity.* Consciousness is one, but it takes many forms. In its "forgetfulness" it can become an atom or an electron, and as the evolution unfolds itself it can reemerge as a person, as an animal, or as a plant. Within a single human being, consciousness can find its home within the body, emotions, cognition, and our spiritual strivings. It enters and exits at its own free will.

Aurobindo refers to "polarities" of consciousness as those aspects, which have opposite characteristics. We would like to explore this point in this exercise. Given below is a sample list of some of the identified polarities based on the above characteristics:

Reactive	Proactive
Microcosmic	Macrocosmic
Internal	External
Personal	Universal
Surface	Deeper
Visible	Invisible
Verbal	Silent
Routine	Creative
Emotional	Mental
One	Many
Withdrawn	Projected

Process

While you refresh your understanding of the seven levels framework, identify "points" of polarities in the matrix below which are found at each level of consciousness. After completing this part of the exercise, draw a "consciousness spiral" rising from the ground level to the universal level using suitable labels to identify different points in the spiral.

Levels	*Different Points of Polarities*
Universal Self-Actualizing	
Spiritual Intuitive	
Creative Self-Expression	
Heart Love & Compassion	
Power Self-Esteem	
Emotional Relational	
Ground Feet on the Ground	

Your Consciousness Spiral

15

Outer, Inner, and Innermost Layers of Being

Background

According to Sri Aurobindo, there are three layers of our being which we normally fail to recognize—the outer, the inner and the innermost. The outer being is the façade or the mask that we wear for a number of reasons. We want assimilation with a group or a community. We behave in ways that others expect of us. We often suppress our true feelings because saying what's on our mind may not be appropriate. What we are most consciously aware of is our outer being, or our exterior self. What others see about us is also our outer self and they make judgments and assumptions based on what they see. In fact, we run the risk of being labeled in a certain way based on an appearance that's "deceptive" because it's not representative of our true inner self.

Our inner being is our subconscious or subliminal self that is also a center of our most cherished memories and experiences. The exact size and scope of our inner being is hard to define because it is the center of what Aurobindo calls obscure unconsciousness or half-consciousness or a submerged consciousness. There is a wall between our "outer and inner beings" and if we break this wall the flood of submerged consciousness can expand the reservoir of our outer consciousness manifold. What is in our subconscious mind can find release in several other ways too: through dreams, intuitions, inspirations, hunches, and insights.

The innermost being is also known as the psychic being. It is like a bridge between our physical existence and our deeper connection with the universe. We can say that this is the seat of our soul. It is the place that spirit visits from time to time. A realization of our innermost self is the start of our spiritual life. If there is spirit within us, the innermost being is its most likely natural habitat. The innermost self is always present, mostly covered up by our material cravings. It grows with our own spiritual evolution, though we may not consciously know about this.

Process

According to Aurobindo, these "three layers of being" have physical, mental, and emotional dimensions. Looking at the following matrix, identify aspects of your own "being"—namely, strengths, weaknesses, issues, potentialities, emotional sensibilities, psychological hurts, etc. The second part of the exercise relates to transforming potentialities or unresolved issues into usable strengths. For example, how can you use your hidden skills (which you know is your strength) to make you more effective at the outer level? Similarly, how can you put the issue of, say, childhood trauma (which is a deep seated emotional issue) behind you and lead the rest of your life without this emotional hurt? How can you positively bring out your innermost compassion to give a new meaning to your outer life?

	Outer Being	*Inner Being*	*Innermost Being*
Physical			
Mental			
Emotional			

16

I Have a Body But I Am Not My Body

Background

One important objective of meditation is to build a foundation of self-awareness and self-knowledge and discovering the "reality" of one's being as a center of Pure Consciousness. Two versions of such a self-awareness meditation by Ramana Maharshi and Roberto Assagioli are presented here. You may select any one or both for your meditation and reflection.

Process

Read the selected meditation one or more times. Reflect deeply on its key messages. What are you identifying with?.What are you dis-identifying from? Use the following questions for your reflection.

1. You are not your body, but what is your connection with your body?
2. You are not your mind, but your thinking has great impact on your behavior. Reflect on the ways in which your thinking has shaped your personality.
3. What is your consciousness free of thoughts, ideas, viewpoints, perspectives, etc.?
4. Watch every "I" thought that arises. What does it say to you?
5. Repeatedly ask yourself the question "Who am I?" Capture your experiences and insights in a learning journal.

Meditation by Ramana Maharshi

Who Am I?

The gross body, which is composed of the seven humors, I am not; the five cognitive sense organs, i.e., the senses of hearing, touch, sight, taste, and smell, which apprehend their respective objects, i.e., sound, touch, color, taste, and odor; I am not; the five conative sense organs, i.e., the organs of speech, locomotion, grasping, excretion, and procreation, which have as their respective functions speaking, moving, grasping, excreting, and enjoying, I am not; the five vital airs, prana, etc., which perform respectively the five functions of in-breathing, etc., I am not; even the mind which thinks, I am not; the nescience too, which is endowed only with the residential impressions of objects, and in which there are no objects and no functions, I am not.

If I am none of these, then who am I?

After negating all of the above-mentioned as "not this, not this," that Awareness which alone remains—that I am.

Source: *The Spiritual Teachings of Ramana Maharshi* (1988, p. 3)

Meditation by Roberto Assagioli

Dis-identification Exercise

I put my body into a comfortable and relaxed position with closed eyes. This done, I affirm: "I have a body but I am not my body. My body may find itself in different conditions of health or sickness; it may be rested or tired, but that had nothing to do with my self, my real 'I'. My body is my precious instrument of experience and of action in the outer world, but it is only an instrument. I treat it well, I seek to keep it in good health, but it is not myself. I have a body, but I am not my body.

I have emotions, but I am not my emotions. These emotions are countless, contradictory, changing, and yet I know that I always remain I, myself, in times of hope and despair, in joy or in pain, in a state of irritation or of calm. Since I can observe, understand and judge my emotions, and then increasingly dominate, direct and utilize them, it is evident that they are not myself. I have emotions, but I am not my emotions.

I have desires but I am not my desires, aroused by drives, physical and emotional, and by outer influences. Desires too are changeable and contradictory, with alternations of attraction and repulsion. I have desires but they are not myself.

I have an intellect, but I am not my intellect. It is more or less developed and active; it is undisciplined but teachable; it is an organ of knowledge in regard to the outer world as well as the inner; but it is not myself. I have an intellect, but I am not my intellect.

After this dis-identification of the 'I' from its contents of consciousness (sensations, emotions, desires and thoughts) I recognize and affirm that I am a Center of pure self-consciousness. I am a Center of Will, capable of mastering, directing and using all my psychological processes and my physical body."

Identification Exercise

When one has practiced the exercise for some time, it can be modified by a swift dynamic use of the first three stages of dis-identification, leading to a deeper consideration of the fourth stage of self-identification, coupled with an inner dialogue along the following lines: "What am I then? What remains after discarding from my self-identity the physical, emotional and mental contents of my personality, of my ego? It is the essence of myself—a center of pure self-consciousness and self-realization. It is the permanent factor in the ever-varying flow of my personal life. It is that which gives the sense of being, of permanence, of inner security. I recognize and I affirm myself as a center of pure self-consciousness. I realize that this center not only has a static self-awareness but also a dynamic power; it is capable of observing, mastering, directing and using all the psychological processes and the physical body. I am a center of awareness and of power."

Source: *Psychosynthesis* (2000, pp. 104-5)

17

Unconditional Love from the Unknown

Background

J. Krishnamurti used to say that it is impossible to create anything new, something really creative from the old. If we wish to create something new, we have to get rid of our memory, our thoughts, and our mind, because mind is a container of everything that is "known" and it has no clue about the "unknown." We can discover the unknown only when we are in a state of complete tranquility, experiencing the moment that is alive, cherishing the feeling that is coming and going. In that tranquility, we can discover the purpose of our being, what we need to change, and how to change.

Process

Picture in front of your closed eyes the flame of a candle that is burning slowly but steadily. Now let this candle recede as if some invisible hand is taking the candle away from you. As the candle continues to move away, the space becomes darker because of the fading light. The candle soon disappears creating complete darkness. With this disappearing candle let all your personal memories fade away, good as well as bad memories, everything including the usual signs of your identity like your name, position, possessions, rank, awards, et al. As your mind becomes quiet and clear, let this darkness too slowly disappear and in its place let there be light—a light that slowly grows in its intensity until the whole space looks new and very bright. You do not know or try to guess from where this light is coming. In this bright space do not search for any images, but do look for the warmth of this bright light and slowly let this warmth enter your entire being as if someone was injecting this warmth through a mechanical device. As you feel the warmth you feel compassion arising, you feel love arising, and you also feel calmness arising in your whole body. Hold this feeling as long as you can.

The important part of this meditation is that you do not ask for anything specific, yet you get everything. When we become a container of love and compassion, we gain everything that is worth having. And this love and compassion is of the "unknown", and not of the "known" because things of the known are always part of our conditioning, one way or the other. What comes to us from the unknown is truly unconditional love and compassion.

18

Level 5 Leadership

Background

Jim Collins' *Good to Great* (2001) is one of a kind business book. While most business books look upon the business world through the lens of models and theories, Collins gathered a brilliant research team to look at historical performance data of companies in America and selected 11 companies based on very tough benchmarks. What made these companies great? Collins' answer has several parts to it, but his basic notion is that these companies won because they had Level 5 Leadership during the pivotal transition years. If leadership is viewed as a pyramid, then Level 5 is the highest segment of that pyramid.

What is Level 5 Leadership? According to Collins (p. 39), these leaders are:

- A paradoxical mix of personal humility and professional will.
- Ambitious, to be sure, but ambitious first and foremost for the company, not themselves.
- Busy preparing the next generation of leaders.
- Displaying a compelling modesty, are self-effacing and understated.
- Fanatically driven, infected with an incurable need to produce sustained results.
- Displaying a workmanlike diligence—more plow horse than show horse.
- Looking out of the window to attribute success to factors other than themselves.
- Not dazzling celebrities.

Process

From a personal development perspective, Collins looks upon "Professional Will" and "Personal Humility" as two sides of Level 5 Leadership (p. 36). The attributes mentioned by him are transformed below into 8 questions for the purpose of self-reflection. The idea is not to seek yes or no answers to any of these questions. Rather, each question is an invitation for individual reflection. Am I doing enough? What more can I do? How can I achieve more? How can I cultivate some of the qualities that make up "Personal Humility"?

- Do I create superb results?
- Do I demonstrate an unwavering resolve to do whatever must be done to produce the best long-term results, no matter how difficult?
- Do I set the standard of building an enduring great company?
- Do I look in the mirror, not out of the window, to apportion responsibility for poor results, never blaming other people, external factors, or bad luck?
- Do I demonstrate a compelling modesty?
- Do I act with quiet and calm determination to motivate others?
- Do I set up successors for even greater success in the next generation?
- Do I look out of the window, not in the mirror, to apportion credit for the success of the company—to other people, external factors, and good luck?

19

Fighting Corporate Corruption

Background

The mega-corporate scandals like Enron and WorldCom shook the ethical foundations of corporate America and businesses around the world. People wondered how could this happen, especially with the amount of Federal oversight that should make any large-scale corruption impossible.

In an innovative study of corporate corruption entitled "Business as usual: The acceptance and perpetuation of corruption in organizations" (Academy of Management *Executive*, Vol. 18, No. 3) researchers Vikas Anand, Blake Ashforth, and Mahendra Joshi attribute wrongdoing to what they call the "rationalization phenomenon." Rationalizations are mental strategies that allow employees (and others around them) to view their corrupt acts as justified. Further, there are socialization tactics through which newcomers entering corrupt units are induced to accept and practice the ongoing unethical acts and their associated rationalizations.

The study authors mention six broad categories of rationalizing actions:

Denial of responsibility: The actors engaged in corrupt behaviors perceive that they have no other choice than to participate in such activities. Typical reactions: "*What can I do? My arm is being twisted.*" "*It is none of my business what the corporation does in overseas bribery.*"

Denial of injury: The actors are convinced that no one is harmed by their actions; hence the actions are not really corrupt. Typical reactions: "*No one was really harmed.*" "*It could have been worse.*"

Denial of victim: The actors counter any blame for their actions by arguing that the violated party deserved whatever happened. Typical reactions: "*They deserved it.*" "*They chose to participate.*"

Social Weighting: The actors assume two practices that moderate the salience of corrupt behaviors: (1) Condemn the condemner. (2) Selective social comparison. Typical reactions: "*You have no right to criticize us.*" "*Others are worse than we are.*"

Appeal to higher loyalties: The actors argue that their violation of norms is due to their attempt to realize a higher-order value. Typical reactions: "*We answered to a more important cause.*" "*I would not report it because of my loyalty to my boss.*"

Metaphor of the ledger: The actors rationalize that they are entitled to indulge in deviant behaviors because of their accrued credits (time and effort) in their jobs. Typical reactions: "*We've earned the right.*" "*It's all right for me to use Internet for personal reasons at work. After all I do work overtime.*"

Process

Corruption harms everyone. Therefore, fighting corruption within a corporation or within any branch of government is everyone's job. But what can you do about it at personal level? Here are some questions for your self-reflection:

1. If I see something wrong happening, do I turn my attention the other way or do I pick up my phone and call the Ethics or Ombuds office?
2. Can I look into the mirror and say, "I have not been party to any act of bribe giving or bribe receiving and I have not knowingly done anything that violates the company policy or the laws of my country?"
3. If I see a senior company executive engaging in corrupt and unlawful actions, do I raise an alarm or do I look the other way because I don't want to get hurt?
4. Do I engage in right action due to fear of punishment or due to an internal moral conviction that taking advantage of one's position for personal gain is plain wrong?

5. Am I prepared to stand-alone and fight back instead of being part of a pack trying to justify a wrong action?

20

Conscious Business

Background

In his new book *Conscious Business* (2006), Fred Kofman defines a conscious business as the one that "promotes mindfulness for all of its stakeholders." (p. 4) He further identifies seven attitudes called "conscious attitudes" that are the hallmarks of conscious business. (p. 17) These are:

Unconditional Responsibility—*taking responsibility for one's actions.*

Essential Integrity—*not focusing only on one's own needs.*

Ontological Humility—*seeing things as others see it.*

Conscious Behaviors—*awareness of consequences of one's actions.*

Authentic Communication—*speaking our truth.*

Constructive Negotiation—*win-win negotiations.*

Impeccable Coordination—*honoring everyone's contribution.*

Conscious Responses—*responding productively to situations.*

Emotional Mastery—*demonstrating emotional self-awareness.*

Process

There are many ways to put this model into practice. I would suggest that you apply it to your current business challenge (something that you want to accomplish in the face of many difficulties). To start with, write down a brief statement of the challenge. Once you have done that, you need to answer the following questions. Each question must be answered specifically and only with respect to the challenge in view:

1. Am I taking full responsibility for all planning, decision-making, implementation, and expected outcomes?
2. Am I working for the well-being of all the stakeholders?

3. Am I seeing the reality as it is, independent of my own biases and prejudices?
4. Am I using authentic communication to share all relevant ideas and informations?
5. Am I trying to build consensus and shared viewpoints rather than having it my way?
6. Do I keep my promises? Do I show my commitment? Do I support those who need help?
7. Do I display emotional mastery in terms of my self-awareness, especially the way I treat other people?

Bibliography

Allen, David. 2003. *Getting Things Done: The Art of Stress-Free Productivity*. New York: Penguin Books.

Assagioli, Roberto. 2000. *Psychosynthesis*. Amherst: The Synthesis Center Inc.

Aurobindo, Sri. 1990. *The Life Divine*. Twin Lakes: Lotus Press.

——. 1993. *The Integral Yoga*. Twin Lakes: Lotus Press.

Beck, Don and Chris Cowan. 1996. *Spiral Dynamics: Mastering Values, Leadership and Change*. Malden: Blackwell Publishers.

Bergson, H. 1907. *Creative Evolution*. Lanham: University Press of America.

Bohm, D. 1980. *Wholeness and the Implicate Order*. Boston: Routledge and Kegan Paul.

——. 1985. *Unfolding Meaning: A Weekend of Dialogue*. New York: Routledge.

——. 1990. *On Dialogue*. Copyright © 1990 by David Bohm.

——. (1994) *Thought as a System*. New York: Routledge.

Boyatzis, Richard and Annie McKee. 2005. *Resonant Leadership*. Boston: Harvard Business School.

Branden, Nathaniel. 1992. *The Power of Self-Esteem*. New York: Barns and Noble Books.

——. 1997. *The Art of Living Consciously: The Power of Awareness to Transform Everyday Life*. New York: Simon & Schuster.

Bruyere, Roslyn L. 1989. *Wheels of Light*. New York: Fireside.

Casse, Pierre and Surinder Deol. 1985. *Managing Intercultural Negotiations: Guidelines for Trainers and Negotiators*. Washington, D.C.: SIETAR.

Campbell, Joseph. 1976. *The Hero with a Thousand Faces.* Bollingen XVII, 2nd edition, revised. Princeton: Princeton University Press.

Collins, Jim. 2001. *Good to Great.* New York: Harper Business.

Combs, Allan. 2002. *The Radiance of Being.* St. Paul: Paragon House.

Cooperrider, David L. and Diana Whitney. 2005. *Appreciative Inquiry: A Positive Revolution in Change.* San Francisco: Barrett-Koehler.

Covey, Stephen. 1993. *7 Habits of Highly Effective People.* New York: Simon & Schuster.

Deol, Surinder and Daler. 1998. *Japji: The Path of Devotional Meditation.* Washington, D.C.: Mount Meru.

Deol, Surinder. 2006a. *The Summit: A Fable about Integral Transformation.* Lincoln, NE: iUniverse.

——. 2006b. *A Moment in the Universe.* Lincoln, NE: iUniverse.

Eden, Donna. 1998. *Energy Medicine.* New York: Jeremy P. Tarcher/Putnam.

Frantz, Roger and Alex N. Pattokos. Eds. 1996. *Intuition at Work: Pathways to Unlimited Possibilities.* San Francisco: Sterling & Stone.

Gardner, Howard. 1983. *Frames of Mind: The Theory of Multiple Intelligence.* New York: BasicBooks.

Gebser, Jean. 1985. *The Ever-Present Origin.* Translation by Noel Barstad with Algis Mickunas. Athens: Ohio University Press.

Gilligan, C. 1982. *In a Different Voice.* Cambridge: Harvard University Press.

Goleman, Daniel. 1995. *Emotional Intelligence: Why It Can Matter More Than IQ.* New York: Bantam Books.

Goleman, Daniel, Richard Boyatzis, and Annie McKee. 2002. *Primal Leadership: Realizing the Power of Emotional Intelligence.* Boston: Harvard Business School.

Goleman, Daniel. 2006. *Social Intelligence: The New Science of Human Relationships.* New York: Bantam Books.

Greenleaf, Robert. 1977. *Servant Leadership: A Journey into the Nature of Legitimate Power and Greatness*. New York/ Mahwah: Paulist Press.

Harvey, Andrew. 1996. *The Essential Mystics: The Soul's Journey into Truth*. New York: HarperCollins Publishers.

Hunt, V. 1977. *Project Report: A Study of Structural Integration from Neuromuscular, Energy Field, and Emotional Approaches*. Boulder: Rolf Institute of Structural Integration.

Huxley, Aldous. 1944. *The Perennial Philosophy*. New York: Harper & Row Publishers.

Jantsch, E. 1980. *The Self-Organizing Universe*. New York: Pergamon.

Johari, Harish. 1987. *Chakras: Energy Centers of Transformation*. Rochester: Destiny Books.

Judith, Anodea. 1996. *Eastern Body, Western Mind: Psychology and the Chakra System as a Path to the Self*. Berkley: Celestial Arts.

——. 2003. *Wheels of Life: A User's Guide to the Chakra System*. 2nd edition. St. Paul: Llewellyn Publications.

Kabat-Zinn, Jon. 1990. *Full Catastrophe Living: Using the Wisdom of Your Body and Mind to Face Stress, Pain, and Illness*. New York: Delta.

——. 1994. *Wherever You Go There You Are*. New York: Hyperion.

——. 2005. *Coming to Our Senses*. New York: Hyperion.

Katie, Byron with Stephen Mitchell. 2002. *Living What Is: Four Questions that can Change Your Life*. New York: Three Rivers Press.

Kegan, R. 1982. *The Evolving Self*. Cambridge: Harvard University Press.

——. 1994. *In Over Our Heads: The Mental Demands of Modern Life*. Cambridge: Harvard University Press.

Kofman, Fred. 2006. *Conscious Business: How to Build Value through Values*. Boulder: Sounds True.

Kohlberg, L. 1981. *Essays on Moral Development*. Vol. 1. San Francisco: Harper.

Kotter, John P. 2002. *The Heart of Change: Real-Life Stories of How People Change their Organizations*. Boston: Harvard Business School.

Krishnamurti, J. 1954. *The First & Last Freedom*. New York: HarperCollins Publishers.

——. 1969. *Freedom from the Known*. New York: HarperCollins Publishers.

Leonard, George and Michael Murphy. 1995. *The Life We Are Given*. New York: Jeremy P. Tarcher/Putnam.

Lovejoy, A. 1936. *The Great Chain of Being*. Cambridge: Harvard University Press.

Maharaj, Nisargadatta. 2003. *The Wisdom Teachings of Nisargadatta Maharaj*. Carlsbad: InnerDirections Publishing.

Maharshi, R. 1988. *The Spiritual Teaching of Ramana Maharshi*. Boston: Shambhala.

——. 2001a. *Talks with Ramana Maharshi*. Carlsbad: InnerDirections Publishing.

——. 2001b. *The Essential Teachings of Ramana Maharshi*. Carlsbad: InnerDirections Publishing.

Maslow, A.H. 1970. *Religions, Values, and Peak Experiences*. New York: Penguin Compass.

——. 1971. *The Farther Reaches of Human Nature*. New York: Penguin Compass.

——. 1998. *Maslow on Management*. New York: John Wiley & Sons, Inc.

Mohan, A.G. 1993. *Yoga for Body, Breath and Mind: A Guide to Personal Integration*. Boston: Shambhala.

Myss, Caroline. 1996. *Anatomy of the Spirit: The Seven Stages of Power and Healing*. New York: Harmony Books.

——. 2001. *Sacred Contracts: Awakening Your Divine Potential*. New York: Harmony Books.

Osborn, Diane. 1991. *Reflections on the Art of Living: A Joseph Campbell Companion*. New York: HarperCollins Publishers.

Owen, Harrison. 1997. *Open Space Technology: A User's Guide.* 2nd edition. San Francisco: Berret-Koehler.

Paul, Marilyn. 2003. *It's Hard to Make a Difference When You Can't Find Your Car Keys.* New York: Penguin Compass.

Pearson, Carol S. *Awakening The Heroes Within.* 1991. New York: HarperCollins Publishers.

Prabhananda, Swami and Christopher Isherwood. 1947. *Shankara's Crest Jewel of Discrimination* [Viveka-Chudamani]. Hollywood: Vedanta Press.

Prabhananda, Swami and Frederick Manchester. 1947. *The Upanishads: Breath of the Eternal.* Hollywood: Vedanta Press.

Quinn, Robert E. 1996. *Deep Change: Discovering the Leader Within.* San Francisco: Jossey-Bass.

Ray, Michael and Rochelle Myers. 1986. *Creativity in Business.* New York: Doubleday.

Salzberg, Sharon. 1995. *Loving-Kindness: The Revolutionary Art of Happiness.* Boston: Shambhala.

Senge, Peter. 1990. *The Fifth Discipline: The Art & Practice of the Learning Organization.* New York: Doubleday.

Senge, Peter, Richard Ross, Bryan Smith, Charlotte Roberts, and Art Kleiner. 1994. *The Fifth Discipline Fieldbook.* New York: Doubleday.

Smith, Huston. 1976. *Forgotten Truth: The Common Vision of World's Religions.* New York: HarperCollins Publishers.

Stone, Douglas, Bruce Patton, and Sheila Heen. 1999. *Difficult Conversations: How to Discuss What Matters Most.* New York: Penguin.

Trungpa, Chogyam. 1984. *Shambhala: The Sacred Path of the Warrior.* Boston: Shambhala.

——. 1993. *Training the Mind and Cultivating Loving-Kindness.* Boston: Shambhala.

Wade, Jenny. 1996. *Changes of Mind: A Holonomic Theory of the Evolution of Consciousness.* Albany: State University of New York Press.

Walsh, Roger. 1999. *Essential Spirituality*. New York: John Wiley & Sons, Inc.

Wauters, Ambika. 2002. *The Book of Chakras*. New York: Barron's.

Weisbord, Marvin Ross and Sandra Janoff. 2000. *Future Search*. San Francisco: Berrett-Koehler.

Whitney, Diana, Amanda Trosten-Bloom, and David Cooperrider. 2003. *The Power of Appreciative Inquiry*. San Francisco: Barrett-Koehler.

Wilber, Ken. 1996. *A Brief History of Everything*. Boston: Shambhala.

——. 2000a. *Sex, Ecology, Spirituality: The Spirit of Evolution*. 2nd edition. Boston: Shambhala.

——. 2000b. *A Theory of Everything: An Integral Vision for Business, Politics, Science and Spirituality*. Boston: Shambhala.

——. 2004. *The Simple Feeling of Being: Embracing Your True Nature*. Boston: Shambhala.

——. 2006. *Integral Spirituality*. Boston: Integral Books.